TOWARDS THE LEARNING COMPANY

Concepts and Practices

CRPYK

TOWARDS THE LEARNING COMPANY
Concepts and Practices

John Burgoyne,
Mike Pedler,
Tom Boydell

McGraw-Hill Book Company

London · New York · St Louis · San Francisco · Auckland
Bogotá · Caracas · Lisbon · Madrid · Mexico · Milan
Montreal · New Delhi · Panama · Paris · Sân Juan · Sao Paulo
Singapore · Sydney · Tokyo · Toronto

Published by
McGraw-Hill Book Company Europe
Shoppenhangers Road, Maidenhead, Berkshire, SL6, 2QL, England
Telephone 0628 23432
Fax 0628 770224

British Library Cataloguing in Publication Data

Burgoyne, John
  Towards the Learning Company: Concepts and Practice
  I. Title
  658.407124

ISBN 0-07-707802-0

Library of Congress Cataloging-in-Publication Data

This data is available from the Library of Congress, Washington DC, USA.

12345 BL 97654

Typeset by Datix International, Bungay, Suffolk
and printed and bound in Great Britain by Biddles Ltd.

Contents

Part III Further thoughts

Preface

In 1991 we published, and made accessible in convenient form, the main interim conclusions of our work on the 'Learning Company',[1] a theme that we had been researching since 1986.

That event marked, for us, the beginning of a much broader debate, sharing of ideas, experience and experimentation. This has involved two major conferences, working with a consortium of companies on the application of the ideas, and numerous workshops, seminars and discussions.

This volume shares some of the fruit of this work, and in particular the first conference in 1992, where many of the chapters here have their origin. At that time, and since, there has been both a demand to visualize better the application of the ideas, and to develop these ideas further. This volume addresses both of these issues.

We wish particularly to acknowledge the help of Gloria Welshman who has helped us in running these further activities.

This book is about concepts and practices associated with the Learning Company and is set out in that order. Starting at the beginning will be a good approach for those who want to stretch their thinking first and then reconsider managerial and organizational change problems in the light of this. Others may wish to start with Part II, on applications, to get in touch with contemporary organizational experience in a number of settings, as a background for thinking about the concepts in Part I. Sutton (Chapter 7) would be a good starting point for those who want to begin in the middle with a synthesis of many of the existing models of learning, and explore from there both ways, into ideas and practices.

Contributors

David Ashton is Chief Executive, The Cable and Wireless College, and Professor of Management Learning in the Management School at Lancaster University where he was Dean from 1987–93.

Margaret Attwood is a consultant in individual and organizational learning.

John Belcher is Director of South Yorkshire Housing Association.

Peter Binns is Lecturer in the Department of Philosophy, University of Warwick.

Chris Blantern is a management learning consultant and researcher.

John Burgoyne is Professor of Management Learning in the Department of Management Learning, the Management School, Lancaster University.

Jim Butler is Director of Training and Development, The Post Office.

John Coopey is Lecturer in Management in the Department of Economics and Management, University of Dundee.

Julia Davies is Senior Teaching Fellow in the Management Development Division of the Management School, Lancaster University.

John Edmonstone is a consultant in Manpower, Training and Development Services, Senior Research Associate, Centre for Health Planning and Management, University of Keele, and Associate Consultant Management Development Group, NHS in Scotland/Management Executive.

John Gunson is a consultant specializing in the facilitation of personal development and organizational change.

Maggie Havergal is a Director at Havergal Associates, and Associate Consultant Management Development Group, NHS in Scotland/Management Executive.

Peter Hawkins is a member of the Bath Consultancy Group.

Hilary Lines is a Human Resource Consultant with Coopers & Lybrand.

John Mackmersh is Quality Development Manager, Intercity, British Railways.

Chris Minett is Chief Executive of the Mid Essex Hospital Services NHS Trust.

Michael Pearn is a Senior Partner in Pearn Kandola, Occupational Psychologist.

Robert Wood, Johanna Fullerton and **Ceri Roderick** are Associate Partners.

Mike Pedler is Senior Research Fellow in the Department of Management Learning, The Management School, Lancaster University, an Affiliate of Transform, Individual and Organisation Development Ltd, UK.

Alan Phillips is a freelance consultant in management development.

Bob Ricketts is Director of Performance Management, East Anglia Regional Health Authority.

David Rooke and **Jackie Keeley** work at Teamwork Associates.

Malcolm Stephenson is Director of the Northern Regional Management Centre.

David Sutton is a Director of System Six Strategic Systems Consultancy.

Paul Tosey is Lecturer in the Human Potential Resource Group, Department of Educational Studies, University of Surrey.

1
Established and emergent learning company concepts and practices [1]
John Burgoyne

The aim of this book is to broaden, deepen, relate and apply the concept of the Learning Company, and in particular to take further the ideas we put forward in 1991.[1] In the spirit of George Kelly's proposition,[2] that a theory should apply to itself, we pointed out then, and do so again now, that a theory of learning is itself likely to move on as a result of a learning process. This volume brings together reports of ideas and experiments which move on the Learning Company concept in various ways.

One of the many themes that can be drawn from this collection is that learning is, or has become, as part of the era shift sometimes labelled with the term 'postmodernity',[3] multi- rather than unidirectional. The terms 'broaden', 'deepen', 'relate' and 'apply' describe some of these main directions in work, thought and action related to the Learning Company concept. *Broaden* implies the opening up of adjacent issues, like environmental issues in the ecological sense (see John Gunson, Chapter 21). *Deepening* is the examination of core concepts in greater depth, particularly the very concepts of learning, and organizations as entities capable of collective learning (Hawkins and Binns, Chapters 2 and 3). *Relate* means establishing the connections of learning company thinking to other well established areas of thought and action, both to see how they compare and what critical insights they bring to bear on each other (Coopey, Chapter 4, Butler, Chapter 16). *Application* covers putting the learning company ideas to work, or interpreting current practice of organizational change in these terms (see Part II).

---

1. Some of the thinking in this chapter, particularly as it relates to the N.H.S. case studies in part II, draws on preliminary work on the organizational learning theme carried out as part at an Economic and Social Science Research Council funded project (Award no. L114251025) which is part of the Contracts and Competition Programmme.

In our original formulation[1] we suggested that organizations are shaped by three interacting forces:

1. the era in which they exist in their macro cultural/economic/political context (e.g. pre- or post-industrial/developed), bearing in mind both the globalization of business and the fragmentation of (some) nation states;
2. the life stage or phase of the particular organization;
3. the current ideas and vision of the people 'running' the organization, including both their 'new' ideas and the ones they carry forward as the heritage of their predecessors and the organization's culture.

We particularly suggested that training and development work has progressed through a number of eras, and that concern for the learning company can be seen as part of this pattern. In developing countries and post-war Europe and America we have seen various attempts at systematic training as a response to skill shortages creating problems of lack of transfer and application. This leads to more person- and task-centred approaches to learning which can be characterized as the self-development movement. This in turn, we argued, created or revealed the problems of organizations rather than individuals as constraint, and a concern for organizational solutions in the form of the 'Excellence' movement,[4] the 'Quality' movement,[5] and, more recently, applications of the ideas of organizational learning[6,7] which have been in circulation for some time as a research interest and theoretical perspective.[8] Our argument has been that systematic training, self-development and creating learning companies are approaches that have responded to contemporary problems, and either created, or revealed, the next problem. It is therefore tempting to ask, even though it may seem premature, what the next problem and consequent organization development focus might be. The uncertainty over purpose and direction, the fragmentation and pluralization of ambition and desire in the context of an ever-increasing ability to communicate, create and control mutual visibility, have already been mentioned.[3] The era of organizational solutions seems to beg the same questions: excellence at, quality in, learning for: *what?* The regimentation of systematic training gave way to the individualized freedom of self-development but constrained by the rigidities of institutional and organizational forms, to which organizational flexibility and learning have been the answers, but again, for what? It seems that organizations now have to respond, more than ever before, to people's needs for meaning, identity and purpose to be met through their transactions, from whatever stakeholder position (employee, owner, supplier, customer, neighbour) with organizations. Although the term may have some dangerous connotations, the more obvious, overt and intimate involvement of organizational processes with the search for essence and meaning in life, manifest in designer culture for customers and vision, empowerment and commitment for employees, concerns with ethical governance for owners, can be thought of as the *spiritualization* of organizations. In this volume, this is addressed directly by Davies (Chapter 5), but also by Hawkins (Chapter 2), Binns (Chapter 3), Rooke and Keeley (Chapter 10), and Tosey (Chapter 6). Sutton (Chapter 7), as a practitioner drawing on a number of the well used frameworks for understanding learning, discusses the relationship between these frameworks, and in particular notions of 'levels' of learning. Lurking in this way of thinking is the question of what is the dimension of 'higher-ness' that distinguishes levels.

It may be that, just as the divisions of labour between people are shifting and breaking down in the post-industrial era, the era of the flexible firm,[9] so this is also the case in terms of the roles of organizations in our lives. Just as building societies, insurance companies and banks now offer us each other's traditional services, so perhaps firms, universities and church(es) are mixing the satisfactions of our material, intellectual and spiritual desires.

However, another source of the 'essences' of the desires and interests that organizations provide the processes to interrelate, maintain and create is in history. Organizations and events can be interpreted not as the product of some permanent essence, or as a step on the way towards some terminal utopian order, but as products of their histories. Some of the notions of *era* as long-term history have been explored here, but short-term history, the biographical pattern of the organi-zation in question, represents the immediate, more personal, contextual history. Pedler (Chapter 12) explores the notion of organizational biography, relating it to issues of organizational ecology, the 'unit' of learning (what is the entity that learns), and the possibility of commonality of phases in the biographies of organi-zations (which may themselves be absolute, or tending to standardization only within particular eras or macro economic, nation state, cultural/social con-figurations). Pedler (Chapter 12) goes on to explore this way of thinking in the context of a specific organizational biography case study, which also begins to suggest ways in which these ideas might be used in an active sense by those whose concern it is to help organizations and those who travel (live out part of their biographies?) in them.

In our earlier work on the learning company[1] we described it, on the basis of our research, in two different ways: first, in terms of eleven characteristics which seemed to be associated with organizational practices of learning; and secondly, in terms of a model of the process which we thought, as we tried to look behind these characteristics, was key to the organizational learning process.

The eleven characteristics were:

1.   a learning approach to strategy;
2.   a high level of participation in policy making by organizational members and stakeholders;

3. use of information technology for sharing knowledge and mutual awareness;
4. accounting and control processes which give feedback helpful to understanding the effects of action, to learning and decision making;
5. internal 'customer/client' relationships feeding mutual adjustment and adaptation;
6. reward systems consistent with an employment philosophy which included the incentivization of learning;
7. forms of structure which both enabled learning and could shift, adapt and accommodate change resulting from it;
8. boundary workers—people working at the formal boundaries of the organization, collecting and passing in 'environmental' information, involving external stakeholders in improving organizational processes;
9. willingness and ability to learn with and from other organizations and companies;
10. a culture and climate which encourage responsible experimentation and shared learning from successes and failures;
11. mechanisms and employee relationships which encourage and support self-development.

Behind these eleven characteristics, we suggested, lies a process linking company policy making, company operations, individual thinking and individual action in a process of flowing ideas and information that allows directed purposeful mutual action which is coherent, flexible, involving all of the people concerned—see Figure 1.1.

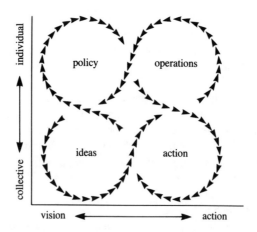

Figure 1.1   Individual/collective/action

Our proposition was and is that all of these four activities need to be *balanced*, i.e. present in reasonable proportions (no one or pair dominating or atrophied), and *interacting*, i.e. each activity influencing the others. Taken as pairs, the activities which may be crucial to balanced company learning and functioning are:

1. individual thought and action = *individual learning*;
2. alignment of collective operations and individual action = *managing*;
3. aligning policy and operations = *directing* (and where the two inform each other this is collective learning, a learning approach to strategy);
4. relating individual ideas to collective plans = *participation*.

The Applications section of this book deals with attempts to change or interpret organizations as learning companies either directly, using these ideas, or using methods that can be interpreted in these terms. In addition, Alan Phillips (Chapter 8) explores the culture, climate and structural issue of the 'space' for learning. Chris Blantern and John Belcher (Chapter 9) consider in depth the issue of participation. The question of whether participation can be anything other than token, or truly give weight to all stakeholders' interests, or how this is likely to be contained and constrained by existing power configurations, opens up a critical perspective on the Learning Company concept explored by John Coopey (Chapter 4). Much of the apparently humanistically informed practice of human resource development work in the past, which has championed 'participative' approaches, can be interpreted as giving organizational members the illusion of participation, freedom and involvement while actually subjecting them to a more subtle form of control. Whether this is or will be the fate of the Learning Company concept is an important question to be considered.

We call our core model of the Learning Company (Figure 1.1) the 'energy flow' model. This seems appropriate because it must be an energizing force rather than cold data that flows between ideas, policy, operations and action to animate the company. What energy means, however, is not entirely clear, and several of the contributions to this book address this problem, particularly Rooke and Keeley (Chapter 10) and Tosey (Chapter 6). The question of organizational energy, its source, nature and intrinsic direction (if any) may be the next frontier, a question to which we can collectively learn the answer, through and beyond this book.

References

1. Pedler, M., J. G. Burgoyne and T. Boydell (1991) *The Learning Company: A Strategy for Sustainable Development*, McGraw-Hill, London.
2. Kelly, G. A. (1955) *The Psychology of Personal Constructs*, Norton, New York.
3. Fox, S. and G. Moult (eds) (1990) 'Post modern culture and management development', *Management Education and Development* **21** (3).

4. Peters, T. J. and R. H. Waterman (1982) *In Search of Excellence*, Harper and Row, New York.
5. Deming, W. E. (1986) *Out of the Crisis*, Cambridge University Press, Cambridge.
6. Senge, P. (1990) *The Fifth Discipline, The Art and Practice of the Learning Organisation*, Doubleday, New York.
7. Garratt, R. (1987) *The Learning Organisation*, Fontana/Collins, London.
8. March, J. G. and J. P. Olsen (1976) 'Organizational learning and the ambiguity of the past', in: March, J. G. and J. P. Olsen (eds) *Ambiguity and Choice in Organisations,* pp. 54–68, Universitetsforlaget, Bergen, Norway.
9. Atkinson, J. (1984) 'Manpower strategies for flexible organizations', *Personnel Management*, August, 28–31.

Part I: Ideas and issues

2
The changing view of learning
Peter Hawkins

Introduction

There is a change at the heart of our understanding of learning. A shift from viewing learning as being abrupt facts to learning as a far more multi-faceted and dynamic process.

We are beginning to learn more about how we really learn. It's not that we, as humans, actually learn differently now than before, but that our understanding of how we learn has begun to catch up with what happens in practice.

No longer is learning being seen as something that happens to children or the ignorant in classrooms. Learning is a process that permeates not only all of our individual lives but can also be seen as a process which is critical for the lives of teams, organizations and communities.

This chapter describes some of the important shifts in our thinking about learning and explores implications for organizations.

The final section looks at some tentative ways of integrating the various shifts in learning—not in any attempt to provide a final model of learning, but as further exploration about the heart of learning itself. I would like to acknowledge the contribution of John Chesney in writing this section.

From learning facts to learning being dialogical

Traditional learning was seen as 'knowledge banking',[1] where learning was storing information, which could be measured by exams. In this view of learning there is a learner and an objective world that is learned about through breaking down the world into digestible facts.

Most of us were taught about how the Battle of Hastings took place in 1066, and as children we imagine that this is one of those objective truths. Yet the people who were involved in the event did not think 'We are now fighting the Battle of Hastings of 1066'. Some of Harold's men were probably exhausted at the end of a long campaign and saw this as another bloody engagement. The Normans probably saw it simply as the day they invaded England. What we are actually learning about is a cluster of events, which at some later date a historian has called the Battle of Hastings and which has been dated by means of the Gregorian calendar as 1066. We are not learning a fact, but our learning is part of a relationship between a series of events, how these have been labelled and framed by past historians and our own perspectives. The learning resides in the relationship, not in the label, which is a shorthand for exchange within the relationship. The history of a period changes over time, not because the events that took place in the past change, but because the way they are perceived and understood changes, as historians always see history through the lens of their own perspective which is shaped by their own present history. Thus history can be viewed as not residing in the past events, nor just in the heads of the historians, but in the three-way relationship between the events, previous historians and present historians.

How does this dialogical perspective change how we work with organizations? A good example is team development, where team learning was seen as an internal aspect of the team's functioning. Some organizations would take their teams off by themselves for 'wood meetings' or 'away-days', for the team to explore their process and learn how to function better. These events can still be useful, but taking a dialogical perspective it can be seen that the learning of the team does not just reside within the team, but also in the relationships of the team to those stakeholders, customers, suppliers, etc., with whom their work is inextricably linked. Thus, to change the team without facilitating learning on its boundary, between the team and its significant others, is like trying to change a marriage by only working with one partner.

From learners as recipients to learning being a co-creative process

I invite you to stop reading and do a short exercise. I would like you to look at your left hand and write down exactly what you see. Now you can compare your observations with those of others with whom I have tried the exercise:

'Five fingers, a palm and a wrist.'
'Lots of lines.'
'I see ageing and wrinkled skin.'
'I see three rings.'
'I see nails that need cutting.'

Each of these statements probably tells you more about the personality of the person observing than they do about the nature of hands, for much of what we see is a projection of our current concerns, be it about ageing, adornment, how we are seen, etc. What we see is also created by our expectations and the way we have been trained to look. Bateson[6] has long argued that we are trained to see separate objects, like five fingers, and not to see pattern and relationship. Very few people who do this exercise observe the relationship between the eye looking and the hand moving into a position where it can be seen at the right distance from the eyes, opening itself up for inspection, turning around, etc.

Others will project their own feelings upon the object, such as I see ageing, or tiredness. What we see is co-created by our looking. There is the story of the tribe who believed that the world ended a mile beyond their village. When taken to this boundary and shown the world beyond, the villagers said: 'But there is nothing there.' We see what our belief system trains us to see.

Thus it is important that organizational learning is seen as a reflexive process. I am not just learning about the world out there, but also about my own way of construing the world, which co-creates the reality in which I live. This has implications for personal learning in organizations and for how the whole organization learns.

The redundancy stores

A manager in an action-learning set had recently been given the task of reorganizing the redundancy stores of an aircraft manufacturer. He described visiting this large aircraft hangar which was a veritable museum of parts of aeroplanes, going back over forty years, which had been rejected as unserviceable and sent down to the redundancy store. He wanted help in strategically redesigning this store so that parts were properly catalogued and located, and the man-hours in storing and reaccessing parts could be made far more efficient.

The group eagerly engaged on this issue with him and began to chart up an Ishikawa fish of the problems presented and brain-storming possible solutions. It was only when the set facilitator stopped them and asked them about the purpose of the store that the learning went in a new direction.

The manager explained the process of how parts arrived at the point of aircraft assembly and those that are damaged or incorrect are labelled 'redundant' and assigned to the store, to be kept there in case bits of them can be used later or the part as a whole can be reserviced to make it useful. The 'set' began to turn its attention away from the product problem and to explore and chart the process. The eventual solution was to aim to dispense with a redundancy store altogether, by a process which ensured that parts that were not usable at assembly were either immediately redirected, to be corrected by the parts production division, with clear information of what needed amending and by when; or labelled, sold and removed from the site as scrap.

The managers had to learn about how they were co-creating the problem by the way they were framing it, and how to switch from trying to reorder a specific place or unit, to understanding how the problem was an assumption of the wider process.

Organizations also co-create their own reality. This has been written about by Morgan in applying the ideas of Maturana and Varela on 'Autopoesis' to organizations. He illustrates how we are affected not just by changes in the environment, but by our way of construing the environment.[2]

From seeing learning as residing in individuals to understanding that it also resides in systemic patterns

You may have had the experience of returning to your family of origin many years after leaving home. Each member of the family may have greatly changed and hopefully matured since the time you all lived together, and their ways of relating are now very different. However, gradually, as the reunited family spends time together, it gradually slides back into old ways of relating: teasing each other, indirect put-downs, arguing intensely about issues that you are not really concerned about. Each member of the family may dislike the fact that this is happening and wish that they were relating more from how they are now in the rest of their lives. But each feels as if he or she is being sucked into a vortex of old patterns of relating, and may well blame the others for causing this. This process is dramatically portrayed by T. S. Eliot in *The Family Reunion* and also by J. B. Priestley in *Time and the Conways*.

One way to understand this phenomenon is to realize that each member of the family may have learned and developed, but the family system itself is at the same stage of learning that it was previously in ten years or more ago. The relationship pattern of the family has not evolved and is strong enough to pull the individual back under its influence.

When I worked as a psychotherapist and met with couples, I learnt that the number of clients I had to attend to had not just doubled, but trebled. Instead of working with the psyche of an individual, I was dealing with two individuals and a third client, which was their relationship or couple system—the psyche of the system that they had both created, but which also constrained them. Their couple system, like that of the family, may be partly created by its members, but it also constantly affects not only the behaviour, but also the perceptions and the emotional flow of feelings that happen within its orbit.

The family or couple system has no material form. It cannot be seen or touched, but we can witness its effects. It will be reflected in the material artefacts of the couple: the decoration of their home, their car, garden, clothes, etc. It can be seen mirrored in the rituals of how they divide up money, allocate tasks, entertain others, and in their private verbal and non-verbal language. It is also represented in the stories they tell and in how they construct their private history.

But the couple system does not reside in these artefacts, rituals or stories. Nor does it reside in the individuals. It can be considered as a force-field which surrounds and flows through the individuals who both create it and reside within it.

This collective psychic field is similar to Rupert Sheldrake's notion of 'the morphogenetic field'[3,4,5] and also Bateson's 'circuits of mind'[6,7]. Sheldrake was by no means the first scientist to use the term and describe the nature of morpho-genetic fields, for since 1923 work on these fields has been produced by such scientists as Weiss, Waddington and Thom. However, his major contribution has been in exploring how these fields are not eternal transcendent entities, but immanent evolving entities. Not, for example, eternal scientific laws that transcend time, but entities that evolve and therefore learn in their own right. This has been formulated by Sheldrake in his theory of 'formative causation'.

These psychic fields have no known material form, but they have a pattern and rhythm, which constrain and influence the patterns and rhythms of behaviour, thought, perception and feeling of those within their orbit.

The psychic fields are co-created by the members within the field, although clearly some have more influence than others, such as parents in relation to children. But the fields are not just created by those within its realm: they will be directly influenced by the patterns of families and couples in the social peer group. These social norms exist in a higher psychic field of the cultural norms concern-ing families and couples which is carried in the stories, films, unwritten rules, written laws and rituals of the culture. These in turn exist in an archetypal field, for cultural patterns are acted upon by the archetypal patterns of the family, the couple, mother, father, child, etc.[8,9,10]

This systemic perspective radically shifts the perspective of the organizational change agent. Instead of focusing on the parts of the organization, they start to focus on the patterns that connect the parts: the interfaces, relationships and contacts between individuals, teams, departments and between the whole organi-zation and those with whom it relates.

This perspective requires a new language, a language which is more analogic, metaphorical and stems from the right brain, rather than the scientific defining of parts that stems from the digital thinking of the left brain. It focuses on the wave-like connections that flow throughout the whole organizational processes, rather than on the functioning of the parts.

From learning is linear to learning is cyclical

Old concepts of learning were often one-dimensional: I would meet a problem I could not solve or something I did not know and through learning I would acquire the knowledge or skill necessary for my needs or to solve the problem. Learning is seen as an acquisition to meet a felt or recognized deficiency.

Unfortunately, or fortunately, learning is not that straightforward and is often a complex process of continual trial and error. Learning is an ever-present element in all we do, woven into the very fabric of action. Stop reading and take up a pencil and place the pencil point on the dot beneath as if you are about to write.

If we now slowed down the process of what you just did onto a slow motion film, you would discover that the journey of the pencil point was not in a straight line aiming for its target, but that you were creating a zig-zag path as you constantly corrected your trajectory from going off course, a bit like a sailboat tacking against the wind, or a heat-seeking missile. You hopefully got to the right place, but you got there not by aiming for it, but by avoiding going to the wrong place. You were constantly learning all the way down.

It is as if you are relearning the simple art of placing a pencil on a specific point every time you start to write. Bateson[11], Kolb[12], Revans[13] and many others have shown how learning is a constant process of moving around the cycle:

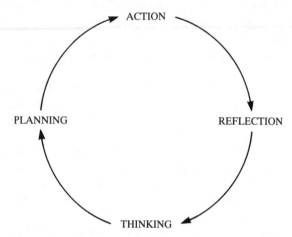

Sometimes people talk as if they are engaged in a cyclical process because they go through all four stages, but what they have followed is a linear process with the ends joined up. This is particularly relevant in the design of training and development in organizations. Often such design still creates a split between doing 'on the job', and thinking in the lecture room or at the training workshop. Even some of the better designed training events, involving a short sandwich course with an action learning project back at work between parts one and two of the course, only achieve one cycle of the learning process. In my forthcoming book *AQ*, I look more fully at how training can be designed to create a process of multiple learning cycles so that participants are moving around the cycle both during the training event and back in the workplace. This enables action to become a key part of training and reflection, thinking and planning become key in action 'on the job'.

From all learning is of the same level to double-loop learning

If the concept of cyclical learning shifts our understanding of learning from one dimension to two, then the notion that there are different levels of learning moves us on to a three-dimensional model. It was Bateson, in his classic paper of 1964[14] in which he used the theory of logical types of Whitehead and Russell[15] to explore different types of learning, who most forcibly showed how all learning is not of the same level. This was taken up by organizational theorists, most notably Argyris and Schon,[16] in their theory of single-loop and double-loop learning, and more recently by Garratt in his two books on the learning organization.

Bateson chose to see learning in an evolutionary context and define it as a process that led to change in the learning organism. Thus the receipt of facts may lead to learning, but is not learning in itself, and thus he termed it 'zero learning'.

Learning Level I

This is the area of skill learning, as described in the cyclical learning section above. It is about making choices within a simple set of alternatives, and is the basis of Argyris's single-loop learning and Garratt's operational cycle learning.

Learning Level II

This happens when we move the level of learning to that of choosing between sets within which Level I learning takes place. This, in conjunction with Level I learning, is Argyris's double-loop learning and Garratt's strategy cycle learning.

Argyris's distinction between single-loop and double-loop learning is based on Bateson's seminal work. He combined Bateson's notion of levels with the principle of learning being cyclical to produce his theory of single-loop and double-loop learning.

Garratt's[17] development of the Argyris theory represents the double loop of organizational learning in a very useful and simple model, which I colloquially refer to as Garratt's egg-timer (see Figure 2.1).

In this model operational learning (Argyris's single loop) begins with a plan, which, like all plans, never turns out quite as you expect it to. The deviations from the intended results are monitored and learnt from and the plan is redrawn and freshly implemented. So it continues, the stochastic cycle of trial, error, correction and retrial. But in this cycle one only learns to carry out the initial plan in a better way. There is no room for questioning the plan itself. One is constantly focusing on *how* to carry out the operation more efficiently, never on whether one is carrying out the right operation.

Sooner or later any organization needs to move into the strategic learning cycle, where the focus moves from efficiency to effectiveness and from the *how* to the *what*. In operational learning the focus is on how to do things more quickly and how to ensure a closer alignment of what is produced with what was planned. In the strategic learning cycle the focus shifts to whether we are heading in the right direction at the moment. The strategic cycle involves reflecting on operational performance and relating that performance to the requirements of the changing external environment. This includes changes in customer needs, the supply chain, the law, health and safety and public attitudes and preferences.

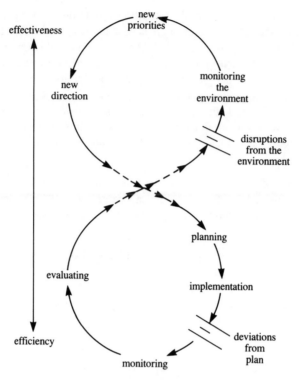

Figure 2.1   Integrating operational and policy learning

By focusing on the alignment between the external environment and the internal organizational processes, organizational leaders can develop new visions, directions and priorities. These new approaches then need to be processed back through the next operational cycle. Double-loop learning only occurs when both the operational and strategic cycle are involved. Working at the strategic level alone, without looping the learning back into one operational cycle, is single-loop learning at the strategic level. Similarly, working at the operational level alone without looking to see whether the current operations are still of value in the environment, is single-loop learning at the operational level.

I find this model particularly useful in the way it pictorially represents the stress in the middle of the organization. The business brain in the Garratt model is not at the head of the organization, but at the heart; it is not carried by the directors, but by the people who need to straddle the domains of strategy and operations. These are the people who are the life-blood of the learning organization; the people who need to be effective at educating upwards as well as translating new vision and direction into operational reality.

Unfortunately, this critical area is absent in many organizations. In one large manufacturing company where I am acting as consultant, the middle managers do not 'educate upwards', but merely pass operational problems up the line; the senior managers usually fail to give time to strategic thinking as they are constantly 'descending' to manage the single-loop operational cycle.

In another leading organization, this time in computing, there is initially a very impressive picture of a great deal of learning. Much time and resources are given to learning at all levels. Many project groups are exploring new strategic approaches to organizing the business, and they are constantly engaging in future scenario scanning, attempting to keep one step ahead of the game.

In terms of Pedler's, Burgoyne's and Boydell's[18] definition of the learning organization, I might conclude that here is a true learning company, for it is indeed one which actively promotes the continual learning and development of all its members, and also attends to trying to transform itself.

However, looking a little closer we find that there are important flaws. First, there is little harvesting of the learning of individuals back at work. Managers go on many personal and skills development courses, but their learning often stays within them and is not networked back into their teams, divisions and organization. They may achieve many new insights on the culture of the organization when they attend a course, but these insights are not feeding back into the two separate projects, one internal and the other external, that are looking at the organizational culture.

This leads me on to the second problem. There are a myriad of strategic project groups, all of which constantly redesign aspects of the organization, without there being either a structure for these strategy groups to dialogue and co-create the new organization together, or an over-arching vision that holds together the diversity of these endeavours.

The greatest danger lies not in the lack of integration within the operational learning or strategic learning loops, but in the lack of the 'business brain' that integrates the two cycles. Without this linkage the most likely outcome is that there will be single-loop learning within both domains.

A similar phenomenon of the strategy domain and the operational domain working effectively within themselves but in isolation from each other was found by my colleagues Adrian McLean and Judi Marshall in their study of the Wrekin District Council.[19] Here was a local government organization that was clearly one of the most progressive and forward-looking in the country. It had a visionary chief executive, was interested in getting close to the customer, in quality and in constant self-improvement. Yet:

A concern expressed most frequently by those in the middle of the organisation is that the Chief Executive and his team of Directors form an elite that is separated from middle level management by a sort of vacuum. The fear, in the form of speculation, is that the team may be prone to a form of 'group think'.

I worked briefly with a police authority who wished to develop themselves as a learning organization. The first step in moving forward was to be to bring together the internal management development team and the organizational development team and help them develop a joint understanding of their interlocking task.

From double-loop to transformational learning

This dimension of learning in the individual, group or whole organization transcends the level of skill acquisition and operational learning (Argyris's single loop) and personal development and strategic learning (Argyris's 'double' loop). This is the level of spiritual development in the individual and of purpose and service in the organization. I have previously written about this level[20,21] based on the explication of Bateson's learning level III.

Double-loop learning helps us move from asking operational efficiency questions such as: 'How can we carry out this process more efficiently?', to asking strategic questions about effectiveness: 'What should we be concentrating our efforts on to be most effective?', or 'Where is our competitive advantage?'

Treble-loop learning takes us even further and poses teleological questions about purpose: 'To what end or for what purpose are we doing this work?', or, 'Who or what are we serving in this endeavour?' Transformative learning is about aligning the operational, strategic and service levels of learning. Greater efficiency without effective strategy can become self-defeating, as it might be achieving greater productivity of goods no longer needed; better strategic effectiveness which is divorced from higher purpose may be effective at winning competitive advantage in the short term, but will lose its reason for being and in time will become an alienated organization, making money but with no sense of relatedness and of doing something worthwhile.

In this dimension of learning on the individual level it is necessary to move into exploring the fundamental perspectives through which we view the world and the paradigms which shape our understanding. Level III learning is not just about personal insight and reframing our experience, but involves a fundamental 'metanoia', a turning around of where we look from, a shaking of the foundations of our beliefs and perspectives.

At the organizational level it involves change in the collective mind-sets of the organization's culture and the emotional ground in which these are rooted. In Bath Consultancy Group, through which I do my consulting, one of the main areas in which we have applied learning organization approaches is that of facilitating change in organizational culture. Many of the companies we have worked with had jumped on the 'excellence' bandwagon and had tried to keep up-to-date by changing their culture. They had invested in new logos, published glossy mission statements and had their leaders make fervent exhortations to the workers about quality, customer care and new attitudes.

On some occasions we have been invited in when the senior management were wondering why this approach had not produced the hoped-for change in performance and instead had given rise to increasing cynicism and suspicion among the workforce, with glossy mission statements ending up in the waste bin.

The approach we have used to help them reflect on and learn from this experience has been to show how their culture change was at the level of changing the high-profile symbols of the culture, the cultural artefacts, rituals and ceremony, while leaving the low-profile symbols of everyday 'lived' behaviour untouched. This inevitably widens the rift between the rhetoric and the reality and creates a breeding ground for cynicism.

These two levels correspond with zero learning and learning level I, for in changing the outward face of the culture there is no real learning. Real learning only begins when the leaders of the company change not what they preach, but what they do; when, in Argyris's terms, there is a change not just in the 'espoused theory', but in the 'theory in action'.

In running culture change workshops we found that even when senior managers made real commitments to a shift in the organizational culture and also in their own behaviour—in how they carried out the culture—some of the changes were short-lived. For a while managers would be managing by walking about, rewarding positive behaviours, speaking with images and vision and not just facts; but soon the old culture would begin to reassert itself, despite good intentions.

We discovered that it was important in culture change work to help those within the organizational culture step outside their normal perception and assumptions and view their organization with fresh eyes. The work required a change in their mind-sets, their personal and collective way of viewing what is around them, so that they could once again see aspects of their culture that they no longer noticed. An old Chinese proverb points out that 'the last person to know about the sea is the fish'.

This required us to develop a new range of learning methodologies[22] to help those in organizations to become flying fish, to step outside their taken-for-granted ways of viewing reality and see their organization with new eyes. By so doing they discover the spectacles they were previously using.

We also discovered that even attending to the collective 'mind-sets' was not enough, for these mind-sets were not something that one could take out and replace at will. They were firmly rooted in the emotional and motivational ground of the organization. Without attending to this underlying emotional ground, mind-sets would only be tinkered with, not transformed.

I worked with a large aircraft manufacturer where most of the staff, from senior managers to shop-floor fitters, had grown up reading 'Biggles' books and making 'Airfix' aircraft models. They were in love with planes and with building them. The particular site where we worked had shifted from building supersonic 'high-tech' aeroplanes to being an assembly plant putting together bits of aeroplanes. We were there to help the organization change its culture to become much more commercially orientated, but the emotional ground of the company was still in mourning for the beautiful aeroplanes it used to build. Without working through this mourning process and helping the organization find a new fundamental purpose, any attempts to change the culture were going to run aground on deep-seated emotional resistance.

From learning as utilitarian and value-free to learning with an ethical dimension

Learning takes place in a network of interconnection. In the third dimension I explored how seeing learning as systemic involved working with the learning of a team and organization in relation to its key stakeholders, its suppliers, customers, shareholders, competitors, etc. In this dimension it is necessary to take the systemic interconnectedness much further and see that the learning of an organization is related to and part of its aesthetic and ecological environment. How we learn impacts on our environment, and our environment pervades every aspect of our work.

Transformative learning cannot be value-free, for how we see and construe the world affects how we live and relate to our surroundings. If we see the world as a limitless store of resources to be exploited we will act exploitatively. If we perceive animals as having no feelings we will relate to them unfeelingly.

Once we move from instrumental learning to transformative learning, then we have to consider the ethical dimension, which asks to what purpose or end are we learning and how does our purpose disturb the aesthetic and ecological balance of the environment in which it happens? Is the disturbance creative or destructive?

There are four dimensions of the ethical perspective that I use to help organizations explore this aspect of their learning organization. These are:

1. *Utilitarian*   Does it provide the greatest good to the greatest number? Does it meet the needs of the customers?
2. *Aesthetic*   Is it pleasing to the senses and does it provide an increase in beauty and harmony to the world in which it resides?
3. *Ecological*   Does it use resources (energy, material and human) in a way that is sustainable and renewable? How do we become aware of it and limit the damage caused?
4. *Spiritual*   Does it serve a higher purpose and contribute to the universal good?

From learning being for kids to learning being a lifelong but discontinuous process

Lifelong learning has become a necessity.[23]

If we are not learning and teaching we are not awake and alive. Learning is not only like health, it is health.[24]

Earlier in this chapter I commented on the now outdated notions that learning was something that happened prior to doing; that learning was for children before they entered the grown-up world and that only the ignorant needed to learn. This reminds me of my cousin who, when younger, said that he did not need a bath, for only dirty people washed!

As fast as we learn so our ignorance increases too, for the more we know the more we become aware of how much more there is to learn. Moreover, any field of endeavour is changing and developing at such a rate that it is easy to find that as your own learning stands still the whole world is changing around you and that you are unable to do the work that your changing job now requires.

Success is often a time of great danger, when the individual or organization thinks that it now knows how to perform and is confirmed in its perceptions of the world. This leads to complacency and less emphasis on learning. Being cited by Peters and Waterman as an 'excellent company' was probably to be cursed, for as the research showed,[25] many of those 'excellent companies' started to go downhill.

As I have previously emphasized, learning is not just adaptive to external circumstances, but also creates the circumstances that constrain it. In my doctoral research[26] I discovered that personal learning and development was often at its most intense at times of transformation. At work many people described their learning as being the most intense when they first joined the team, or when they were promoted and had a whole new range of relationships and skills to contend with. When asked about important learning in their personal lives, many talked of times of personal transition or even times of crisis, such as leaving home, being made redundant, getting divorced, or suffering personal bereavement.

Life transitions often take away our comfortable set patterns of acting and perceiving, our set ways of coping with the world. They provide the disconfirmation that initiates a new cycle of learning. To put it another way, crisis creates the heat in which new learning is forged. I have elsewhere developed a model of short-term counselling that has been used in work-placed counselling services, for helping individuals focus on the life transitions they are currently engaged in and how these are being affected by unfinished issues from previous life transitions.[27]

Life transitions are also key foci of learning in teams and organizations. Pedler *et al.*[28] provide a very useful system for helping organizations look at their 'company biography', the life transitions and the key learnings at each stage.

From learning being a means to an end to learning being at the heart of all we do

Many of us were brought up in school to see learning as a means of passing exams.

Some of the excited interest about the learning organization means learning as providing 'the leverage for competitive advantage'. Learning becomes viewed as always a means to an end.

However, it is also possible to reverse this perspective. Exams exist in order to focus and increase learning. True competition is not about winning, but about the engagement between both parties creating an atmosphere in which both learn to perform at a higher level than would be possible without competition. It is possible to see how, in our Western culture, many activities that were originally routes to learning have become ends in themselves.

There is an old Sufi story about creation, which states that God was complete unto itself and knew itself completely in its own 'oneness' or 'ipseity'. However, it did not know itself in its form of particularization or fragmentation. 'I was a hidden treasure and I longed to be known.' Thus God embarked on creation as a way of learning about itself through its fragmented and particularized self. The hunger for learning was at the core of creation.

In order to complete the cycle of creation, God needed an aspect of creation to know God not just in its own aspect, in the way a blade of grass knows the blade of grassness of God. The story tells how God offered this covenant to the mountains and the mountains refused. He offered it to the birds of the air and the birds refused. He offered it to the animals and they too refused. Finally he offered it to humans and they, in their foolishness, accepted the covenant.

This covenant which is both a blessing and a curse gives us the ability and responsibility to be self-reflective and self-aware. All aspects of creation are part of the evolutionary learning process. Some species may also learn how to learn, sometimes referred to as 'deutoro learning'. But for us as humans, learning and constantly attempting to improve the quality of this learning is a central responsibility of our lives.

As learning resides not just within us, but in circuits of mind of which we are part, so our responsibility is to constantly attend to improving the learning of the worlds in which we exist.

The motto of my children's junior school was 'learning to live'. In the new learning epistemology we must equally focus on 'living to learn', to see living and learning as inseparable processes.

Integrating the new thinking on learning

In this chapter we have noted a shift in thinking about learning:

From	To
1. learning facts	being dialogical
2. learners as recipients	being co-creative

3. learning resides in individuals	also residing in systemic patterns
4. learning is a linear process	being cyclical
5. all learning is of the same level	integrated loops
6. learning to be efficient and effective	transformational learning
7. learning is utilitarian and value-free	having ethical dimensions
8. learning is for 'kids' and beginners	a lifelong, but discontinuous process
9. learning is a means to an end	at the heart of everything

As we assimilate the new thinking it can help us to spot our current assumptions about learning and help us to open up to different perspectives and focuses for further exploration. We can double-loop our learning about our current learning operations and strategy to see how new shifts in our thinking may warrant shifts in what we do in practice.

It is also possible to begin to play with putting some of these factors together. What might it be like to be involved in dialogical double-loop learning within a functional system in an organization? What would be the result of running several cycles of co-creative action learning within a department? The permutations are many.

It would, of course, be premature and dangerous to offer an overall synthesis of the new thinking that trapped the further expansion of our thinking within the confines of some grand meta-model. However, it can also be constructive to engage in creative cartography—playing with possible schematic maps rather than searching for 'the Holy Grail'.

One such model comes from a colleague in the Bath Consultancy Group which I offer as an illustrative example, to encourage you to play with your own maps (Figure 2.2).

What the model suggests and offers
1.   It may be helpful to use this tentative map as a way of locating current styles of learning within organizations to see what the next step forward might be. For example, we were recently invited to give a workshop on change management to a public sector organization. They were looking for a one-off event run for middle managers aimed at informing them about change management practice. At the same time, the organization, a district council, were using consultants to help them think through ways of becoming more proactive as an organization. We were informed that they did not want to have any flow of ideas or new learning from the

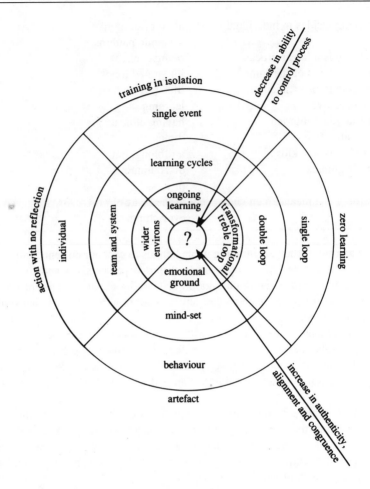

Figure 2.2   Learning circles

policy group to the workshop on change management, or vice versa. Locating this proposal on the map (Figure 2.2) suggests that this was aimed at individuals as a single event and would most likely lead to zero learning, as no follow-up or action was envisaged from the training. Further discussions implied that the main focus for the organization was at the level of changing artefacts rather than behaviour. Their attention appeared to be focused on demonstrating that they were a proactive district council, through events such as the workshop, rather than by exploring the lived reality of employees' working experience.

Referring back to the model then, this would place the suggested event at the perimeter. The map suggests possible ways forward, through spiralling in towards

ncouraging cycles of learning, involving functional teams and
nt behaviour. The model suggests that it would have been too
to have gone from the perimeter into the centre in one quick
iralling-in may be more possible and helpful.

of learning moves towards the centre, two factors come into play,
e. First, the momentum for change moves from being mainly
sultants) to being mainly internal (i.e. employees at all levels).
in which you know that change has really taken hold when you
ontrol of what happens next. In some ways it is a similar process
car. Once the engine fires up, it takes over in a way that no
l 'pushing' could achieve. Secondly, as learning nears the centre,
e in the alignment between what is espoused and what is enacted,
ppen and what happens in people's experience. As the learning
national and in tune with individual and organizational purpose,
increased alignment between aspiration, vocation and actual
learning involves more and more of the people who have a
ship with the organization, there is an increased alignment, or
en different people, teams and departments.

to speculate from the model on some of the links in learning
approach. For example, it seems common sense to see double-loop learning as
benefiting from a learning cycle approach, so that the learning process goes round
the operational and strategic cycles more than once. It also makes sense to talk
about double-loop learning being associated with learning at the level of mind-
sets, since reviewing strategy often calls for a review of current perceptions and
assumptions. It also seems reasonable to think about this level of learning involving teams and functional systems, because reviewing which operations and strategies to pursue is likely to have an impact on a wide range of people within an
organization. You may care to look at some of the other links the model offers and,
equally importantly, some that it misses, for example transformational learning
with the individual.

4.   It is possible to map a schematic representation of a period of organizational
learning on the chart. This would most likely begin at the perimeter, concerned
with individual requests for development and policymaking about new structures
within the organization. To produce the possibility of a real and sustainable shift
in learning, the process would then need to spiral in towards the centre until clarity
was reached about the emotional ground that might otherwise resist further
change, and the implications of the new learning were seen in the context of the
organization's purpose and environmental setting. Then, most importantly, the
learning would need to begin to spiral out again, so that the impact of the full
learning was finally enacted in individuals and had a lasting impact on the artefacts
that echoed the new lived reality.

What the model does not do

1. It does not cover all the nine points outlined in this chapter; it is only a partial model.
2. It does not encourage the reader to view the myriad of relationships that may exist between the outlined factors, for example, the possible dialogical nature of work at the level of mind-set. In short, it is not a comprehensive overview, but an interesting example of one way of viewing the learning process. The fact that it has shortcomings is reassuring. It would be a contradiction in terms to pretend that we could give some inclusive and authoritative metamap of learning. Learning is, after all, ultimately a continuous journey of exploration. This journey is exciting and interesting and involves us all. You may like to contribute now by summing up your thinking from this chapter in your own way, using the space provided below. Whether it is by 'playful cartography' or some other form, I would invite you to continue your own double-looping of learning now.

References

1.   Freire, P. (1972) *Pedagogy of the Oppressed*, Penguin, London.
     Freire, P. (1972) *Cultural Action for Freedom*, Penguin, London.
2.   Morgan, G. (1986) *Images of Organisation*, Sage, California.
3.   Sheldrake, R. (1981) *A New Science of Life: The Hypothesis of Formative Causation*, Blond & Briggs, London.
4.   Sheldrake, R. (1988) *The Presence of the Past*, London, Fontana.
5.   Sheldrake, R. (1990) *The Rebirth of Nature*, Rider, London.
6.   Bateson, G. (1979) *Mind and Nature*, Dutton, New York.
7.   Bateson, G. and M. C. Bateson (1988) *Angels Fear*, Century Hutchinson, London.
8.   Hillman, J. (1973) 'The Great Mother, her Son, her Hero, and the Puer', in P. Berry (ed.) *Fathers and Mothers*, Spring, Dallas.
9.   Hillman, J. (1979) *Puer Papers*, Spring, Dallas.
10. Hillman, J. (1983) *Archetypal Psychology: a Brief Account*, Spring, Dallas.
11. Bateson, G. (1979) *Mind and Nature*, Dutton, New York.
12. Kolb, D. A. (1984) *Experiential Learning*, Prentice-Hall, New Jersey.
13. Revans, R. (1982) *The Origins and Growth of Action Learning*, Chartwell-Bratt, Bromley and Lund.
14. Bateson, G. (1973) *Steps to an Ecology of Mind*, Paladin, London.
15. Whitehead, A. N. and B. Russell (1910) *Principia Mathematica*, Cambridge University Press, London.
16. Argyris, C. and D. Schon (1974) *Theory in Practice*, Jossey Bass, San Francisco.
17. Garratt, B. (1987) *The Learning Organisation*, Fontana/Collins, London.

18. Pedler, M., J. Burgoyne and T. Boydell (1991) *The Learning Company*, McGraw-Hill, Maidenhead.

19. McLean, A. and J. Marshall (1989) *The Wrekin District Council: a Cultural Portrait*, Local Government Training Board, Luton.

20. Hawkins, P. (1986) *Living The Learning*, PhD thesis, University of Bath.

21. Hawkins, P. (1991) 'The spiritual dimension of the learning organisation'. *Management Education and Development*, **22** (3), 166–81.

22. George, M., P. Hawkins and A. McLean (1988) *Organisational Culture Manual*, Bath Associates, 6, Vane Street, Bath.

23. Smith, R. M. (1983) *Learning How to Learn*, Open University Press, Milton Keynes.

24. Ferguson, M. (1981) *The Aquarian Conspiracy*, Routledge and Kegan Paul, London.

25. Pascale, R. (1991) *Managing on the Edge*, Penguin, London.

26. Hawkins, P. (1986) *Living the Learning*, PhD thesis, University of Bath.

27. Hawkins, P. (1992) *A Humanistic and Integrative Model of Short Term Counselling*, a Bath Centre for Psychotherapy and Counselling Working Paper, 1, Walcot Terrace, London Road, Bath.

28. Pedler, M., J. Burgoyne and T. Boydell (1991) *The Learning Company*, McGraw-Hill, Maidenhead.

3
Organizations, values and learning
Peter Binns

Introduction

An assumption which will be familiar to readers of this book goes as follows. Learning, openness, flexibility and proactivity are said to be 'good' things, and are seen as likely to be even better things in the future for individuals and organizations, because in conditions of accelerating change the ability to respond positively to these changes is likely to become the most important—or one of the most important—assets that people and organizations possess. While there is obviously a sound kernel of truth here, there are also a number of problems which arise when attempts are made to articulate and clarify the conceptions of learning and organizational development that are implied by it.

One problem concerns the identification of environmental adaptation—as implied by the notions of 'flexibility' and 'openness'—with learning. It is by no means clear that such an identification should be made; if we look at organisms in nature, for example, we find that environmental adaptation is only a part of the story. All organisms are characterized, rather, by a two-way process in which their accommodation to the environment takes place within a context in which they are actively assimilating the environment to themselves, as Piaget[1] and Gibson,[2] in their different ways, have pointed out. Furthermore, the evolutionarily higher organisms are characterized by the fact that they tend to meet their needs more by adapting the environment to themselves rather than by adapting themselves to fit the environment (amoebas thus respond to dry conditions by adapting themselves into cyst-like forms, but human beings dig wells instead). Thus the higher the organism the more it organizes the environment rather than being organized by it—the more *autopoietic it* becomes in the terminology of Maturana and Varela.[3]

It begins to seem as though we might be looking in the wrong direction by thinking of learning primarily in terms of 'openness' and 'flexibility'; it seems to invite us to move from a higher to a lower level of the learning process, and this surely cannot be right. Learning processes imply processes of change, that much is clear. But what is it that changes, and how does it change? If our earlier reasoning is correct we will need to identify this autopoietic core of the organismic process which then acts in such a way that external change is compensated for rather than adapted to—thus ensuring that the core does not change, but rather becomes more deeply entrenched and immutable. This suggests that learning processes are to be differentiated from processes of mere change by the fact that within them the processes of change are subordinated to, and serve, the goal of preserving—not changing—the autopoeitic core. But what is this core? And how might an organization's core differ from that of a biological organism in general, or persons in particular?

Learning values

One suggestion might be to see this as a question of values. A person's most deeply held values might be thought of as defining what they most want to preserve as the central source of their acting and being in the world. The core values of a company might be seen as playing a comparable organizational role. On this view values become the fixed point around which changes can be organized and evaluated. It would follow that the failure to develop, or develop sufficiently, such a set of core values would lead to a loss of directedness and strategic coherence for the organism in question. The role of such valuational failures in precipitating organismic degeneration has been stressed in a number of recent books, including Drummond and Carmichael,[4] Deming,[5] Handy[6] and Peters[7]; the latter contending, most famously, that what distinguishes the successful company from the rest is the fact that it is 'value-driven'.

This metaphor of values being the source rather than the object of change is an interesting one. Taken literally, it would imply that values are in some sense or other what induces learning to take place rather than being a product of learning itself. It would suggest a linear, non-systemic relationship between valuational and non-valuational elements of the organizational process. In an important sense, values—or at least core values—could not be learned, because opening them up for learning would *ipso facto* remove the possibility of all learning taking place. But if these core values cannot be learned, if they are just given and not open to critical assessment, how could it be rational to assent to them in the first place? If individuals and organizations are just assigned certain values how can they then accept them and claim them as their own? If core values really do have such a degree of autonomy it is difficult to see how they could arise organically within the internal process of the person or organization in question.

Part of the problem derives from the way values have been characterized so far in this chapter and in most of the organizational literature on the subject. Core values have been depicted as moral principles and moral principles have been understood like the Mosaic law—chiselled in stone and unchanging, rather than being part of the complex flow of organismic life. We began this chapter by asking: (a) Are values to be assimilated to the autopoietic core of personal and organizational processes? We moved on to (b) If so, how might valuational processes develop, become learned and owned by persons and organizations? We now see that this too rests on a further question: (c) How are the valuational elements to be related to the non-valuational elements of the personal and organizational process? It is to this question that we now turn.

Values and desires

The non-valuational elements referred to above are various, but if we are looking at the question from a motivational point of view, the major alternative element that appears at first sight is desire; and certainly a central preoccupation of the Western tradition has been the relationship between values and desires. Two major and opposed philosophical traditions have emerged: naturalism and anti-naturalism, and both seem to contain significant elements of truth.

Anti-naturalism, as found in the broadly Protestant and Puritan tradition, and more exactly in the philosophy of Immanuel Kant, is concerned to build a Chinese wall between desire and what is morally right. Kant[8] gives an example of a shopkeeper who never attempts to cheat his customers; according to him the shopkeeper might have adopted this practice either (a) because it is not in his long-term business interest to cheat, or (b) because irrespective of (a) he is concerned to follow the call of duty. In the former case he is simply maximizing his long-run desires, while in the latter he is disregarding them in the name of a higher principle. The former case therefore has nothing to do with morality, which rather is confined to cases of the latter variety. For Kant this is not just an example of one choice versus another; rather, it is marked by a transition from one kind of being doing the choosing to another—from an animal-like organism driven by sensual forces to a rational agent assenting to the call of duty. Within us, therefore, there co-exist two selves, one akin to the animals and the other akin to the angels, and the drama of human existence is played out along the line of *opposition* between them. A full discussion of this viewpoint clearly goes beyond our present scope, but it does seem to present us with a problem that needs addressing: if morality (and therefore the language of values and valuation) is to make any sense it will have to establish for itself a field of operation which is not simply that of desire. But does this demand for a degree of autonomy for moral values imply the *opposition* between values and desires as Kant claims? Does it imply that they are quite different sorts of things, or can we make a valid distinction between a person's ordinary desires and their values without such an opposition?

The naturalist approach, at least as we find it in Aristotle,[9] seems at first sight to meet this latter requirement without creating such an opposition between desires and moral values. For Aristotle too makes morality into something different from the sorts of desires that, for instance, animals might have. The Aristotelian world is one in which there are virtues, and in which the moral learning and development of these virtues requires intelligence, training, instruction and habit. This in turn presupposes that while human beings are a part of nature, they have their own peculiar essence in nature as learning, thinking, contemplative beings, whose special excellence and life-purpose is only achieved to the extent that they are rational agents. Aristotle's point here is that it is only in so far as they become such agents that they can become fulfilled, happy, and thus have their most important desires satisfied anyway, so if morality seems to conflict with certain desires that would imply: (a) the desires in question must be of a lower or more animal variety, and (b) in relatively morally well developed persons, they must have a less powerful influence on the psyche than the desire to act from the virtues.

So Aristotle's answer to the problem about how it is possible to separate the 'moral' from the purely 'self-interested' shopkeeper, is not to deny any connection between them, as Kant does, but rather to try to show how self-interest itself becomes something moral as human beings learn and naturally develop from the more animal to the more personal. Flourishing individuals gain more excellence and pleasure for themselves, and as this at the same time develops their moral stature, others around them benefit as well. The virtues then turn out to be developed, or moderated, desires, rather than opposed to desire altogether.

This naturalist approach has much to commend it, but we are entitled to ask whether such a learning process, in which there is a transition from the pre-moral agent to the moral agent, can ever be viewed as a purely natural event. The learning that is implicit in moral growth seems to involve not so much a change in desires (and beliefs and actions), as the appearance of a different sort of desire, a desire that is not aimed towards external objects and events, but rather inwardly, towards the desires (and beliefs and actions) themselves, as a number of recent philosophers such as Frankfurt[10] and Nerlich[11] have pointed out. Kant's shopkeeper may therefore have both a primary desire to make more money and thus cheat his customer, and also a *secondary desire*, as he reflects on this state of affairs, to change, or at least hold in check, this primary desire. Such desires about my desires (and still higher order desires about my desires about my primary desires ... etc), seem to be a precondition for the learning that is implicit if moral growth is to be possible. If there were no such thing as higher order desires two consequences would follow:

1. All modification of desire (and belief and action) would have to be external and coercive rather than internal and rational; we would notice our desires changing, but we would not feel in charge of this process, and therefore we would have no reason for preferring, or valuing, the later set of desires as

better than the earlier one, or vice -versa. Desires would be *successive*, but not *progressive*.

2.   The corollary of this is that even if we recognized that changes in our desires were rationally necessary, unless we were able to call upon higher order desires to put this recognition into practice, we would never be able to act on them—the only motivators we would possess would be our primary set of externally directed desires. Moral thoughts might be possible, but not moral acts, nor indeed the learning process implied by the moral growth of individuals.

To possess primary desires, as we have mentioned already, we need no more than an agency reflecting our animal or sensual being. But in order to have a set of secondary desires which take the primary desires as the objects to be transformed, these desires have to be able to operate within an entirely new medium reflecting conceptual, linguistic and logical operations. The higher order desires are directed not towards external objects, as are the primary desires, but towards particular *facts* or *propositions*—for instance, if a drug abuser in a rehabilitation centre both desires the relief provided by the drug (primary desire) and wishes to end his desire for the drug (secondary desire), the latter desire is not for a concrete, sensorily defined object, but rather for a state of affairs which can only be articulated or understood through the conceptual medium of language: the desire is a desire *that* something should be the case. With primary desires I am *acquainted* with what it is that I want, but with secondary desires I *understand* what it is that I want.

This means that when people learn to develop higher order desires, this does not just add on a new kind of desire that can be possessed (given the appropriate conceptual/linguistic skills), but requires a new kind of subject to do the desiring. With primary desires the agent does not need to be reflective; he or she does not need to ask the question: 'What kind of person do I want to be?' But where higher order desires are present, the agent takes not just the outside world as an appropriate arena for change, but him or herself as well. (The way such conceptually based, semiotic processes modify the agents using them is interestingly developed in Vygotsky[12] and Voloshinov.[13])

Values: self-denial and self-expansion

Connecting our valuing processes with higher order desires is important. Without a connection with desire in some form or other it would be difficult to show how values could become psychologically rooted in our lives; we would lack any motivation to follow our principles, and therefore—certainly as far as our will is concerned—it would be odd to think of them as 'our' values at all. Equally, desires, while being of crucial motivational significance, may also threaten personal autonomy; when they take on a form which is obsessional or overpowering, or are experienced as alien or 'not me' in any way, it is that same motivational force that they possess which seems to stand in the way of their being experienced or owned by me as part of my value system. Higher order desires seem to solve both problems; they are desires and therefore are capable of activating the psyche, but they are also a special set of desires that only self-reflective, rational beings possess, which turn the rationality of the psyche into an active motivational force. Hume, in *A Treatise on Human Nature*, argued that reason can only be the slave of the passions, but the theory of higher order desires suggests that there is an important sub-set of the passions which are, in their turn, themselves influenced by the processes of reasoning. According to what we have argued so far, the existence of this sub-set is a necessary condition for the establishment of personhood. Values and persons, therefore, presuppose both rationality and its embedding in a matrix of desires that is supportive of such a rationality.

But where does this rationality come from, and how could it create reflective autonomous persons? The problem is that when we look at reasoning processes in practice they seem very often to contradict the requirement of autonomy. Nietzsche[14] explicitly argued this point and went on to assert that the internal dialogue of what generally passes for moral reasoning not only fails to create autonomy, but is actually a major force for eliminating it; it changes us from human beings into slaves, because instead of listening to ourselves we heed an alien discourse which emasculates us. The implication is that it is the very nature of this discourse that ensures that the internal dialogue we have with ourselves is disabling, and it is easy enough to see what Nietzsche has in mind with regard to traditional moralities like Christianity with its injunction to love one's neighbour, to turn the other cheek, and with all its 'thou shalt nots'. The question still remains as to whether there might be alternative sets of values which could be self-expanding rather than self-denying.

A similar point of view can be found in Freud[15] which is, perhaps, not surprising given the influence of Nietzsche on his thinking. Ethics, for Freud, is the province of the superego—the voice of another being, an authority figure—internalized within the psyche. This agency acts against that other part of the psyche which is the repository of desire, the id, in just the same way as a garrison occupies a conquered city. Freud notes 'the severity of its commands and prohibitions', and its false assumption that the ego has unlimited mastery over the id. So while Nietzsche and Freud differ over whether it is a good thing for desire to be repressed in the name of morality, both agree that morality (in the normal way it is conceived) and desire are, and can only be, antithetical to one another.

There is a great deal that I would want to agree with in this. Much of what passes for moral values is indeed the internalization of an alien voice that restricts desire, rather than the expansion of its field to include new, higher order desires. It is also true that many ethical theories depict morality as being opposed to desire, as Nietzsche and Freud claim—Kant's 'stern call of duty' and the utilitarian call to subordinate self-interest to the greatest happiness for the greatest number, are both cases in point. The 'oughts' and 'shoulds', the judgementalism, the guilt and punishment associated with many traditional moral viewpoints cannot plausibly be denied. A major task that twentieth-century psychotherapy has grappled with is getting at what lies behind these moralities.

A common theme in nearly all of the psychotherapeutic approaches is that of personal growth going beyond such traditional moralities. In Freud the superego—the repository of these moralities—is a scaffolding within which the fragile and inchoate form of the ego can begin to come together. The ego, in its turn, is strengthened by the abandonment of certain desires coupled with the attachment to new desires connected with the emerging ego-image (a process Freud referred to as narcissism). Once the ego has gained mastery of the primary desiring processes of the id, the old scaffolding of the superego can be much reduced, and with it the corresponding 'oughts' and 'shoulds'. One might question how thoroughgoing is Freud's critique of traditional morality; certainly he believed in the continued usefulness of what he called the 'cultural superego'—the prohibitions contained in social rules and law—and the very notion of the mastery of the ego over the id would still seem to imply reason ruling passion as in traditional approaches to morality. Self-acceptance and reintegrating the personality seem difficult to achieve on this basis, though it remains true that this is the aim of therapy for Freud.

A more thoroughgoing distancing from traditional morality takes place in Jung[16] and Reich.[17] Both abandon the Enlightenment project for the supremacy of reason and judgement that we still find in Freud's concern with making the ego into the master of the id. Jung does not accept that the self is to be identified with the ego and its processes of judgement; rather, it is much bigger, and it develops by integrating the judging dimension with three other dimensions of equivalent importance: intuition, feeling and sensing. The therapeutic process can often take an expressive, artistic or spiritual form, and will involve at least as much in the way of preventing the 'inflation' of the ego as it will in helping it assert itself to the appropriate degree; the end-point of this process is also one of harmonization between these different elements rather than the battle of one against the rest to achieve 'mastery', as in Freud. Reich, too, although he departs from Freud in the opposite direction from Jung (see Sharaf[18]), also ends up in opposition to the ego-domination view (see Conger[19]). For him, as for Jung, personal growth consists of the integration of all parts of the self, but these parts are to be located through a bodywork-based therapy in which both bodily tensions and free expressions carry with them elements of meaning too. Personal growth only takes place for Reich when we permit these unconscious sources of our personal identity to guide and limit our conscious rational processes.

A similar viewpoint is found in a large number of contemporary psychotherapeutic theories. Many have also raised the role of our affective life to at least equal status with our cognitive, intellectual, judgemental life over questions of personal identity and personal growth. Object Relations theory has been argued to be one of these,[20] and Fritz Perls's development of *Gestalt* therapy[21] can be seen to be another. Furthermore, new theories of the ego itself have been developed where it no longer appears as a seamless unitary subject producing its own linear discourse, but as a complex plurality of many sub-personal subjects or processes, which are the real bearers of contact in interpersonal interactions. In transactional analysis (TA), for example, where just such an analysis is employed, what we have referred to as traditional morality issues from only one of these ego-states, the critical parent, and is received by only one other, the adapted child. The self-emasculation that we referred to above in Nietzsche's account might then be seen as occurring as an internal transaction between these two ego-states, with the former playing persecutor and the latter victim in one of the games made famous by Eric Berne.[22] Looking at values through the framework of TA theory raises an interesting question: must all value transactions take place within such debilitating games as Persecutor–Victim–Rescuer, or can some play a more positive role?

We have so far defended an alternative conception of values which sees them as desires of a conceptually distinct, higher order variety. This has had the advantage of depicting the acquisition of values as a desire-expanding activity, not a desire-diminishing one. It also has the implication that values can only overcome primary desires if the desires embodied in the values are stronger, as desires, than the primary desires they are overcoming; i.e. the net effect of acquiring the values is the expansion of desire even in cases of conflict—however major—with primary desires themselves. But if the humanistic psychotherapists are on the right lines, this can only be a part of the truth. Taken on its own it might imply that values connect with personal growth solely through self-transcendence and change, and it might suggest that this process is essentially a reason-driven one. Yet there are good reasons for denying this, for seeing the acquisition of values as being connected with self-acceptance as much as (or more than) self-change, and for seeing the failure to develop values adequately as involving a feeling-processing disorder as much as (or more than) a reasoning, or information-processing, disorder.[23] Indeed the over-use, or inappropriate use, of reasoning processes may often constitute the problem rather than the solution.

In fact, there is something very odd about the idea of changing oneself. It would seem to suggest the splitting of our own personal processes into two, and designating one as 'good' to be identified with and brought into victorious battle with the other, the 'bad' side, which is somehow to be eliminated from our personal processes. Karl Jung has shown some of the psychological disasters that arise from an attempt to deny the negative or 'shadow' side of ourselves, and although the language is different much current psychotherapeutic and personal growth theory says similar things. Contemporary theories of values have to take this on board too.

The problem with the theory of higher order desires is, then, that it is too one-sided. It sees the learning of values as deriving from the ego rather than the wider sources of our being; it characterizes the linkage between the ego and the rest of our personal processes in terms of just one element, reason; and it depicts this connection in unilateral and mechanical terms—reason is seen as *driving* moral learning and development.

If moral growth and learning are to be seen within the context of self-acceptance, reason can still play an important role. There can be no self-acceptance without self-awareness and self-discovery, and while contact with, and enrichment of, our emotional and spiritual lives provides the source for this self-awareness, reflection and reason are important clarifying elements in its development.

Learning and the 'value-driven' organization

We began this chapter by referring to the general view that an organization's values might function as its autopoietic core, and the specific view of Peters (and others) that the more this happens and the more the organization becomes 'value-driven', the better this would be. It is time to return to these points in the light of our intervening discussion. Two questions seem to arise: (a) is it right to see values as having the sort of autonomy that this view might suggest; and (b) in the best organizational practice (whatever that might be) do values appear only as the drivers of that practice, or are they also the end result of a process of development and learning?

Living organisms, as we have seen, organize their environment (within certain limits) so as to perpetuate themselves. But what it is that gets perpetuated exists at a number of distinct levels: first, and most obvious, there is the development that preserves the individual member of the species; secondly, there is the preservation of the species itself; thirdly, there is the preservation of the network of cyclical inter-species and species/nature interactions which provide the environment for the species. Self-preservation therefore involves (at least) three simultaneous levels of activity directed at the individual organism, the species and the ecological niche. Conflicts can appear within each of these levels, and organisms which flourish must obviously be well provided with learning mechanisms appropriate to them and to the resolution of conflicts between them. Living organisms which, for instance, adopted a strategy of sacrificing the species for individual gain, or sacrificing the environmental niche for the gain of the species, can only be found on the dead branches of the tree of life, not in its living core.

Sometimes this is seen as a balance between self-assertion and harmony within living systems, and in a way this is a correct characterization. But the balance takes place within a hierarchy in which the need for environmental harmony is primary because it is this which provides the necessary context for self-assertion to take place.

Organizations are not natural organisms, so how much do the above considerations apply to them? To answer this question it is helpful to look at the relationship between natural organisms and the inorganic world. In a distant lifeless galaxy it may be a plausible assumption that inorganic processes are governed only by physical laws, but within our own biosphere further considerations apply. As James Lovelock[24] has shown, when inorganic processes become elements in the systems through which life-forms express and reproduce themselves, they acquire (or induce) new principles of development. Today we are very aware of the way that past life forms have counteracted the increasing strength of the sun and have regularized ambient global temperature by converting carbon dioxide into fossil deposits—here life-forms have profoundly influenced physical processes. By contrast, the switch from anaerobic to aerobic, oxygen-breathing life-forms some three thousand million years ago shows us the reverse scenario of physical changes affecting life processes. The point here is that both scenarios are governed ultimately by the need for harmony if the plurality of life-forms had been unable to stabilize temperatures our planet would be as lifeless as Venus, and if they had not adapted themselves to new atmosphere they would all have perished from oxygen poisoning

This ultimate requirement for harmony of the inorganic processes that participate in the systems of the expression and reproduction of life-forms obviously applies equally to all necessary elements in these systems. The modern organization clearly plays such a role; in its corporate form it is the protagonist of the contemporary social and economic order. As such, organizations must also be bound by the requirements for long-term harmony between themselves and their context too. Organizations have human resources as their input and human needs as their output. They participate centrally in the life-form of human beings, and therefore stand or fall with them—as individuals, as members of a species and as part of the intricate network of life on Earth.

A number of implications follow from this about the place of values in organizations and their role within learning processes.

1. The assumption that for organizations 'value-driven' = good must be seriously questioned. If what we have been saying is correct, part of the problem is the very 'drivenness' of organizations as such.[25] If the ultimate requirement is for long-term harmony between organization and environment, the appropriate role for moral sensitivity would have more to do with increasing an awareness of the current reality for the organization in question and for the global context within which it operates. On the other hand, to locate values as drivers is to coopt them behind an essentially task-oriented approach to which the context of the task is subordinated; an approach which mirrors what is happening in relatively undeveloped personal processes where the psyche is still dominated by an over-inflated ego (as in Jung's theory), or is conquered from within by abstract principles which prevent genuine self-assertion (as in Nietzsche's account).

2. If values are not to be seen simply as drivers of organizational learning and change, then they can be as much a consequence of organizational learning as they are a condition for it, in which case the very idea that there could be any uniquely specifiable set comprising 'the values of the learning organization' seems mistaken. To be sure, learning processes imply reflective self-awareness, and when these flow from the heart the evaluative dimension is involved, but exactly which values are invoked by this process cannot be predetermined in advance; nor can they be summarized as a set of bullet points on a checklist of the 'oughts' that need to be swallowed whole in the attempt to become a learning company. And no such list could plausibly be identified with the organization's autopoietic core, which rather should be seen as the systemic archetype provided by the dynamic relationship between organism, species and niche.

3. If we need to think of values in organizational contexts as involving self-awareness, self-realization and harmony in place of a 'drivenness' by abstract principles, then many of the features we noted earlier for personal values apply here too. With regard to personal life we noted a grounding for values in desires and also their subsumption under a general process of self-realization which included self-acceptance as much as it did self-assertion. For organizations this would suggest that the grounding of their values is to be found in the culture, or affective life, within the organization itself or its wider stakeholder grouping, and an approach which is process-oriented and starts from an internal phenomenological account of the subjective experience of what it is like to be part of that organization. It would also imply that an organization's values become part of its learning process when it pursues a process of self-reflective development along the same sort of lines as that of personal forms of growth, of which certain forms of psychotherapy provide the most obvious model.

Towards transorganizational shamanism?

If psychotherapy is the most obvious personal model for the sort of organizational moral development referred to here, it is not quite the best. What gave organizations their valuational significance was the fact that they played an essential role in the expression and reproduction of life processes, and with regard to the latter we noted a hierarchy of levels. At the most fundamental level there was the ecological niche; next there was that of the species, and finally that of the individual. Psychotherapy, however, has traditionally confined itself to the latter level only, so it provides us with a model that is of limited use. At the same time, in more recent years many psychotherapists have sought to expand its scope so as to include the dimension of meaning of the context within which the individual person resides, creating a transpersonal approach to the psyche, and in doing so moving closer to the concerns of religion or spirituality. This seeking of connections between the personal psyche and the cosmic order recalls the approach of shamanism, particularly in its native North American hunter-gatherer form; furthermore, placing the psyche in its total cosmic context implies a method which operates at each of the levels referred to above, and therefore a more appropriate model for approaching processes of valuational change in organizations.

This suggests that change agents seeking to help organizations undergoing processes of valuational learning might need to play a role that is as priestly as it is scientific. The latter would be concerned with the spheres of values insofar as they apply to (a) the individual organization; (b) the organization as part of the system of interorganizational linkages; (c) as part of the wider system of life on Earth. These correspond to what Peter Hawkins[26] has referred to as efficiency thinking, effectiveness thinking (helicopter vision), and planetary thinking (satellite vision or evolutionary consciousness—for instance, thinking about sustainable development) respectively, and they are objective in the sense that they deal with determinate needs (though of course there can be differences in subjective belief about what these needs actually are). In addition to this objective side, and in parallel with it, there is the subjective, or spiritual, side; here people search for ways of enacting or living these three levels of objective need in ways that are meaningful to them. Within organizations this side is carried on by daily life and the idioms, folklore, narratives, myths and rituals that are enacted within it, and through which the organization's values are transferred from person to person. Many process-oriented organization development consultants are well aware of these meaning-carrying enactments, and see it as part of their job to help bring out some of the less conscious forms that are getting in the way of good communication; and there is no doubt that such facilitative skills are a necessary part of the spiritual role. But just as traditional forms of psychotherapy have to be broadened in a transpersonal direction to deal with the systemic relationship between individuals themselves and between people and the cosmos, so too is it necessary within organizations for new meanings to be created and nurtured which reflect all these levels of objective valuation process too.

Such learning would be the product of the engagement of the total organizational process, its heart and its soul as well as its head. Current organizations are obviously, in the main, at an altogether different and lower level of spiritual development; too often they are characterized by impoverished and hostile cultures which would have to change radically to get anywhere near to this picture. And yet there are powerful commercial forces that are already pushing organizations towards reconstituting themselves as continual learning structures. The literature is also in general agreement that such structures require, and are beginning to create, humanized, person-centred cultures in which values appear more and more on centre stage. What has been outlined here is the beginnings of an account of what the implications of this process might include for the role of values in such organizations.

References

1. Piaget, J. (1954) *The Construction of Reality in the Child*, Basic Books, New York.
2. Gibson, J. (1979) *The Ecological Approach to Visual Perception*, Houghton Mifflin, Boston.
3. Maturana, H. and F. Varela (1992) *The Tree of Knowledge*, Shambala, Boston and London.
4. Drummond, J. and S. Carmichael (1989) *Good Business*, Hutchinson, London.
5. Deming, W. (1986) *Out of the Crisis*, Cambridge University Press, Cambridge.
6. Handy, C. (1990) *The Age of Unreason*, Arrow, London.
7. Peters, T. (1988) *Thriving on Chaos*, Macmillan, London.
8. Kant, I. (1959) *Foundations of the Metaphysics of Morals*, Bobbs-Merrill, Indianapolis.
9. Aristotle (1955) *Nichomachean Ethics*, Penguin, London.
10. Frankfurt, H. (1971) 'Freedom of the will and the concept of a person', *Journal of Philosophy*, **68**, 81–95.
11. Nerlich, E. (1989) *Values and Valuing*, Oxford University Press, Oxford.
12. Vygotsky, L. (1978) *Mind in Society: The Development of Higher Psychological Processes*, Harvard University Press, Cambridge, Mass.
13. Voloshinov, V. (1973) *Marxism and the Philosophy of Language*, Harvard University Press, Cambridge, Mass.
14. Cf. Nietzsche, F. (1966) *Beyond Good and Evil*, Vintage, and (1969) *On the Genealogy of Morals*, Vintage, New York.
15. Freud, S. (1985) 'Civilization and its Discontents', Pelican Freud Library, Vol 12, *Civilization, Society and Religion*, Penguin, London.
16. Jung, K. (1988) *On the Nature of the Psyche*, Ark, London.
17. Reich, W. (1975) *The Mass Psychology of Fascism*, Penguin, London.
18. Sharaf, M. (1984) *Fury on Earth*, Hutchinson, London.
19. Conger, J. (1988) *Jung and Reich: The Body as Shadow*, North Atlantic Books, New York.
20. Modell, A. (1968) *Object Love and Reality*, International Universities Press, New York; Hundert, E. (1990) *Philosophy, Psychiatry and Neuroscience: Three Approaches to the Mind*, Clarendon, Oxford.
21. Perls, F., R. Hefferline and P. Goodman (1972) *Gestalt Therapy*, Souvenir Press, London.
22. Berne, E. (1968) *Games People Play*, Penguin, London.
23. Eagle, M. (1984) *Recent Developments in Psychoanalysis: A Critical Evaluation*, McGraw-Hill, Maidenhead.
24. Lovelock, J. (1989) *The Ages of Gaia*, Oxford University Press, Oxford.

25. This drivenness of many contemporary organizations is discussed in Schaef, A. and D. Fassel (1988) *The Addictive Organization*, Harper & Row, New York.

26. Hawkins, P. (1991) 'The spiritual dimension of the learning organisation', *Management Education and Development*, **22** (3), 172–87.

4
Power, politics and ideology
John Coopey

Introduction

In this chapter notions of the transformative potential of individual and collective learning are related to those of power, political activity and ideology.[1] The term 'learning organization' is used, encompassing not only 'companies'—i.e. private enterprises whose shareholders enjoy a legal monopoly over their governance—but also public and voluntary sector bodies representing directly and indirectly the interests of various stakeholders, often through democratic processes.

Several arguments are put forward:

- The relatively apolitical assumptions which underpin the notion of learning organizations tend to obscure the amount of political activity likely to be experienced within them.
- Greater employee empowerment promised by the learning organization will probably be vulnerable to strategic retrenchment and, in any case, be very modest compared to that of managers and other professionals, especially those at the apex of the organization enjoying preferential access to the extra knowledge and understanding generated.
- Those same senior managers are in a position to use the language of the learning organization to create an ideology which helps to ensure competitive advantage and safeguard their own prerogatives while ensuring the continued obedience of other members despite lower levels of 'empowerment' than seems to be promised by the proponents of the learning organization.

Control and political activity

In the learning organization literature explicit discussions of control seem to relate almost exclusively to the learning process. There seems little disagreement, however, as to who should exercise overall control of collective learning processes or control in a more general sense: for example, Pedler's 'workbook' advice is addressed to managers; Hawkins entrusts governance to 'men and women of wisdom'; and Garratt allocates the key strategic 'brain function' to his audience of directors.[2]

Any plurality of interest occurs within the learning context where differences between a learning organization's members provide the challenge that aids discovery. Conflicts are settled via constant dialogue within trusting relationships. So, while control is an essential element of the learning organization it does not constitute an overtly political process. Implicit is a unitarist framework in which shared goals are persued in a climate of collaborative high trust and a rational approach to the resolution of differences.

This contracts with Giddens's view of institutional life.[3] People engage in political activity, using power to pursue individual wants and collective interests through a 'dialectic of control'. Attempting to maintain some semblance of control over their work, they take advantage of imbalances in personal capabilities to draw on existing resources and to create new ones, exploiting the mutual dependencies which exist within all human relationships. Such an analysis fits Clegg's argument that political activity is premised on organizations as loci of decisions and action.[4] Decision making and political activity are correlated because decisions generally affect allocation of resources and, consequently, power relationships.

Within this dialectic, managers attempt to operate disciplinary practices designed to ensure that employees perform allotted tasks within constraints of formal rules while exploiting sanctioned forms of creativity. Such creativity-enabling processes are essential for managers of learning organizations, seeking to construct consent without recourse to bureaucratic forms of control. Pedler's rational approach to organizational design, based on fairness, mutual respect and trust, might well yield unobtrusive control devices, mitigating the level of political activity.[5] As such, it could be a form 'of high discretionary strategic agency ... for which power will be less prohibitive and more productive ... the classical conception of the professional discipline as a vocation'.[6] In effect, the mutual investment in the process of learning on the part of management and other employees should enable the former to relax the frontier of control which separates them.

But in constructing more permissive forms of control managers have to deal with various underlying tensions. First, managers seek in the employment relationship to minimize unit labour costs in the owners' interests as against the employees' interest in maximizing the price of labour. This conflict complicates managerial efforts both to ensure that employees are committed to the organization while making contributions to match, and to constrain their behaviour to accord with economic realities.[7] Pedler's notion of 'reward flexibility' within a learning organization does not seem to deal with these economic issues.[8] Openness is not enough; where are the real checks on managerial power to determine rewards?

Secondly, in circumstances of external turbulence which have prompted the learning organization, the volume of decisions is likely to increase considerably. It is difficult to visualize how decisions could be made less numerous and less salient without sacrificing the purpose of collective learning—organizational transformation via decisions based on new knowledge and understanding. In this case, political activity will probably increase as employees defend themselves against the potential effect of resource reallocation.

Thirdly, given the turbulence and the requirement to realize the potential for competitive advantage, we should expect managers to be under considerable pressure to compromise the extent of employee autonomy and the scope for learning and creative action. Senior executives consulted by Pedler *et al.*[9] expressed these pressures in their focus on the need for increased productivity. Garratt's advice to his director audience[10] to monitor monthly performance indices is probably typical of the time-related techniques that will continue to dominate senior management motivation in controlling operations, in managing people generally and in making strategic decisions.

In this context of greater uncertainty and potential dissensus, despite the devices embodied in the learning organization to construct consent, action is still likely to 'result from bargaining and compromise (where) those individuals or groups with access to the greatest power will receive greatest rewards from political interplay'.[11] Kanter provides supporting evidence in her review of managerial work within new organizational forms designed to deal with external turbulence.[12] Political action increases considerably and political skills are at a premium as decisions are made under ambiguous conditions, calling for regular trade-offs between competing goals and values.

An understanding of these environmental pressures on managers and other employees to behave in traditional ways might moderate expectations of how far displacements of the frontier of control within learning organizations will, in practice, lead to real employee autonomy and, hence, to learning. This is consistent with Keenoy's critique of strategic human resource management (HRM), placed by Pedler at the centre of their learning organization. Human resource policies which benefit employees will be maintained by management for only as long as 'those policies represent a good fit with the prevailing product and labour market constraints'.[13] So, in terms of the learning organization seen as a flexible HRM strategy, freedom for employees to learn and develop is not a desirable end in itself. The notional moving outwards of boundaries of control which this requires can be seen as a dependent variable, just one of a variety of strategies available to managements in the movement to decentralized production in response to a considerable extension and deepening of global competition and control.[14] Hence the learning organization, like the notion of organizational culture[15] might well be destined to be transformed from a root metaphor, helping to explain the nature of organizational activities and performance, to a mechanism through which to achieve improved managerial control under dramatically changed external circumstances.

Power and agency

As noted, organizational members undertake political activity in order to accrue and use power to satisfy individual wants or pursue collective interests. Our definition of power is summarized in Figure 4.1.[16]

The assumptions underlying the diagram's outer cycle is that institutions (in our case organizations) are constructed by individuals, acting singly or together, and that individual identities are themselves constructed in part through the roles people fulfil within institutions.

At any particular time an organization is constituted out of a fixed resource base which individual members can access according to their roles. But access is not equally available: through the bias in the sets of relationships between organizational roles some people have greater access to existing resources than others and greater capacity to create and control new resources.

The use they make of the resources available to them in influencing the organization's form depends on what Giddens calls *transformative capacity*. The basis of individual power, this capacity has two main elements: *discursive penetration* and *discursive capacity*.

Discursive penetration reflects a person's understanding of the organization's 'logic', based on knowledge of its structures and systems and their likely effect on the behaviour of individuals within it. Included is 'cynical knowledge'[17] of the distribution of interests and power and of decision processes through which power is expressed, enabling an individual to decide where to invest resources and with whom to collaborate in agency building.

Discursive capacity describes people's ability to translate knowledge into discursive forms and, hence, to use it to influence others to accept their interpretations of shared events.

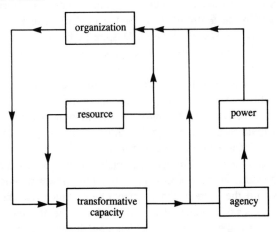

Figure 4.1   Circuit diagram

Those with a high level of transformative capacity, in these two senses, will probably be persuasive, able to create and transmit new knowledge through the skills they bring to the crucial organizational activities of presentation, argumentation and debate.

Through such social processes individuals can exploit the dependency of others in order to recruit those others to their agency, to act on their behalf in pursuing shared interests. This extension of the personal power of transformative capacity into collective power completes the cycle shown in Figure 4.1. It is, in effect, a 'cycle of dispositional power'[18] within which successful agencies create access to further power through their control of knowledge and other resources which others need in order to solve problems arising from their perceptions of the external environment. Agency is used in this way to build the formal and informal structures which constitute organizations.

The learning process within a learning organization creates increments of collective knowledge, as a vital resource to be used internally in building agency and externally in creating competitive advantage. For our purposes it is important to examine how that knowledge, and the potential power it confers, might be used.

First, through the notion of 'informating', Pedler et al.,[19] allow for all individuals to have the potential for penetrative capacity sufficient at least for them to participate competently in production processes within a learning organization. But the incumbents of managerial positions—though fewer than they might be in a more conventional structure—will typically have access to deeper penetrative knowledge than is open to other organizational members. This will be in addition to any formal authority they are granted to command people and exploit other resources.

Secondly since knowledge is such an important resource in a learning organization it will probably be a strong focus of the control dialectic, with members contesting how it is stored and accessed. Despite Pedler's prescription of widely available information, limitations on access are inevitable in all but the smallest cooperatively controlled organizations because of the need to specialize to some extent in order to overcome the constraints of limited cognitive capacities and bounded rationality.[20] Specialization of decision-making roles, for example, is reflected in the development of corporate information systems built up from individual contributions of knowledge, but into which 'the rules expressing hierarchical access to information have come to be incorporated in the provision of levels of access and security, complete with elaborate passwords and gates'.[21] The 'rationality' embedded in the protocols gives potential power to those experts who build the rules into the system and to their client senior managers who make decisions as to access. Together they will probably be the only ones able to penetrate holistically the knowledge which constitutes discursive penetration, knowledge used to provide strategic meaning for the organization's members.

Thirdly, through boundary roles between parts of the organization and into the external environment vital information can be transmitted and controlled. Within a learning organization it is prescribed that all members at the external boundary should act as 'environmental scanners', importing interpretations of external events as potentially useful knowledge. But there are degrees of penetration: it is one thing to import information about the pattern of a competitor's local market prices; but knowledge of their market strategy, or the government's policy on competition within that market, constitutes much more significant knowledge. The implications for differential accumulation of penetrative discourse and the influence which boundary spanning activities promises are considerable.

Fourthly, it is managers who have control of key nodal points between internal parts of the organization and at the external boundary. In particular, business directors or trustees of other organizations are at the most salient nodes linking two circuits of power:

- the internal circuit of dispositional power described above (Figure 4.1); and
- circuits of 'facilitative power' in the wider society through which socially derived forces flow, engendering innovation in techniques of production and discipline.[22]

Circuits of facilitative power consist of influential individuals and organizations, especially those involved in the media, finance, technology development, government and regulation. Scarbrough et al.[23] provide an example of how the power of top management, in this case over technology, is linked to their connection to the circuit of facilitative power, relating them to external constituencies of owners, technology suppliers and providers of capital.

Finally, if learning organizations worked as prescribed, directors would have access to an increasing stock of collective knowledge. If used through their control of nodal points of relationships within the broader circuits of facilitative power, this would enable them to consolidate the membership of existing agencies, to recruit new members to them and to set up new agencies. Sir Adrian Cadbury criticizes the everyday use of such power when he accuses British company executives of relying on the 'old-boy network' to enrol non-executive directors onto their boards.[24] Directors' nodal positions, and the internally derived knowledge and control of discourse which these facilitate, enable them to 'translate phenomena into resources, and resources into organization networks of control, of alliance, of coalition, of antagonism, of interest and of structure'.[25] This conclusion parallels two findings by Kanter:[26]

1. Chief executives of modern forms of organization tend to retain their identity, status and control, occupying positions which still yield considerable power, despite the difficulties they face in creating agency through networks of stakeholders rather than control over subordinates.

2.   While hierarchy might be a thing of the past in the modern organizations she studied, senior managers wielded power in ways which their subordinates perceived as arbitrary.

So those at the apex of a learning organization, despite the difficulties they might face in exerting control, could be expected to have their power enhanced through occupation of nodal points of power and the holistic nature of the discursive penetration which this makes possible. Cooptation and patronage of lower level innovators would also probably enable them to disarm those with expertise critical to the extension of their agency. Others sited less advantageously in a learning organization would probably be active in developing their own agency through similar but less potent tactics. People perceiving themselves to be especially disadvantaged might attempt to exercise control by restricting the scope for their tacit knowledge to be translated into objective collective knowledge which, potentially, others could use to control them.

The learning organization as ideology

The learning organization as a prescription for yielding competitive advantage in turbulent times fits Geertz's 'strain theory' in which ideology is construed as a means of reducing social friction and individual strain.[27] New cultural knowledge helps to renew patterns of shared understanding threatened by the cultural, social and personal disequilibrium caused by high levels of environmental turbulence.

Like science, ideology focuses on problematic situations, but where science 'is the diagnostic, the critical, dimension of culture, ideology is the justificatory, the apologetic one—it refers to that part of culture which is actively concerned with the establishment and defense of patterns of belief and value'.[28] While science provides needed information in language designed to aid intellectual clarity, ideology uses 'ornate, vivid' language which, taken with the psychological pressure of the rituals and settings within which it is employed, helps to construct situations encouraging commitment and motivation.

Strain theory fits the learning organization well, a prescription which offers managements a new formula for dealing with organizational strain prompted by perceived turbulence in the external environment and provides employees with some means of reducing stress caused by that turbulence manifested at individual level. Corporate reassurance lies in the belief that organizational flexibility and responsiveness will be enhanced by collective learning. Its source in the learning of individual members will enable them to feel more secure about their own identity.

Certainly none seem to claim that learning organizations are scientifically based: Pedler[29] acknowledges that the learning company is a sort of scientific hypothesis without empirical evidence. The language, however, is certainly 'ornate, vivid, deliberately suggestive'[30] potential raw material for those senior managers whose power, enhanced by the collective learning process, already gives access to newly generated corporate knowledge and language. For example, through their control of strategic planning activities, senior managers are able to influence strongly insiders' perceptions of the external environment and outsiders' perceptions of the internal environment.

The language of the learning organization available to managers can fulfil an ideological function, mediating between individual members of the organization and the conditions of their existence. People can be positioned as subjects and, as such, assume that they are the authors of the ideology which they speak, as if in control of the meanings which that ideology carries. In the terms and practice of a learning organization, framed in the language offered by its proponents, individuals might 'imagine' that they were the type of subject proposed.[31] Similarly, how managers labelled workers involved in quality circles implied a degree of skill not reflected at the workplace.[32]

How might management use the language of learning organizations? They could embark on a process of resocialization within an overall 'ethos of self-responsibility' fulfilled through collaboration rather than competition. Members would probably be encouraged to see themselves as critical providers of organizational knowledge through their enhanced learning capability; as responsible for experimentation; as wise interpreters of collective knowledge; as honoured participants in decision making; as responsive to the needs of internal and external customers. In imagining themselves as these types of people, members of organizations would be accepting a revised personal identity, taking on more responsibility for providing solutions to corporate problems and for self-surveillance, enforcing norms which constrain the expression of doubts or disloyalties reflecting differing belief structures.

Within the framework of explicit and tacit legitimation which the metaphor of a learning organization provides, those managements who realize its ideological potential will be able to make use of the prescribed language and practices to maintain their hegemony. In the process, employees risk being subjected to further socialization, encouraged to adopt aspects of identity which, as Clegg[33] anticipates, would ensure their continued obedience, not only in a prohibitive sense, but also creatively and productively.

Nor is the ideological potential of the learning organization restricted to its language. Equally important is what is not said, for example, about the competence of directors as currently conceived to manage a learning organization in an ethical way, or in questioning the prerogatives that they assume in carrying out their directorial roles. The learning organization literature tends to be silent on these central issues and on questions of democratic control which they raise.[34]

Given this analysis, it seems that those who propagate the principles and practices of a learning organization within the current economic structures risk opening the latest phase of a long history of social science metaphors which have been used manipulatively[35] by managers with a long pedigree of instrumental interest in social science as a means of solving industrial problems.[36] The force of the metaphors employed stems from the rational, conscious level of explanation and, perhaps even more strongly, at a deeper level at which versions of social science—'the orthodox consensus'—provide commonsense explanations of lived experience which it serves to justify.[37]

Like an earlier metaphor, 'human relations', the learning organization promises to 'transform compliance into cooperation, consent into commitment, discipline into self-discipline, the goals of the organisation into the goals of the employee'.[38] When this happens, when a metaphor is translated into an instrument for control as in the case of 'organizational culture', 'ambiguities are suppressed in favour of a dominant and stable set of beliefs and interests'.[39]

References

1. Coopey, J. G. (1993) *The Learning Organisation: A Critique and Extension*, discussion paper in Management, University of Dundee, Dundee.
2. Pedler, M., J. Burgoyne and T. Boydell (1991) *The Learning Company: A Strategy for Sustainable Development*, McGraw-Hill, Maidenhead. Hawkins, P. (1991) 'The spiritual dimension of the learning organization', *Management Education and Development*, **22**(3), 172–87. Garratt, B. (1987) *The Learning Organization*, Fontana, London.
3. Giddens, A. (1979) *Central Problems in Social Theory*, Macmillan, London.
4. Clegg, S. (1989) *Frameworks of Power*, Sage, London.
5. Pedler, M. *et al.*, op. cit.
6. Clegg, op. cit., p.199
7. Keenoy, T. (1992) 'Constructing control', in J. F. Hartley and G. M. Stephenson (eds) *Employment Relations*, Blackwell, Oxford.
8. Pedler, M. *et al.*, op. cit.
9. Pedler, M., T. Boydell and J. Burgoyne (1988) *Learning Company Project Report*, Manpower Services Commission, Sheffield.
10. Garratt, B., op. cit.
11. Pfeffer, J. (1981) *Power in Organizations*, Ballinger, Cambridge, Mass.
12. Kanter, R. M. (1989) 'The new managerial work', *Harvard Business Review*. November/December, 85–92.
13. Keenoy, T. (1990) 'A case of sheep in wolf's clothing?', *Personnel Review*, **19**(2), 3–9.
14. Whitaker, A. (1992) 'The transformation in work: post-Fordism revisited', in M. Reed and M. Hughes (eds) *Rethinking Organizations*, Sage London.
15. Meyerson, D. E. (1991) 'Acknowledging and uncovering ambiguities in

culture', in P. J. Frost *et al.* (eds) *Reframing Organizational Culture*, Sage, Newbury Park, Ca.

16. Adapted from Giddens, op. cit.
17. Pfeffer, op. cit.
18. Clegg, op. cit.
19. Pedler, M. *et al.*, op. cit.
20. Simon, H. A. (1976) *Administrative Behaviour*, 3rd edn, The Free Press, New York.
21. Scarbrough, H. and J. Martin-Corbett (1992) *Technology and Organization*, Routledge, London p. 140.
22. Clegg, op. cit.
23. Scarbrough, H. op. cit.
24. *The Financial Times*, 28 September 1992.
25. Clegg, op. cit., p. 204.
26. Kanter, R. M., op. cit.
27. Geertz, C. (1964) 'Ideology as a cultural system', in D. E. Apter (ed.) *Ideology and Discontent*, The Free Press, New York.
28. Ibid., pp. 71–2.
29. Pedler, M. *et al.*, op. cit.
30. Geertz (1964), op. cit.
31. Deetz, S. (1992) 'Disciplinary power in modern corporations', in M. Alvesson and H. Willmott (eds) *Critical Management Studies*, Sage, London.
32. Scarbrough *et al.* op. cit.
33. Clegg, S. op. cit.
34. Coopey, op. cit.
35. Giddens, op. cit.
36. Pfeffer, op. cit.
37. Giddens, op. cit.
38. Hollway, W. (1991) *Work Psychology and Organizational Behaviour*, Sage, London.
39. Meyerson, 1991, op. cit. p. 257.

5
The spirit of the learning company
Julia Davies

Introduction

In this chapter I want to explore some of the issues connected with the idea of the spirit of the learning company, in particular the tension and paradox which is evident between the tangible and intangible elements of learning and between objective knowledge and the subjective process of learning. These elements are interconnected and reflect the symbiotic nature of the visible and invisible aspects of learning. At an individual level much has been known of this connection, and at all levels of education stress is laid on learning to learn and the ownership of this by the learners themselves (Roger's,[1] Dewey,[2] Boot and Reynolds[3]).

However, at an organizational community level there is often more stress on the tangible structures and artefacts of learning and this chapter attempts to emphasize the importance of what is so often hidden and becomes forgotten, the spirit of the learning company.

The tension between the concrete and the purpose

The flight to structure
One of the questions asked about the learning company as described by Pedler, Burgoyne and Boydell[4] is, does it exist? The people asking this are looking for the tangible, the verifiable, the graspable. If it does exist 'in the flesh' so to speak, where is it? Can I see it? Can I visit it? How can I make my organization like that? The next questions are, What are the first steps to this? Is there a ladder, a blueprint, and where am I? The questions asked are about the outward signs they emphasize, as Senge[5] indicates the emulation of best practice rather than the process of practising the discipline' of learning itself.

So often the answers disappoint the enquirers. The responses to these eager questions are vague, intangible; the possible organizations appear far from the dreams of what a learning company should be. Is it therefore just a myth, a theatrical concept, a vision without any form? One response is to dismiss the ideas as 'idealistic' and to discard with impatience the 'spirit' because as yet the substance is too vague. This is a pattern repeated many times in human learning and change. The new idea often appears simplistic and formless. As an example, Revans's[6] concept of action learning was too simple and rejected by many in favour of structured knowledge and known facts. Those organizations, academic and managerial, which used action learning began to clothe the deceptively simple idea with complexities, encouraging Revans himself to come up with alpha and beta systems, formulas and divisions of learning into P (applying known solutions) and Qs (dealing with unstructured problems). Around the idea designed to help managers question themselves and their own actions and ask more appropriate questions arose a technology of Action Learning programmes and formulas, sets and set advisors, books and articles, 'how to do it' books. Soon there will be competencies and NCVQs. The spirit of enquiry, discovery and, dare one say, love and caring, will have flown away.

One might almost say that this is happening with the learning company. The simple and seductive idea of an organization in which people are open to learning from one another, with one another in order to achieve a common purpose seems to slip away under the pressure of structure. Yet without structure, discipline and direction can be lost. The question is how to control without controlling.

How to describe the spirit

There is a paradox here which may be at the very heart of the concept of learning. As individuals we have learnt to deal with it in a number of ways, but as a company we need to trust a communal entity rather than our own autonomy. I have called this entity the spirit, and in many ways the paradox is inherent in this chapter where by trying to capture the spirit in the structure of language may result in an emptiness. So I would like to approach the spirit, the essence, in a number of ways, not in the hope of capturing and tying it down, but so that the 'butterfly' aspect may be more fully seen and appreciated.

First, I will return to the paradoxical nature of learning and look particularly at the relationship between form, structure and the essential spirit of enquiry and the form it might take. It is the shifting relationship between the two which creates the greatest difficulty and the tension between them, which is that of the stimulus to learn.

This is true in our everyday life, our work and personal life and in the organizational and wider world of which we are a part. Too often the design is to reduce this tension by focusing on the structure or the content which becomes an end in itself. Thus, as a way of trying to recapture the spirit, there can then be a tendency to focus on the process of learning which becomes a structure in its own right and the underlying purpose—the 'why'—becomes lost. This tension between form and substance is inherent and is part of the learning journey. I will illustrate this through a story related to me by a colleague, Chia.[7]

There was once an American management consultant who was particularly interested in learning from the Japanese experience and, aware of the cultural context, he wished to learn about the tea ceremony. He eventually got himself an appointment with an elderly and renowed teacher and flew in for his lesson. The Japanese Tea Master asked how much time he had to spare and the American, mindful of these pressures, said he had just three hours. The Master smiled and said that what he had to teach took a life time, but that he would spend three hours with this young man. The learning began, and the Tea Master, who was very old, began to pour tea into a little bowl. His hand trembled as he poured, and gradually the bowl filled to the brim and overflowed and still the Tea Master kept pouring. The American thought 'Poor old man, he can no longer control his actions, he doesn't know what he is doing'. Eventually he said 'Master, the cup is already full and flowing over, the tea is being wasted.' The Tea Master turned to the young man and said, 'That is like you, you are already so full of knowledge but you do not know it.'

What this story indicates, both in content and process, is that there is a paradoxical nature to knowledge and knowing. This is particularly highlighted in a time of change when the tensions and stresses of alternative views are sharpest. It is then that there is a dichotomy between fragmentation, chaos, anarchy and structural containment.

In the world of some organizations there has been in some situations a freeing of the human spirit to, in Drucker's[8] words, 'think the unthinkable'. This is often difficult for people; how can they begin to work outside the tight boundaries of working life? Yet many experience profound unease with the way in which life is compartmentalized and the alienation they feel between their beliefs and their actions. How to connect spirit and structure personally and organizationally is a central theme of this chapter. It is the connection, not the emphasis on the spirit[9] which identifies a learning from a 'new age' organization. However, in order to appreciate this connection attention has to be given to both the spirit and the structure. This chapter emphasizes the spirit to balance the public past emphasis on structure.[10]

Alternative ways of learning

One method of freeing the spirit is to approach intuitively what is already known through a wider use of alternative ways of learning. Experiential learning has been one way of accessing the individual's learning.[11] A more public forum is through stories and their role in learning. They have many forms and can be seen as illustrations of personal and organizational learning from biography to the stories told almost as anecdotes, important myths and legends inside and outside organizations.[12]

To access these hidden connections we use a process often described as intuitive. At the moment we are in a transition in which intuition[13] is seen as of growing importance and yet in which emotions and the importance of feelings are often ghettoized and exploited.[14] Intuition is, as Agor and others show, not a new rational panacea to be tapped into by techniques, but is a part of an organization's spirit which can easily be damaged or blocked by structures and forces which are connected to the efficiency, operational dimensions of organizational action, operations as ends in themselves.

Structure as purpose

In order to examine the relationship between spirit and structure it is necessary to briefly consider some of the negative aspects of structure. This is to balance the emphasis of organizational analysis which has often stressed the structure as the content of organizational life.[15] Change is too often seen in structural terms, whether this is about breaking up a company into constituent parts or internal restructuring into new divisions/departments with people being reshuffled into different roles and with new organizational charts. This is not a new development, and Suetonius[16], writing in AD 100, has been widely quoted on this in relation to the Roman army, 'we re-organised and then just when we were about to attack, we were restructured and then again reformed before ever performing our task'. One by-product of such restructuring is to devalue it in the long term as an effective change process, i.e. 'the more things change the more they remain the same'. Many of our large public organizations continue to operate in similar ways despite widely publicized changes.[17] Like the Titanic, despite frequent moving of the furniture on the decks the engine-room is continuing on full power.

The NHS in particular, since the late 1960s, has gone through regular change and reorganization arising from reports, scandals, investigations and concerns about cost. Yet until the latest change in the late 1980s life on the wards remained, despite technological change, fairly constant and familiar to patients, staff and the community. The organization values and spirit were not really touched by surface level upheavals. The present structural changes, which are deeper and begin to affect the culture and values of an organization, are also more deeply resisted. They are both a threat and a potential releasing force for the spirit of an organization which can be buried and be seen to be dead. The defences in ourselves and in organizations are alerted by a challenge to the status quo.[18]

Those with existing investment in a present traditional structure are always likely to resist change even if they do not present it in a self-interested way. The costs of seeing things differently are high, the personal and group pay-offs appear low. This is well documented in Kuhn's[19] work on paradigm change and Lewin's[20] and Argyris and Schon's[21] on change at an individual and conceptual level. In organizational and, indeed, national terms it would seem that energies go into holding systems and structures together long after the purpose has departed, and it is only catastrophes which precipitate change (Davies and Binstead).[22]

Despite this evidence of the resistance of structures to learning and the false reliance we as managers and people place on them, the spirit of learning and enquiry resurfaces elsewhere, often bringing with it challenges and upsets to the existing order. Is the spirit of the learning company any different? Do organizations only provide a temporary home and is it inevitable that growth and change will occur elsewhere?

The dream, desire, vision might be that of a self-knowing, self-transforming company, one which is forever centred on the spirit of enquiry. But enquiry for what? Organizations set up to foster such learning as their main *raison d'être* also have the same tendency to atrophy into structures. New departments in universities have a tendency to gain respectability either through existing channels or by creating their own gates, structures and regulations for harnessing knowledge.

So we have experienced the impact of structures and rules on us. We have worked in organizations which have nearly killed the spirit in us. The effects can be seen in the disillusioned managers, the alienated workforce.[23] Yet the world of the spirit seems so distant from the picture of managerial life and the reality, we often experience how managers will talk in terms of measurement and performance rather than purpose. At the event in which some of these issues were first raised and discussed,[24] the opportunity was given to mention this aspect of organizational life. The joining of the forces of spirit and managerial purpose led to a number of new insights and challenges. The question was remaining, How do we move this forward into action and in a way which does not in itself dispower people? It is here that structure has an enabling role as the servant and vehicle of the spirit, so that it serves to guide and channel the spirit. The spirit of the learning company is thus a channelled and disciplined spirit.[25] One which is not solely the reflection of a guru with all its inherent centralized power, but a shared community spirit. If I can use an analogy, the relationship between spirit and structure is seen in the relationship between water and the boundaries of river banks. Without the banks water spills over and in dry conditions soon evaporates and disperses. In other circumstances in which the banks collapse, chaos, disorder and confusion results. The banks exist for the water, as can be seen in decayed rivers, where stagnant pools replace living eco-systems, and in man-made structures such as canals, where the removal of the water exposes the debris of the waste land.

This analogy is an attempt to indicate the symbiotic relationship between structure and spirit in a learning company. They are like the two strands of the rope as described by Vickers[26] in which the intertwining is a fundamental part of their strength. Without each other there is no rope. In too many organizations structure and spirit have become separated, with individuals being unaware that there is often more to life than the system. The last 20 years have seen an emphasis on strategy and organizational effectiveness. The two-loop model of learning united by the Business Brain (Garratt)[27] has been used to encourage managers to connect thinking with action, to move from efficiency to effectiveness. The more recent development of this by Hawkins[28] has been to emphasize the service aspect of organizational life and the need for the soul of an organization to be activated. It is this action which I have called the spirit and it is something which is often supremely practical. To use Peters and Waterman's[29] phrase it has more than a 'bias to action'; however, the actions which result may appear counter to the old order of efficiency or even effectiveness. How we deal with such challenges as individuals, organizations and as a wider society is the learning challenge of the next century. Moreover, challenges in the wider economic, ecological and political systems of the world suggest that such learning cannot be put off until after the pain has gone.

Conclusion

The spirit of learning in a company is elusive; its capture in a sense would kill it and yet it does manage to live and develop within organizations. One key factor seems to be that of freedom, in particular the freedom to take risks and the freedom to move on. The timing of this is difficult and relies on being in tune with the underlying purpose of an organization's life—this may mean using feelings, intuition and making new connections rather than relying solely on logical rational linear progression. This approach is difficult to justify within the logical paradigm as it often seems to defy logic and may only be used or recognized when all other avenues seem closed.

At this time it is worth recognizing that organizations do come to an end and die.[30] Sometimes this is inevitable, but sometimes it is because of premature ageing (many bodily analogies might be appropriate here!). But what I would stress is the importance of the renewal of organizational purpose by channelling into the essence of the organization rather than into defending the status quo. Such patterns can be seen in the life of voluntary organizations, whereby the purpose of the founder becomes set in the context of the past and change is often resisted because the spirit has been lost (even if only temporarily) and the structure becomes the purpose. This transformation and change in organizations is not easy; the spirit in a sense has to be lived and so much energy is often involved in either resisting change or in trying to keep alive dead and dying organizations. One key element often seems to be missing for us as managers and learners, particularly in the West—that of understanding and discerning the core, which I have called the spirit of a learning organization, and being able to serve it rather than try to control or harness it. We may need to find organizational forms in which the structure can embody the spirit and the spirit internalize the structure and in which both continually change.

References

1. Rogers, C. R. (1969) *Freedom to Learn*, Merrill, Indianapolis.
2. Dewey, J. (1919) (1966) *Democracy and Education*, Free Press, New York.
3. Boot, R. and M. Reynolds (eds) (1983) *Learning and Experience in Formal Education*, Manchester Monographs, Bournemouth.
4. Pedler, M., J. Burgoyne and T. Boydell (1991) *The Learning Company*, McGraw-Hill, Maidenhead.
5. Senge, P. (1990) *The Fifth Discipline. The Art and Practice of the Learning Organisation*, Doubleday/Currency, New York.
6. Revans, R. (1982) *The Origins and Growth of Action Learning*, Chartwell-Bratt, Bromley, Kent, and Lund, Sweden.
7. Chia, R. (1991) *Theory as Practice*, unpublished seminar paper, Lancaster University, Lancaster.
8. Drucker, P. (1985) *Innovation and Entrepreneurship*, Heinemann, London.
9. Helas, P. (1992) 'God's company: New Age ethics and the Bank of Credit and Commerce International', *Religion Today*, **8** Autumn/Winter.
10. Senge, op. cit.
11. Boot, R. and M. Reynolds (eds), op. cit.
12. Davies, J. (1992) 'Careers: biography in action: the narrative dimension', *Management Education and Development*, special issue Vol. **23** (3), 207–14.
13. Agor, W. E. (ed.) (1989) *Intuition in Organisations. Leading and Managing Productivity*, Sage, London.
14. Hochschild, A. (1983) *The Managed Heart*, University of California Press, California.
15. Wilson, D. C. (1992) *A Strategy Of Change*, Routledge, London.
16. Suetonius (1987) *The Twelve Caesars*, Penguin Classics, London.
17. Pettigrew, A., E. Ferlie and L. McKee (1992) *Shaping Strategic Change*, Sage, London.
18. Menzies, I. (1971) 'Social systems as a defence system against anxiety', *Human Relations* **13**, (2) 95–121.
19. Kuhn, T. S. (1970) *The Structure of Scientific Revolutions*, University of Chicago Press, Chicago.
20. Lewin, K. (1936) *Principles of Topological Psychology*, McGraw-Hill, New York.
21. Argyris, C. and D. Schon (1974) *Theory in Practice*, Jossey Bass, San Francisco.
22. Davies, J. and D. Binstead (1981) *Environmental Turbulence and its Effect on Organisation and Management Learning—The Dilemma of the 1980s*, unpublished seminar paper, DML, Lancaster University, Lancaster.
23. Snell, R. and J. Davies (1988) 'Tackling organisational disillusionment

through management development', *Journal of European and Industrial Training*, **12** (6), 5–11.

24. Snell, R. *et al.* (eds) (1992) 'Developing spirituality in organisations', *Management Education and Development*, special issue, **22** (3).
25. Senge, op. cit.
26. Vickers, G. (1984) *Human Systems are Different*, Harper & Row, New York.
27. Garratt, B. (1987) *The Learning Organisation*, Fontana, London.
28. Hawkins, P. (1990) 'The spiritual dimension of the learning organisation', *Management Education and Development*, special issue, **22** (3), 112–20.
29. Peters, T. and H. Waterman (1982) *In Search Of Excellence: Lessons from America's Best Run Companies*, Harper & Row, New York.
30. Lawrence, G. (1992) *Is There a Place for the Spiritual in the Industrial Enterprise?*, unpublished seminar paper, Lancaster University, Lancaster.

6
Energies of organization and change
Paul Tosey

Introduction

The concept of the 'learning company' implies a need for new ways of thinking about organizations, and about how we generate learning and change. This chapter explores an emerging, holistic way of thinking about organizations as energy. It introduces and discusses the concept of energy, and then illustrates how we might view our experience of organizations as flows of energy. The intention is to consider what this view could be like, and what it might reveal conceptually and pragmatically, but not to claim this exploratory framework as an authoritative perspective; nevertheless, dialogue with consultants and others who work with organizational change suggests that an 'energy' approach may have both practical relevance and experiential validity.

I wish to thank all those who have contributed to the ideas in this chapter, particularly those who, following the first Learning Company Conference, met at Sutton Courtenay Abbey in order to explore the theme of 'Energies and Organizations', and those who have participated in the continuing research into these themes.

How is the notion of energies relevant to the learning company?

The notion of the learning company may, and probably should, seek to transform our understanding of organizations. Traditional models, such as those using metaphors of machinery or concentrating on structures and procedures, seem thoroughly incongruent with the notion of learning. Even models that are more organic may not focus on learning.

What several newer perspectives on organizations appear to share, including that of the learning company, is a need for understanding based on energy and flow, rather like the way the 'new physics' describes the fluidity and patterning underlying the material world. For example, Morgan[1] refers to physicist David

Bohm, whose theory views 'process, flux, and change as fundamental, arguing that the state of the universe at any point in time reflects a more basic reality'; Bohm refers to this underlying, basic reality as *implicate order*. In the same way that the study of sub-atomic particles relies on traces of those particles' existence, but never senses the particles directly, perhaps the concrete, sensed reality of organizations is a trace of the underlying phenomenon of 'organizing'? Heider's Taoist perspective expresses a similar notion:

Everything, every behaviour, is a vibratory pattern or process. Such process emerges, develops, and decays, according to the single principle.[2]

This emphasis on process connects well with some personal biases about understanding change,[3] and elsewhere in the field of management and organizations Senge supports 'destroying the illusion that the world is created of separate, unrelated forces',[4] while Pedler *et al.*[5] describe their model of the learning company as essentially about 'energy flow'.

In spite of this, few have attempted to develop more specific models of organizations as process and energy. One example is Ackerman's[6] notion of 'flow state management'. The idea of 'flow state' is useful and relevant to this paper—for example, in the idea that an alignment of energies is desirable. Ackerman whets the appetite for a more detailed and practical analysis, yet continues to link the notion of energy to mechanistic metaphors of force, motion and critical mass— which I suggest is likely to mislead us. Do we not normally associate such concepts with 'energy'? Indeed we do, but herein lies a key point of this chapter's 'energy perspective'. I invite you to suspend, for now, your understanding of energy as a phenomenon that can be quantified and entered into equations—not only as used in the physical sciences, for Freud's notion of 'mental energy' carried similar connotation.[7]

This chapter is concerned with *human experience* of energy, rather than with 'energy as fuel' alone—although exploring the phenomenology of expressions such as 'feeling drained of energy' or 'raising the energy' is highly relevant. The *quality* of our energy feeds back into the systems in which we participate, just as we can imbue a statement with qualities of compassion or anger or joy or boredom and so communicate different messages through the same words. In Neuro-Linguistic Programming (NLP) a view put forward especially by John Grinder[8] is that effective performance arises from entering an appropriate physiological and neurological 'state'—rather than the 'state' being an output of effective performance. In more everyday terms, instead of feeling good or 'on form' as a result of doing well, we do well when we feel 'on form', and so preparation of our state is important. Thus consider, for example, how the New Zealand rugby team prepares their state through the ritual of the *haka*; how Buddhist chanting may literally be experienced as harmonizing people; and the Findhorn practice of beginning meetings with a period of meditation and attunement.

I suggest that most of us already influence the 'states' of our surroundings and of our organizations through our energy in this way, though somewhat blindly and perhaps counterproductively in that it may be towards outcomes different from those we consciously intend to produce. Perhaps we can use this influence more intentionally to maintain or change 'energy states' of organizations. UK-influenced corporate culture seems, however, more inclined to insist that it is only acceptable to 'feel good' after prolonged hard work; suffering must come before joy. We also have objections to 'energy-raising' rituals such as the *haka*, or cheer-leading, or communal exercise and the company song at the start of the working day. My own experience is more redolent of solemnity and obedience—when I recall the kind of state that resulted from morning assembly at school, or from attending church, my first inclination is to shed it before doing anything productive or creative.

These are illustrations of some of the variety of qualities of energy—all sensed through the body yet emotional ('energy' is related to, but not synonymous with, 'emotion'), mental and spiritual as well as physical. Participants in a workshop at the 1993 Learning Company Conference commented that they had previously thought of 'energy' as one thing, typically as 'get up and go', but were becoming open to wider interpretations. There are indeed many approaches which have explored, or are based on, energies; for example, energy as a felt sense is used in contemporary psychotherapeutic and developmental approaches such as Gendlin's 'focusing',[9] and many Eastern approaches to healing emphasize connections between energies, consciousness and well-being.[10]

There are two principles to note about the nature and meaning of energy for the purposes of this chapter. First, I am intentionally avoiding, and advising against, the use of 'energy' as a concept to explain what causes events in organizations.* Undoubtedly we will continue to slip back into that way of thinking, since it is well ingrained, but at least now we might spot when we are doing so. Secondly, I am suggesting that the experience of energy is an obvious, available and reliable 'trace' of the underlying processes, or implicate order, of organizing, which

---

* Gregory Bateson, an influential if not mainstream thinker whose work encompassed and connected anthropology, biology, psychology and ecology, frequently referred to the epistemological error of using a physical science concept of energy as an *explanatory* principle in the world of mind (Bateson, G. and Bateson, M. C. *Angels Fear*, Rider (1988) p. 188). Bateson proposed instead the notion of 'collateral energy' (Bateson G., *Mind and Nature*, Fontana/Collins (1979) pp. 111–14), which is neither causal nor deterministic. He distinguished, for example, between the direct, physical, causal transfer of energy when a billiard ball is struck and the *informational quality* of a kick given to a dog (a somewhat bizarre example, I admit). In the latter case the dog's response is not a direct function of the physical energy used in the kick; growling or biting has no necessary causal connection to the kick. The response is an example of collateral energy from its own metabolism. A related example frequently used by Bateson is that of the letter that is not sent. If I have been expecting a letter from you, I may respond to its non-arrival with sadness and complain of feeling hurt. But there has been no transfer of physical energy to cause this response—nothing physical has hit me and injured me; in fact, there was no letter. It is the *idea*, or what non-receipt of the letter *means* to me, that has elicited collateral energy.

become explicate as events, procedures, structures and so on. Thus energy is an *indicator* of implicate order and (through the information it supplies) an *influence* on, but *not* a cause of, action. What we are talking about is like the *Gestalt* notion of the 'field'[11] as something created by the relationships between people and the context in which they meet—a real phenomenon of 'mind' (in Gregory Bateson's terms) that can be apprehended by our senses. It has been suggested, for example, that corporate cultures can most usefully be thought of as existing as 'fields' in this sense—thus reflecting both their elusive nature and the point that we are the architects, albeit unconsciously and unwittingly, of our own cultures.

What difference might this view of energy make? Well, to begin with, if our experience is a direct, valuable indicator of the state of whatever system(s) we participate in, then our experience is a resource, the use of which we may need to relearn (my own feeling that I am relatively unfamiliar and inarticulate with energy is part of my desire to explore this theme). Nowadays, it seems, we either dismiss our sense of energy as an epiphenomenon—smoke from a factory chimney, a consequence of, but not a meaningful aspect of, events, an example of 'new age speak'—or, at the other extreme, allow it almost to become a demon through believing that feelings are the most authentic part of us and so compulsively take precedence over thought, intuition and so on (curiously, this creates a way in which 'energy' may determine action). This is rather like having an accelerator pedal whose settings are restricted to 'off' and 'full on'. Going back to school for a moment, I used to dislike the ritual of morning assembly; it escalated my sense of being a small and timid part of a stern institution. I never really thought of it as significant in the sense of shaping my energies and my performance; yet now it makes great sense as a 'designed' preparation of state, probably with the best of intentions of developing community, respect, even awe and celebration. And perhaps because I failed to treat this experience of energy as information, it seemed more like something 'out there' that was determining how I acted. We pay a price for remaining unfamiliar with parts of ourselves.

Of course, the influences on our energies come from more than rituals—our surroundings, and the minutiae of our experience, provide continuing sources. I work in the lee of Guildford Cathedral, a landmark for miles around and, in my view, an exceptionally ugly building. Yet I have experienced a profound shift at times when I have walked inside; the dark, squat exterior conceals light, soaring arches that almost pull my heart to the ceiling. Now, if this is an easily noticeable example of a shift in energy, reflect for a moment on what you experience when you arrive at work in the morning, or what you notice when you enter a client's premises. What happens when someone you like (or dislike) enters a room—how do you know that you like or dislike them? What's the difference between being in a group when the atmosphere is tense and can be 'cut with a knife', and when the group is flowing and celebratory? Most people would recognize these experiences—but consider how it is that you tell them apart. When spelt out like this, the notion of energy regains ordinariness and familiarity. Of course, you say, we all experience energy in these ways (and, I suggest, we usually dismiss such experience as insignificant unless it is heightened and overwhelming).

What would happen, then, if we turned our usual perception around, even if for the purpose of playing with ideas? What if, instead of being ephemeral 'smoke from the chimney', these experiences were seen as capable of telling us something important? What if, indeed, these experiences are perceived as direct apprehension of the implicate order of organizing, rather than the residue of its explicate order? A theoretical and philosophical analysis of these points exceeds the scope and exploratory purpose of this chapter, although it would be necessary to move beyond the heuristic and speculative. My intention here is to do no more than sketch out the 'what if' scenario and some of its possible implications.

A framework for 'energies': the nature and relevance of the *chakras*

Everything of importance is already known, a sage said—the only thing is to discover it.[12]

I and other authors have been talking about new perspectives on organization—yet I suggest we already know what we need to know, and that the task may be more a rediscovery and reinterpretation of ancient wisdom within a modern context. In beginning to explore the notion of energies, a perspective that began to resonate for me, feeling insightful but also challenging me enormously in unexpected ways, was that of the *chakra* system, originally a Hindu approach to understanding people and their world as flows of energies. In this chapter, the *chakra* system is drawn upon as a way of illustrating the nature of energies, an ancient 'screen' onto which to project contemporary questions and concerns, encouraging readers to apply the ideas to their own experience and situations. Note, though, that the outline and application presented here give no more than a highly simplified and superficial sense of the *chakras* and the deeper wisdom to which they are connected—at the same time, the choice of this approach is neither arbitrary nor merely an intellectual exercise.

The *chakra* system has existed in various forms, probably for millennia. Principally it is an integral part of Hindu philosophy and spiritual discipline;[13,14] 'chakra' is Sanskrit for 'wheel'. In its simplest form, there are seven wheel-like centres located in the body (see Figure 6.1). Each centre has a real, physical existence in that it is believed that we possess the potential capability of sensing their flows of energy;[15] and each has psychological and spiritual significance too, being associated with different qualities of experience and consciousness. Gerber[16] describes *chakras* as functioning like 'energy transformers', enabling, as in Bohm's notion, implicate order to become manifest and perceptible as an explicate order.

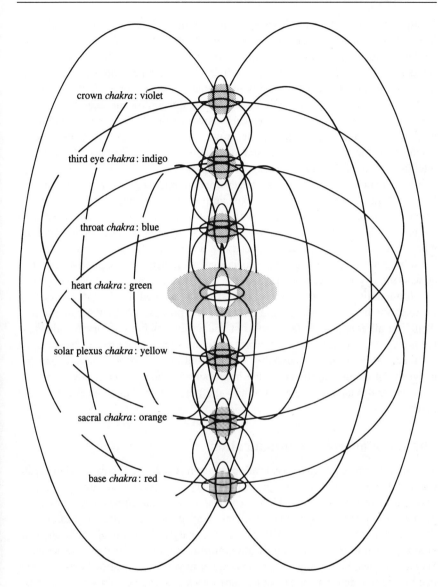

crown *chakra*: violet

third eye *chakra*: indigo

throat *chakra*: blue

heart *chakra*: green

solar plexus *chakra*: yellow

sacral *chakra*: orange

base *chakra*: red

Figure 6.1   The seven main *chakras* and commonly associated colours

Different emphases in various sources give rise to a diversity of interpretation of the 'meaning' and associations (with colours, sounds and more) of the *chakras*—they or their equivalent appear in many other cultures, and nowadays in many approaches to health and spiritual development. The *chakras* embrace multiple facets of human experience in a holistic way: the rational and the irrational, the material and the spiritual, the emotional and the intuitive, and the aesthetic and the pragmatic. As the *chakras* represent levels of vibration so the 'higher' *chakras* represent higher frequencies. There are developmental aspects to this, yet it is not intended as a strictly hierarchical system. For example, the 'base' or 'earth' *chakra* is no less divine or spiritually significant than the 'crown' *chakra*, even though the latter is typically associated with spirit, just as all human activities may have spiritual aspects, however mundane. Gandhi's practice of spinning cotton was both work and meditation, the spiritual and the material integrated through the 'mindfulness' of the spinner.

There are other approaches to management and organizations that have a similar form and qualities.[17,18,19] Here the main purpose is to outline seven energies, or strands of experience, associated with the seven main *chakras* and related to organizational life. For this purpose the strands are highly simplified—there are whole clusters of concepts and associations with each *chakra*, as can be seen by consulting the sources cited. The associations made here—perhaps best described as working hypotheses through which the framework itself continues to evolve— are ultimately personal choices, but strongly related to literature sources. Distinctions between energies are made for the purpose of drawing attention to them, but all energies are taken to exist concurrently within all organizations. In *Gestalt* terms, focusing on one treats it as figure rather than ground, but not as a separate entity. Finally, inevitably in presentation on paper there is tension between the whole and the parts; the impression of the connected flow of Figure 6.1 is therefore useful to keep in mind—the music, rather than the score set out here.

The seven energies of organization

The central themes and main associations of each energy are summarized in Figure 6.2. I will expand on these through an imaginary account of a consultancy project, which also introduces some theoretical and conceptual connections. Since the purpose is to illustrate the themes, and not to debate the validity of any analysis of the situation, the style is discursive rather than analytic. While reading the account, you may wish to relate the strands of organizational life to your own experience. Which energies, for example, are most familiar in your organization? How are they manifested? Which is present but perhaps unacknowledged? Who or what in the organization do you associate with each energy? Alternatively, work analogically by, for example, exploring associations with the main colour associated with each *chakra* (Figure 6.1).

Estelle, a consultant, had returned from an initial meeting with Frank, a middle manager involved in a quality improvement project in a large service organization. Frank managed a personnel section which served a national head office site, and

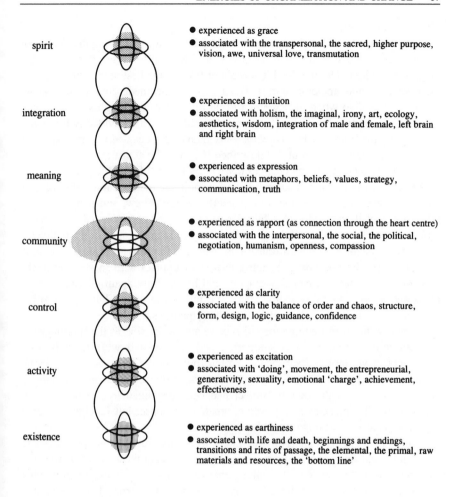

spirit
- experienced as grace
- associated with the transpersonal, the sacred, higher purpose, vision, awe, universal love, transmutation

integration
- experienced as intuition
- associated with holism, the imaginal, irony, art, ecology, aesthetics, wisdom, integration of male and female, left brain and right brain

meaning
- experienced as expression
- associated with metaphors, beliefs, values, strategy, communication, truth

community
- experienced as rapport (as connection through the heart centre)
- associated with the interpersonal, the social, the political, negotiation, humanism, openness, compassion

control
- experienced as clarity
- associated with the balance of order and chaos, structure, form, design, logic, guidance, confidence

activity
- experienced as excitation
- associated with 'doing', movement, the entrepreneurial, generativity, sexuality, emotional 'charge', achievement, effectiveness

existence
- experienced as earthiness
- associated with life and death, beginnings and endings, transitions and rites of passage, the elemental, the primal, raw materials and resources, the 'bottom line'

Figure 6.2 The seven energies

was participating in a wider quality project led by Estelle's principal client. Their meeting had been a chance for them to get to know each other, and to begin to explore issues potentially relevant to the section. Her intention had been to work conversationally to gain a sense of the underlying patterns at play and not to rush into a solution. Estelle then met with Archie, a fellow consultant, to debrief. As well as reviewing information about Frank's situation and the organizational context, Archie encouraged Estelle to attend to her own sense of energy both during her meeting with Frank and now, during the debrief. This was treated as potentially valuable data about the field.

The energy of existence

Estelle explained that Frank appeared keen for help with improving the quality of his section's service to internal customers, and wanted to know more about the project as a whole. He imagined it was about finding the best approach to quality improvement, and implementing it. But Frank had seemed cautious, defensive, Estelle felt, and so when they seemed to be relating well enough she had asked what was the bottom line; what if nothing changed—so what? Evidently Frank felt under pressure from the HR Director—his manager's boss—to deliver a better service or, perhaps, to get out. He described it as a survival issue.

Archie reflected that many changes involve issues of 'life' and 'death'—at least in the sense of beginnings and endings, of bringing something into existence, or letting something go. Thus the project itself was fairly new, and people needed time to accept it and feel safe. Change is often framed or perceived in terms of crises or transitions,[20] such as the growth stages of organizations[21] or even directly as birth and death.[22] Although transitions may feel traumatic and unsafe, people also thrive on the grounding, earthing energy of contact with these 'life-death' issues—to learn that we can slay dragons and live to fight again, or endure birth pains and survive to enjoy motherhood. We talk about earthy humour, positive aspects of which include elemental, nourishing qualities.

In organizations, this energy may also be related to money, as the 'bottom line' that determines what is to be supported and survive and what is to be cut; metaphors of warfare and survival are often found in the language of corporate finance and the business pages of the newspapers. In Frank's company, as in many other organizations, the quality project had been prompted by the need to cut costs—certainly intended as a positive, creative response, but Estelle wondered what the perceived message might be.

Frank's concern with survival was likely to be hooking into his personal and even biological fears of ceasing to exist. Acknowledging these could be the first step in releasing his capacity for making changes; conversely, clinging on to what we think is life for fear of dying is, writ large, like the inertia of organizational dinosaurs that lumber around in desperate need of an Ice Age. Archie asked how else Frank might be protecting himself, and Estelle reflected that his section seemed relatively large for its function. Had Frank perhaps been building up a small empire to inflate his importance?

The energy of activity

Archie asked Estelle about her sense of the level of energy—what kinds of activity did Frank prefer to engage in, and how did he compare with others in the organization? What was currently 'felt' in relation to this situation? What was exciting, and how was the flow of excitation blocked? Estelle had picked up little in the way of excitement or entrepreneurial urge as they had talked, and sensed that Frank was turning his fears of survival inward rather than outward. They had also talked of the frustrations of staff and customers, as if it were niggling away and not yet cleanly or clearly expressed. The predominant culture of the organization appeared to be professional, with bureaucratic and technical aspects, not a place for emotional outbursts.

Frank had said that people in the company typically seemed expected to handle crises without making a fuss. The engineers were an exception, expected and allowed to be a bit wild, but people took notice of Frank and his section when something went wrong, not when it went right. They would go in and get their hands dirty, though he took greater pleasure in things running smoothly. And when he wanted to be noticed? Frank had paused and acknowledged, a little reluctantly, that he resented being 'unseen' and that crises gave him an opportunity to be appreciated, so long as he did not over-dramatize.

So he did have a way of letting off steam, noted Archie, wondering too what frustrations and resentments about Frank and his section might be voiced by others in the organization. Apparently, continued Estelle, a difficulty Frank felt with the current situation was that he was being asked to become more proactive and entrepreneurial; that was not 'him', and he doubted his ability to deliver in that way. His preference, it seemed to her, was to damp down excitement rather than to raise it. The management literature that celebrates corporate heroes and heroines—perhaps much of the spirit of the 1980s—extols the entrepreneurial, action-orientated manifestation of this energy, and perhaps the drive for excellence.[23] It is also related to energies of group process, in the sense that a psychodynamic approach,[24] for example, is to do with the ways in which creative, active energy is manifested, utilized and blocked. Frank was reactive rather than passive; there was a lot of frustration around now—from his customers, from his staff, and from management. It was brewing and simmering rather than boiling over (yet), and he gave the impression of putting more and more effort into keeping the lid on it. Estelle concluded by observing that she felt joyless, and that this part of the project currently seemed like hard work.

The energy of control

Archie noted that the first two strands involved what most people naturally associate with the word 'energy'. Now there was a shift into looking at other qualities of consciousness, starting with the emergence of conscious intent; control, in a wide sense, since there are many ways in which thought creates forms, designs, plans and rules which structure events—clarity and direction which guide the energy of activity (often this *chakra* is also associated with intuitive knowledge in the sense of 'gut feeling', and with ego).

Although contained chaos suited him from time to time, Frank had seemed most comfortable with control and order; the principal task of Frank's section was to maintain an infrastructure of systems that enabled the organization to operate, and in fact his 'activity energy' seemed geared to maintaining control more than achieving end results. Certainly he was trying to get the systems 'right', but through design rather than through a perhaps more chaotic process of dialogue and feedback with his customers. Frank had agreed, when Estelle questioned him, that he and his staff did spend a lot of time focused on systems—designing them to do a job, aiming to gain long-term value in that once they were set up people did not appreciate constant changes. At the same time, they would complain about the system's deficiencies, which seemed unfair—another resentment. And now he was trying to guess the 'right answer' to the 'problem' of his section's quality of service.

At one extreme, the energy of control has as its archetype the rational organization—a prominent metaphor[25] is of the organization as machine—which can ignore human aspects of organizations and lead to management-as-exact-science and the view that the primary task of management is to control the deviations and disorder introduced by people's irrationality. Indeed, a huge proportion of organizational theory could be associated primarily with this energy.[26] However, the energy is not only about rationality and rules, nor is there an assumption that control in itself is a 'good thing'; in essence it is to do with managing the balance of order and chaos, and how control is manifested and experienced in relation to this.

The energy of community

It seemed, then, that Frank liked to relate to others through formal and technical aspects of work. What else was there? He had talked about having been around for a few years, and he had a good network of contacts at middle management level. They seemed to form a cadre: Frank had said it was not in any of their interests to let senior management think they were weak, so most of them tended to support each other by letting them get on with their jobs and not making trouble. Senior management were given quick service since it was they who were the most influential people.

He knew that other customers sought favours from his staff, and so liked them to stick to the policies and his own guidelines. In effect, it seemed that Frank required his staff to follow the rules while working more on a 'you scratch my back and I'll scratch yours' basis with his peers, and bending the rules for senior managers. He had portrayed this as the 'reality' of the organization—there was no point in operating in a way that was counter to his interests.

Archie said he wondered what kind of consultancy relationship would develop as the project continued. Would Frank be involved so long as it was meeting his interests, rather than having his heart in it? Estelle herself had felt little sympathy with Frank, and had worked hard to empathize. Frank had seemed reasonable enough on the surface, but not warm, and her impression was that he would retreat behind his defences if the going got tough.

The 'heart' *chakra*, the central energy, is often treated as being highly influential in the way the whole being functions. An open heart or centre facilitates flow of energy and health; a closed heart may offset the advantages of openness in other fields. The energy is about the sense and quality of connection with other people, experienced in how we relate to other people and create a co-existence with them. Sometimes we trust; sometimes we achieve intimacy and belonging; sometimes we create community through conflict and negotiation. In organizational theory, this energy is reflected, for example, in Human Relations theories of management and organizations;[27] perhaps in MacGregor's terms,[28] Theory X is an expression of 'controlling' energy, while Theory Y emphasizes 'community'. Social and political dynamics—the ways in which people relate to each other and create community—come to the fore. A traditional organization development approach to change could be seen as emphasizing especially the control (a rational, planned approach to change) and community strands (values of openness and honesty, and emphasis on interpersonal skills and relating).

For Frank, the energy of control seemed again to spill over into relating (illustrating, Archie remarked, that energies are interdependent and mutually influential, not neatly attributable to discrete features of organizations), in at least two ways. First, he appeared to relate to his own staff and other people in the organization through roles and rules; secondly, he seemed to be using his network as an aid to managing. The organization as a whole had a backcloth of rules, but from day to day Estelle had experienced an easy, informal style with people showing each other respect, whatever their status. The politics of the organization were probably more tacit than overt, but overall people appeared friendly. Frank, in contrast, seemed more isolated and had allies rather than friends.

The energy of meaning
The wider project was a story of how to improve quality, and Frank appeared enthusiastic about this—but to what extent was it a public rhetoric? Frank seemed to have assumed that 'quality' would provide a solution to the 'problem' he had perceived the HR Director to have defined, and revealed that he was still waiting to discuss the issue in detail with his own management team. He began to talk about the characters he managed. There was a secretive quality to this, which reinforced Estelle's sense of Frank isolating himself—the meaning of the quality project to him was more threatening, and he was not opening up to other interpretations and options. He seemed unwilling or unable to take his team into his confidence; he was concerned with his private meanings, rather than sharing ownership through dialogue. Estelle wondered how other people's truths might compare with Frank's perceptions.

Archie asked about the tone of what Frank was communicating. Estelle said that as she recalled it now, her own voice felt constricted. But, they noted, he could also be doing no more than echoing ambiguity in the organization's approach to the programme, in the way that it was couched in terms of quality and appeared to be driven by costs. Frank had told Estelle that the report which had set up the quality initiative had been referred to by managers at his level as the 'day of judgement' paper.

In relation to this energy, organizational culture approaches[29,30] would be concerned with exploring 'truths', beliefs, values, metaphors and symbols—the ways in which meaning and significance are created and maintained. Mission and strategic overview are relevant, too: as 'future-orientated stories'; symbolic tools for managing collective effectiveness. Finally, total quality[31] could be seen as emphasizing the meaning of each person's contribution within the whole system (it could also, noted Archie wryly, be seen in many other ways).

The energy of integration

Towards the 'higher' chakras, the energies refer to less concrete aspects of the outer organization, although they are still accessible through felt senses. They are less familiar to our usual ways of thinking, explained Archie, but are still recognizable. This is the energy of integration of principles such as left brain and right brain, mind and body, male and female, conscious and unconscious, and may be experienced through our intuition in the sense of apprehending wholes and patterns—an aesthetic awareness of people no longer as separate individuals, and organizations no longer separate from their environments. Irony is also related to this—ironic humour often signifies a reconciliation of opposites. Our sense of the whole picture may also draw attention to contradictions, paradoxes and dilemmas.[32]

Estelle said she recognized something like this as a kinaesthetic and visual sense of wholeness, a three-dimensional quality to her image of a client's situation. She suggested that they review some of the contradictions and incongruities they had picked up so far. For example, there was Frank's espoused values of quality and his apparent emphasis on control; and discrepancies between expecting others to keep to the rules while he got around them informally. Key points around which patterns seemed to have formed included status, which made a difference to the quality of Frank's response, and his concern with his own survival. They acknowledged that so far they were focusing a great deal on Frank as an individual, and reminded themselves that he was acting in relation to other people, all creating and maintaining together organizational patterns. The situation could be seen as a fractal, potentially a local example of a widespread pattern; they were not yet sure what this might look like.

Stafford Beer[33] raises the issue that our brains may not even be designed to apprehend this holistic level and its complexity, but perhaps it is this energy that models such as the learning company (that is, assuming that 'learning' is intended in an integrated, holistic, systemic sense) are aiming to access. 'New paradigm' ideas[34] and concepts such as chaos and fractals become incorporated into thinking about organizations. Some relevant approaches use ecological and sophisticated cultural metaphors to view organizations as complex, evolving systems which are both artistic and scientific[35] and, in a sense, conscious.[36] Approaches to change may emphasize processes of learning or inquiry[37,38] within the system itself—very different from the transfer of learning from a consultant to an organization, and not necessarily analogous to ways in which individuals learn.

The energy of spirit
Some people might dismiss the relevance of spirituality to work organizations; others claim that organizational change work is already embracing the spiritual realm. 'Organizational Transformation'[39] is a familiar label now—spiritual in intention and rhetoric, but perhaps a more unknown quantity in practice. Experientially, spirit might be described as a sense of grace, or of the sacred;[40] but these are words that might refer to very different experiences for different people. Harman[41] refers to 'potentially universal spiritual experience', which is 'sometimes referred to as "perennial wisdom"'. Here we meet more transpersonal aspects of experience.

The extra dimension here, Archie continued, was of universality and higher purpose—vision in a sense, but perhaps more than the strategic level that may be described in organizations' vision statements. Estelle and Archie were aware that it is not usual to talk directly about spirituality in organizations, especially because of its connotations of religion. She did note that the organization's sense of its own purpose was on a global scale, and had asked Frank how he felt in relation to that. He replied that it rarely occurred to him—his aim was to do his job effectively, and that what was most important to him was his home and his family. At this point Estelle had begun to feel more sympathetic again.

Archie remembered, in relation to the presence of concern with making cuts, reading a book by Richard Moss,[42] about surgery as a transformational experience. Moss suggests we are mistaken if we believe that only some 'natural', ideologically whole approaches to healing are valid and that medical practices such as surgery are necessarily harmful. Even the mundane brutality of surgery can be transformed or transmuted, given a spiritual approach. This reminded them that spirituality is not necessarily pure, and certainly not removed from everyday experience—the energies of 'spirit' and 'existence' are very much connected. In contrast, they were aware so far of a sense of disconnection in Frank's situation. Perhaps, they concluded for now, there was potential for learning here.

Conclusion: overview and implications

The purpose of this brief concluding section is to point to some implications, rather than to explore them in detail. A summary of Archie and Estelle's review is shown as Figure 6.3. This gives a sense of how the issue began to unfold when mapped out as energies; it was not, of course, a technical diagnosis, although it has proved

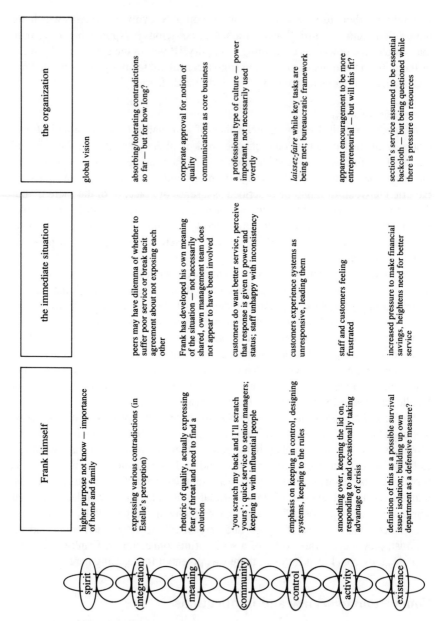

Figure 6.3   Summary of Frank's situation

a useful reflective process in its own right for some people wanting to clarify their experience of comparable situations.

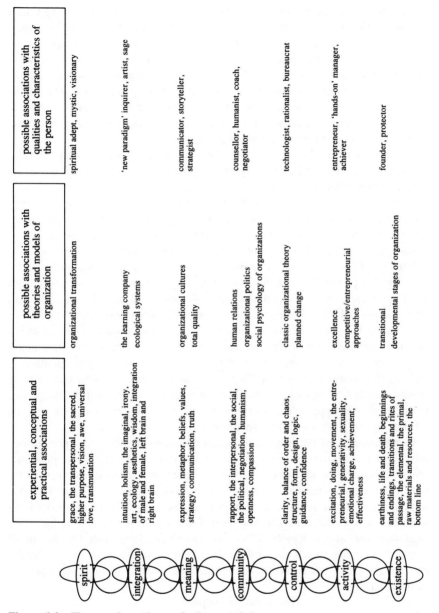

Figure 6.4   The energies and some further associations

There have been references to various approaches to understanding organizations and change where their principal concerns or assumptions seem 'figural' in relation to the energy in question. These associations are summarized in Figure 6.4, in which form this framework has been used as a learning tool. We should remember that its neatness is false, and useful principally for stimulating debate.

The account also intentionally leaves open the question of choices about 'what happens next', although an energies perspective introduces potential ways of working by aligning or balancing the energies; or by creating analogies of the *haka*, for example—contexts, rituals, spaces and structures which allow energy to flow appropriately and enable learning to take place. Current research is exploring how consultants 'work with energy' in practice.

In reading through the account, you may have noticed yourself being drawn to explore further one or more energies, or perhaps being convinced about the diagnosis and action you would take. Which features do you perceive to be most significant here? How would you describe your own 'energy profile', and how does this relate to the models or technologies you might choose to introduce to this situation? How might approaches to performance and change adopted in organizations be related to culturally valued or emphasized energies?

Finally, an energies perspective might also question how influential technologies for change can be in themselves. Typically, we are more concerned with models, strategies and programmes which we hope will provide solutions than with qualities of consciousness. But is any technology inherently capable of determining the 'state' of an organization, or of producing learning—or might outcomes be dependent at least as much on the consciousness through which a programme is approached as on the technical skills of implementation? Ackerman's own description of 'flow state management'[43] emphasizes state of being rather than competencies. Might we not benefit, therefore, from deepening more 'explicate' approaches with a sense of how our own energies may be influencing our work and our organizations?

In conclusion, understanding organizations as flows of energy, in a non-quantitative and non-deterministic sense, equips us with an emergent metaphor that seems relevant to the idea of the learning company. It also indicates potential for relating our direct, sensed experience to organizational processes. This chapter has superimposed contemporary questions onto the 'screen' of the *chakra* system, so providing a heuristic for exploring further the theme of energy. It has been suggested that as we reawaken to such knowledge, and with the advent of emphasis on organizations as processes of learning, it may be time to consider the effectiveness of change strategies and technologies more in relation to people and their energies.

> Energy is for support
> of
> the human soul
> as
> it moves towards its freedom.
> (Virginia Satir [44])

References

1. Morgan, G. (1986) *Images of Organization*, Sage, Beverly Hills, p. 233.
2. Heider, J. (1986) *The Tao of Leadership*, Gower, Aldershot, p. 101.
3. Tosey, P. (1993) 'Interfering with the Interference', *Management Education and Development*, **24**(3), 187–204.
4. Senge, P. (1990) *The Fifth Discipline*, Doubleday, New York, p. 3.
5. Pedler, M., T. Boydell and J. Burgoyne (1991) *The Learning Company*, McGraw-Hill, Maidenhead, p. 29.
6. Ackerman. L. (1984) 'The flow state: a new view of organizations and managing', in J. Adams (ed.) (1978) *Transforming Work*, Miles River Press, Virginia.
7. DeBoard, R. (1978) *The Psychoanalysis of Organizations*, Tavistock, London.
8. For example, Bandler, R. and J. Grinder (1979) *Frogs into Princes*, Real People Press, Moab, Utah p. 55.
9. Gendlin, E. (1981) *Focusing*, Bantam Books, New York.
10. Soo, C. (1983) *Taoist Yoga*, The Aquarian Press, Wellingborough, Northamptonshire.
11. Parlett, M. (1991) 'Reflections on field theory', *The British Gestalt Journal*, pt 1 69–81.
12. Ferguson, M. (1982) *The Aquarian Conspiracy*, Paladin/Granada, London, p. 296.
13. Ozaneic, N. (1990) *The Elements of the Chakras*, Element Books, Dorset.
14. Vaughan, F. (1985) *The Inward Arc: Healing and Wholeness in Psychotherapy and Spirituality*, New Science Library, Shambhala, Boston.
15. Brennan, B. (1988) *Hands of Light*, Bantam, London.
16. Gerber, R. (1988) *Vibrational Medicine*, Bear and Co., Santa Fe, p. 128.
17. Boydell, T. (1990) *Modes of Being and Learning*, Transform Working Paper no. 8.
18. Lessem, R. (1991) *Total Quality Learning: Building a Learning Organization*, Blackwell, Oxford. This describes Lessem's 'Spectral' system, a comprehensive approach to management learning and development.
19. Torbert, W. (1991) *The Power of Balance*, Sage, Beverly Hills, pp. 42–7.
20. There are copious version of 'transition curves'—see, for example, Adams, J., J. Hayes and B. Hopson (1976) *Transition: Understanding and Managing Personal Change*, Martin Robertson, London.
21. In Pedler, M., J. Burgoyne and T. Boydell (1991) *The Learning Company*, McGraw-Hill, Maidenhead, p. 6.
22. Wasdell, D. (1990) *The Roots of the Common Unconscious*, Meridian Monograph, Urchin, London.

23. Peters, T. and R. Waterman (1982) *In Search of Excellence*, Harper & Row, New York.

24. DeBoard, R. (1978) *The Psychoanalysis of Organizations*, Tavistock, London.

25. Morgan, G. (1986) *Images of Organization*, Sage, London, pp. 19–38.

26. Pugh, D. (ed.) (1971) *Organization Theory*, Penguin, London, (see, for example, parts 1 and 2).

27. Ibid., (see part 3).

28. McGregor, D. (1960) *The Human Side of Enterprize*, McGraw-Hill, New York.

29. Frost, P. et al. (eds) (1991) *Reframing Organizational Culture*, Sage, London.

30. McLean, A. and J. Marshall (1988) *Cultures At Work*, Local Government Training Board, Luton.

31. Walton, M. (1990) *Deming Management at Work*, Mercury, London.

32. Hampden-Turner, C. (1991) *Charting the Corporate Mind*, Blackwell, Oxford.

33. Beer, S. (1974) *Designing Freedom*, John Wiley, London, p. 59.

34. Harman, W. (1988) *Global Mind Change*, Knowledge Systems Inc., Indianapolis.

35. Marshall, J. and A. McLean (1985) 'Exploring Organisation Culture as a Route to Organisational Change', in Hammond V. (ed.) *Current Research in Management*, Frances Pinter, London.

36. For example, the notion of autopoiesis (see Morgan, G. (1986) *Images of Organization*, Sage, London pp. 235–40).

37. Reason, P. (1988) (ed.) *Human Inquiry In Action: Developments in New Paradigm Research*, Sage, London.

38. Torbert, W. (1991) *The Power of Balance*, Sage, Torbert, W. op. cit.

39. Owen, H. (1987) *Spirit, Transformation and Development in Organizations*, Abbott, Potomac, MD.

40. Bateson, G. and M. C. Bateson (1988) *Angels Fear*, Rider Books, London.

41. Harman, W. (1988) *Global Mind Change*, Knowledge Systems Inc., Indianapolis, p. 83.

42. Moss, R. (1985) *How Shall I Live?* Celestial Arts, Berkeley, CA.

43. Ackerman, L. (1984) 'The flow state: a new view of organizations and managing', in J. Adams (ed.) *Transforming Work*, Miles River Press, p. 125.

44. Satir, V. (1985) *Meditations and Inspirations*, Celestial Arts, Berkeley, CA, p. 49.

7
Levels of learning in organizations
David Sutton

Overview

This chapter has been written to share some frameworks and models of learning that I have used and developed over more than twelve years in consultancy and management development. In the course of trying to help others with their problems, and to make sense of what seemed to work, I often found it useful to look into the literature which dealt with learning. The search has not been an academic one; it has always been grounded in the need to help a specific client or group as they grappled with a current practical problem. The search has been fruitful, and I hope to give you some feel for the flavour of what I have found useful.

The frameworks and models which I will discuss here may seem neat and well thought out now, but they did not spring out fully formed in the manner of Athena from the brow of Zeus. It is more true to say that they slowly crystallized out of reflection, upon numerous flipchart sketches hastily scrawled in the heat of discussion, and debate, in many situations with many different groups working upon many different problems.

The materials were used and refined in the course of working on individual self-development and creativity sessions, training and facilitation in group and inter-group processes, the development of computer systems and expert systems, work on human–computer interaction, the design of new organizational structures and systems, and in the debate of significant and contentious issues such as 'What business are we in anyway?'

The frameworks are introduced here in their general form; in use, they are interpreted into the client's domain and populated with facts and perceptions that correspond to the specific situation of concern. The real benefit of the frameworks lies in going through the process and developing the increased clarity of vision. Any model interpreted and constructed by a group of participants is not necessarily 'true' so much as more or less useful. Such models are better regarded as a condensed record of the ideas formulated; they are essentially icons which have most meaning for those who participated in their development.

No reporting of the framework in its interpreted form can convey the sensations of success and confidence which those involved felt. To paraphrase the scripture: 'To know what it is to dance, you must have danced yourself', the spectator may see more of the game, but he or she will never experience what it felt like to play in that particular game. So, the frameworks which I am about to describe must be viewed in the light of, say, an essay on the rules and principles of a game. (If you would like to know about what it feels like to play, and be caught up in, the game, that is, as they say, another story.)

Introduction

In my view, all organizations are learning systems. Learning embraces the capacity to respond to change; if organizations are not learning they are dying, or dead. Unlike with people, however, it is not so obvious when an organization is in a terminal condition. Different parts of a dead organization decompose at different rates and they may appear to be operating in an apparently normal way. However, I have experienced working in an organization from which the soul had clearly departed, and have heard others talk of similar feelings.

If, therefore, all viable organizations are learning, the learning company debate, as I see it, centres on finding ways to understand the *quality* of the learning that is present in an individual organization, how we assess whether that quality may be improved and how we may usefully intervene. To do those things, we need to be able to understand that there are many different types of learning, to be able to evaluate the extent to which a given organization supports the repertoire of learning faculties its environment necessitates and, ideally, to understand how to intervene in ways which are constructive, feasible and acceptable.

I view people as the fundamental constituent of organizations, and in trying to help with organizational issues I have generally found it necessary to start with some aspect of people at an individual level. Of the possible people-focused starting points, the most generally useful that I have found is, as I said before, that which highlights learning and problem solving.

Models of learning for an individual

Learning styles
One of the most powerful models of learning that I have found is the learning cycle model as described by Kolb and Fry.[1] It was developed from a synthesis of experiential learning[2,3] and the psychology of human information processing.[4,5,6] All these sources converge on similar conclusions, namely, that there are four princi-

pal stereotypes of human behaviour when it comes to modelling the way we learn, solve problems and communicate information.

These four styles may be briefly described in terms of orientation to particular aspects of situations and behaviour:

1. *Ideas*   This style is very open to new ideas, easily seeks and adopts new perspectives, is very comfortable with uncertainty and is oriented to the people side of things.
2. *Frameworks*   This style is always after the underlying principles, looks for the generalizable aspects of situations and seeks rigour and objectivity.
3. *Plans*   This style seeks to select and close down, to follow procedures, make decisions and is uncomfortable with uncertainty and untidiness.
4. *Actions*   This style is concerned with acting on current situations rather than being objective, passive or dealing with generalities, preferring interacting with people.

The underlying framework to which all these authorities subscribe views learning as a cyclic process. In learning or problem solving, the focus of attention and approach will, ideally, pass sequentially through the different styles. The basic framework (illustrated in Figure 7.1) relates well to other models of learning and problem solving such as medical examinations and the scientific method.

A key assumption of this model is that all people have some facility in all four styles, otherwise they could not learn. However, individuals are seldom equally at ease in all the modes of processing and in most cases people have a strong preference for focusing on one or two of these styles or orientations. We use this model to develop people's awareness of the different behaviours that make up effective learning and so we give it the name of the learning style preferences model (LSP).

Persistent use of inappropriate styles or refusal to acknowledge the merits of the other styles causes many organizational problems. An important lesson from this

Figure 7.1   Phase of problem-solving and learning

work is that there is no 'right' style, all have merit and appropriate times for employment. Generating respect through appreciation of the value of each style is a valuable aid to interpersonal communication and cooperation.

It is important to view these distinctions as modes of behaviour and focus rather than as labels for individuals. They are not describing personality 'types' as such, but attitudes which relate to learning and problem solving in general. Although the psychological explanations for these preferences are complicated, it is not difficult to take account of them; all that is really needed is to be given a language with which to recognize, differentiate and understand the characteristics of the archetypes.

We make considerable use of this framework in our work; it is able to explain and guide us through many of the situations that arise when individuals and groups have preferences which do not correspond with the styles of those with whom they have to work.[7] It is also found to be very helpful to anyone who has to manage research or problem-solving teams.[8]

The basic learning style model assumes a cyclic process of learning. We continuously receive data from the outside world, assimilate them into our models and theories and respond in accordance with our beliefs and intentions. Learning refines those beliefs and intentions in a process which may be viewed as a spiral as we cycle through the styles and progress through time.

While this model has very great explanatory and diagnostic power, far beyond that mentioned here, it does not tell the full story of learning. Learning is more than just refinement driven by stimulus-response; whence come new models, new beliefs, inspiration or motivation? The LSP model does not explain the difference between knowledge and understanding.

Learning levels

The term 'double-loop learning' was coined[9] to highlight the distinction between learning and problem solving that simply refined existing knowledge and skills and that which deliberately sought to develop new knowledge or capabilities. The term was used to distinguish the approaches of organizations and their managements to problems. Some focused on efficiency, and when problems arose they tried to do 'more of the same'; other organizations recognized the need to consider effectiveness as well and, when problems arose, were prepared to ask themselves 'Should we be doing this anyway?' In that work Argyris may be said to have created the notion of organizational learning.[10]

However, there were others who, in examining how individuals learned, developed models of learning which posited more than just two types of learning. As with the cyclic model, workers from a diversity of starting points all came to similar conclusions. For example, Bateson,[11] a psychologist, and Gagné,[12] an educationalist, both proposed many more than two levels of learning (these are featured in Figure 7.2). (In fact, Argyris[9] acknowledges that he was influenced by

	Bateson	Gagné
L0	(detection)	signal
L1	reflex	stimulus—response
L2	skill	chaining
L3	learning	discrimination
L4	learning to learn	problem solving
...	learning to learn to learn	concept learning
...	...	...

Figure 7.2   Levels of learning

the early work of Bateson.) The levels of Bateson and Gagné correspond quite closely and may be explained as follows.

If we accept that, at root, learning is recognized by a change in behaviour, we can distinguish different categories of change, each of which is held to correspond to learning of a different type. This does not mean that the process of learning is necessarily any different, just that the quality of the change, and the nature of the entities affected, are different.

An obvious change is to respond to a stimulus, such as when we snatch our hand back from a plate which was hotter than we anticipated. This reflex is an automatic response, but it is still a change in response to a change in circumstances. This corresponds to L1 in Figure 7.2. While we might see this as the most elementary form of change, there is one even more fundamental, shown as L0 in the figure. The point of level 0 is that, for us to be aware of any stimulus, one of our senses must itself have detected some disturbance in the first place and this involved a response of an even more basic kind. This is still learning, in that we 'learn' that the sun has just come out through the increased signalling rate of the light-detecting cells in our eyes. This is a different order of learning from our response to the realization that the sun has come out of putting on our sunglasses.

The reason we make the distinction between level 0 learning and level 1 learning is that sensory detectors are 'hard wired'; they must, by their very nature, respond in the same way to a given stimulus. Their response may never change, but they still do respond. On the other hand, our larger scale responses to stimuli, while often automatic, are changeable. For example, we can decline to put on our sunglasses or we can train ourselves to walk upon burning coals.

Further orders of learning are recognized in the same way. While we use our reflexes to respond to low-level stimuli more or less automatically, there are situations where we wish to make use of our reflexes to achieve more controlled or coordinated action, for example, to learn to play tennis or to ride a bicycle, we need to train our muscles and hand–eye coordination. This is the realm of skills, which can be learned by training and practice. Bateson characterized the skill (L2) type of learning as learning to select and combine reflexes. For example, if we snatch back our hand every time we put it in the fire, we are using L1 learning, whereas if we decide to stop putting our hand in the fire, we have used L2 type learning. L2 type learning may be characterized as 'learning not to make the same mistake twice' and would match with the second loop of the Argyris model, while companies which respond to failure by doing 'more of the same' are using type 1 learning.

Of a different order again is learning to select and combine skills. You may be able to ride a bicycle and drive a car. The decision as to which to use requires a different order of thought from that of developing either of the individual abilities. Bateson characterized L3 as the type most commonly viewed as learning, but, observing that some people seem better able to learn than others, he speculated that higher levels of learning must exist, for example, 'learning how to learn'. He suggested that the series may go on through learning to learn, learning to learn to learn, and so on. The Gagné model, grounded in direct observation and experience of the way children learn, provides more tangible labels for the higher levels of learning.

There have been many other suggestions of multiple levels of learning. Hess,[13] when studying the ways fighter pilots handled the complexity of information processing and action priorities in their work, identified multiple levels of problem solving and cognitive processing, and the objects and considerations being addressed at each level. Beer,[14] when offering guidance to the management of complex business operations, offered a series of different levels of perspective and purpose. These two writers' models are illustrated in Figure 7.3.

Other studies of problem solving and communication have found it helpful to assume multiple levels of processing. Linguists posit seven levels[15] and Sutton[16,17] has developed a framework for modelling human communication which harmonizes with these and other sources in a recursive system of learning cycles known as Cognitive Transactional Analysis.

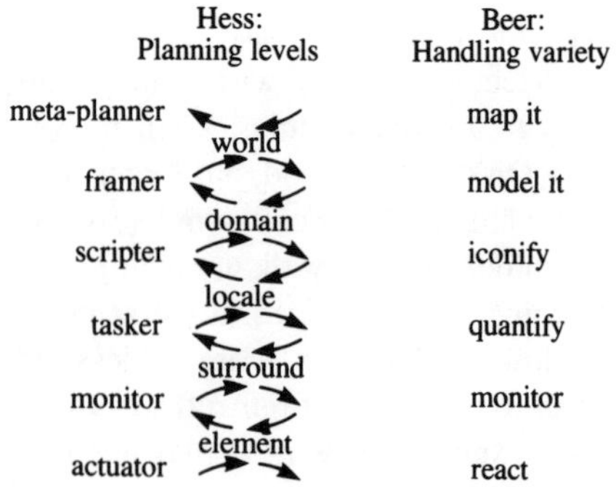

Figure 7.3

The aim is not to assert that there is any number of learning levels that is particularly 'right', simply that many sources have found that differentiating multiple levels of learning has been helpful. It is important to recognize, however, that the levels are not arbitrary distinctions; they separate aspects of our world which are of different logical type. Objects and issues at one level are of equal status, while the relationships between the contents of different levels are like those between components, sub-assemblies and finished items. The conventional taxonomic approach in which families have species and species have sub-species is a typical application of this way of structuring ideas. In essence, learning how to do something better is not at all the same as deciding when or if to do it.

These models in combination answer a number of questions that have been raised about the nature of learning. For example, learning may be viewed as a spiral if we consider the type of learning that is concerned with refinement over time. The refinement of a skill, the refinement of ideas within a fixed context or the type of non-revolutionary research characterized by Kuhn[18] will all be essentially single-loop learning proceeding as a spiral.

On the other hand, learning may also be discontinuous if it entails recognizing novelty or shifting to a new level of awareness. The revolutionary type of scientific development cited by Kuhn or the 'aha' type of discovery will be examples of this type of learning. These models also extend our understanding in other directions, for example, certain types of personality conflict and communication breakdown can be explained in terms of these two models, and the models of Kelly[5] and Pask[19] can, among others, be seen to harmonize with these essential features of learning. Issues such as these are explored more fully in Sutton.[17]

A final point which will be featured later is that when we concentrate on any topic we tend to direct our attention to one level of focus at a time. This is not to say that we cannot move rapidly from one level to another, or that we cannot 'see' the relationships and contents of more than one level at a time. The point is that, when we need to fill in or refine details, the limits to our cognitive capacities cause us to deal with one level at a time.

The learning of organizations

If we combine and distil what all these studies of individual learning tell us, it looks as though it would be useful to view learning as a process which cycles through a limited number of perspectives and which operates at multiple levels. Each level will represent a point of view which focuses upon objects of a particular logical type. The rest of this chapter will discuss what emerges when we take these core elements and broaden their scope into the realm of a whole organization.

The essential features of cycles, styles and levels that characterize individual learning *are* relevant in the context of an organization. The difference lies in what the levels, etc. represent and in the mechanisms whereby learning will be manifested. For example, our reflexes are automatic muscular or mental responses, whereas the automatic responses of an organization will be encoded in its structures, rules and procedures. At a higher logical level, we change our behaviour by changing our desires or our view of the world, whereas an organization will change its behaviour by changing its mission, rules or structures.

The first step towards organizational learning is to identify a useful and logical way of differentiating organizational processes into levels. A framework which we find very useful is that of Socio-technical systems design (STS).[20] This embodies a very participative approach to organizational learning which has many significant benefits and guidelines for action. However, the feature I want to highlight here is the way STS differentiates four main levels of concern in an organization.

An organization must be clear what it is trying to achieve in global terms and what are the factors that will influence its definition and pursuit of its objectives. These are issues of *Vision and Mission*. It must also be clear about how it is to actualize the mission, what activities it must engage in, how they are to be organized, supported and managed. STS classifies this aspect as identifying the *Major Activities*. Each activity must be understood in terms of exactly how it must be performed, what is the nature of each step, what are its inputs, outputs and the transformations it must achieve—these are the *Tasks*. Finally, any task may necessitate the use of some tool or the preparation of some artefact. These are issues of the *Tools and Technology*.

Within each of these levels of issue, there are many subsidiary divisions and structures, but it is fair to say that each of these four represents topics of different scope and scale. Each of these levels requires many processes to be performed, and whole professions have grown up around and within them. Each level has an associated design activity which addresses recognizably different objects and issues: these are the design areas of strategy, structure, work, and technology. We have often found it very useful to link the STS viewpoint with the design levels and they are illustrated together in Figure 7.4.

I have found it useful to view the process of design as another form of the learning or problem-solving process. I will illustrate this by showing how the

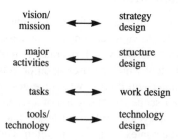

Figure 7.4 Socio-technical systems design: levels of organizational issue

conventional models of the design process may be transformed into the LSP framework introduced earlier.

There are many models of the design process, but they can all be viewed as versions of the basic scheme shown in Figure 7.5. *Requirements* are specified by the customer, and the designers then *analyse* those requirements against the known laws and capabilities governing the type of application. For example, if the requirement was for a building, then the reference disciplines would be those of architecture, civil engineering, geology, etc.; if for some machinery or plant, the reference disciplines might be metallurgy, mechanical engineering, etc., and so on.

The analysis would, in effect, translate the performance specification expressed in the language of the client into the technical specification expressed in the language of the designers and engineers who are to make what is required. The stage of *design* then proceeds to prepare all the detailed drawings and instructions which, when followed in the *implementation* stage, will ensure the satisfactory construction and operation of the finished product.

When initially developed, design models were presumed to proceed in a linear fashion, with each stage having a definite finished output and being completed before work started on the next phase. It has gradually been realized that this is no more true of what happens in reality than is the idealized version of the scientific method true of how scientific discoveries are made. In fact, design should be viewed as an ongoing process which must allow for alterations at every stage.

It is being realized that designers in many spheres must accept that user requirements are necessarily going to change over the lifespan of any project. Given the turbulent nature of today's world, users' business priorities will change faster than systems can be designed and delivered. To go further into this area is beyond the scope of this chapter but it was precisely in the course of helping clients to face up to such challenges as these that we developed and made use of the learning models featured here.

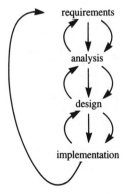

Figure 7.5   Stages of technical design

When we brought the cyclic model of learning together with the stages of design featured above, we found that the design phases fit very well with the four learning style stereotypes. *Requirements* correspond very well to the *Ideas* and opening-up phase, and the others, Analysis, Design and Implementation, fit with *Frameworks*, *Plans* and *Actions* phases respectively. This linking yields further fruit when we look into the behavioural orientations that support the activities of each design phase, but again, in the interests of brevity, this aspect cannot be discussed here in any more detail.

We next brought in the multi-level aspect of learning in the form of the four organizational levels of issue identified by STS and their design analogues. If we consider the activities addressing the design of an organization's *strategy*, we can see clearly that establishing the requirements at this level deals with very different objects and issues from establishing the requirements at the level of *structure*. The same is true for analysis and design; however, I want to focus next on the nature of the *Implementation* phase.

It is clear that, to implement a strategy, you must design an organization. This may entail designing a whole new operation, or simply modifying an existing one. Without defining an organizational structure and procedures to support operational (implementation) activities, no effective work can be done. Therefore, we proposed that the implementation phase of strategic design is, in fact, structure design. This is represented in Figure 7.6.

Figure 7.6 illustrates the relationship between the different processes and issues addressed by strategic design and structure design. By structure design, we mean all institutional aspects of an organization, that is to say, the structure and relationships within and between operating departments and service departments together with all formalized procedures.

Our representation, even in the simple form shown in Figure 7.6, brings out much that can be overlooked in the day-to-day turmoil. First, structure, as the

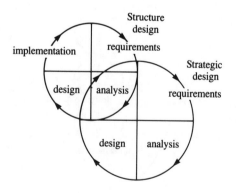

Figure 7.6

implementation phase of strategy, cannot proceed in isolation from it; indeed, the strategy design has set the requirements for the structure. Secondly, the strategy level, while setting the requirements for structure, also receives valuable information from the structure design process concerning issues of feasibility and opportunity. So structure sets constraints upon strategy just as much as strategy sets constraints upon structure. These are dynamic processes and their interaction is two-way.

We need to emphasize further the special status that is given to implementation at any level. The complexity of considerations and actions in the implementation phase is always higher than for any other phase at the same level. This is because implementation is where 'the rubber meets the road'. The idealized and formalized abstractions and generalizations that were the currency within the deliberations over requirements, analysis and design are required, in the implementation phase, to meet the variety and uncertainty of the concrete, physical world of action.

So, while implementation is a fourth phase, to deal properly with its complexity and dynamism, we must enter more deeply into it. It is the act of focusing upon implementation at any level that drops us into the more detailed and restricted domain which encompasses it. As we seek to resolve it into its parts, we enter upon another cycle of learning, with the same four phases but with more narrowly defined issues and objects of concern. Thus, what the encompassing perspective sees as 'attending to the fine details of implementation', the encompassed perspective sees as simply the beginning of consideration of the 'statements of requirements'.

This minimal model helps to remind us that changes in strategy are very likely to change the requirements for structure. Although implementation may be considered as the jumping—off point to a more detailed level of resolution, it must be emphasized that it is not a one-way flow. Admittedly, the implementation has a duty to implement the design specified by the strategic design process, however, the strategic design process has a duty to listen to the messages provided by the strategic design debate. The requirements, analysis and design *must* take account of what it is feasible to implement, and it is the strategic design level which provides the information as to what has been before and is now feasible. The model helps to remind us that there must be two-way interaction between adjacent levels of design.

This means that, if we want to survive, we must not fix our organizational structures or procedures—we must ensure that they can be changed. We must also ensure that the strategic design process is informed of the actualities encapsulated in the structure design and *its* implementation. We must not miss opportunities to enhance or improve our strategy that are afforded by the way our structure performs. Using this framework we can confirm and enhance the total quality message that highlights the importance of measurement; it is not just for statistical process control of current operations, but to keep strategy informed as well.

A further fundamental message from this model is to cause us to reflect upon the forms which stylistic preferences will take at the organizational level. As Kolb[1] and others found, members of disciplines and professions tend to share dominant learning style preferences. We have found that departments and groups within organizations share style preferences which characterize the context and focus of the function concerned. We also find that many operational problems can be seen to have their source in the failure to cope with a mismatch of styles between groups or departments.

In fact, the LSP framework can be used to distinguish not just learning styles, but the underlying values and world views that are held by individuals and groups. This provides many powerful insights and has been a core component of many of our facilitative interventions. The implications of stylistic and world view mismatch in and between departments and interest groups is featured at greater length in Sutton.[17,16]

Reflection upon Figure 7.6 also leads to the question of what constitutes implementation of organizational structure. If the structure defines the standard and formal operations, implementation must address the actual operation of the procedures and execution of the tasks. These are the areas addressed by work design. This can embrace the necessary coping and adjustment which is entailed in the performance of any operation, or the working out of the details of new tasks. This is the realm of resource allocation, scheduling, job specifications, etc.

Just as work design is the implementation phase of structure design, so technology design may be viewed as the implementation phase of work design. Taken together, these different learning processes address the four sets of concerns in

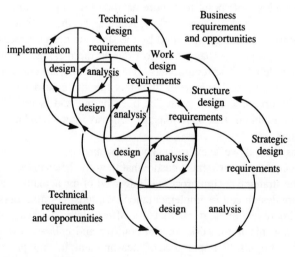

Figure 7.7   Enterprise Design Framework

the development and functioning of an organization as originally defined by STS. However, this model goes further than the STS distinctions in that it represents both the logical relationships and their nature as dynamic processes grounded in learning principles. We give this model the title of the Enterprise Design Framework (EDF) and the full set of relationships is depicted in Figure 7.7.

Strictly speaking, there is a fifth level to be considered which sets the context for the strategic design process. That fifth loop would represent the underlying culture, values and ethical issues which define what may count as an acceptable mission and as acceptable ways of pursuing such a mission. At general management level these are often the dominating considerations. However, we find that handling aspects of culture, power, values, etc. is an issue of process facilitation for which other tools and techniques are more helpful.

Implications of the Enterprise Design Framework
This is a framework to assist deliberations; it is not 'true' in any sense beyond its usefulness. We call it a framework to emphasize that it is representing features which underlie learning processes rather than defining processes which are distinct, observable activities. That said, we find the framework to be very useful. First, it reduces the confusion that arises when groups have overlooked the multiplicity of perspectives and issues that impinge upon the problem which is the current focus of their attention. Secondly, it clarifies the nature of the misunderstandings that arise because the groups have different dominant learning styles, world views or systems of values. Thirdly, it reinforces the recognition that the contact with everyday practicalities, the customers, new technology, etc., is engaged in the learning cycle that is represented by the implementation of the technology. It is therefore a most valuable source of information about constraint and opportunity: it provides constraint and opportunity to the work design level of the enterprise and, appropriately interpreted, to the more global levels as well.

Using this framework we can show that too often information is passed down ('cascade briefing') without recognition and support of the reciprocal flows of information that are vital. It would be more helpful to talk in terms of 'cascade listening' or 'two-way briefing'. In addition, too often information is passed down without interpretation into the languages and goals of the more focused levels of the organization. We have been able to radically improve institutional design methodologies simply by operationalizing such simple insights as these, although it was only by use of this framework that they appeared as articulatable insights at all.

If we proceed further in considering the implications of the need for two-way mutual briefing processes in organizations to support the different design and learning processes, we see a role for the middle managers displaced by advances in information technology (IT). While IT is able to carry out the gathering, exchange and filtering of data that used to be a major component of the role of middle management, it is not able to interpret the language or significance of information in the personal context of each individual.

This is exactly what two-way briefing entails. Constraints and opportunity at each level of focus must be communicated to the adjacent levels. However, communication alone is not enough; different levels deal with different concerns and speak different languages. It is only by translation that the implications for and from adjacent levels can be identified. This translation can only be carried out by people and, furthermore, by people who speak both languages. This should be a challenging and satisfying role, one for which middle managers should be well qualified and one which is essential to support the learning processes of an organization. For example, a company vision or mission statement is useless if individuals cannot see how it relates to what *they* do.

As emphasized above, the framework in Figure 7.7 is not a model of specific organizational processes, but an illustration of the principles and features which will underlie and characterize certain organizational processes, namely those which support learning. An essential feature of frameworks is that they can be

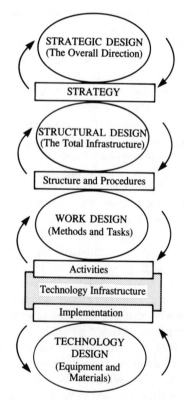

Figure 7.8   Enterprise Design Framework

interpreted into different domains. However, after interpretation, they can look quite different from the core model. Figure 7.8 illustrates a version of the EDF that was used when helping a group concerned with the design of computer-based information systems. It is simplified in that it does not emphasize the styles and cycle within an individual level of learning, but is focusing upon the interaction between levels. In addition, to fit the greater detail required in the domains of work and technology, it has been modified to convey the operational fact that the implementation of the organization's work actually takes place through the simultaneous implementation of work design and technology design.

The interactions with the real world actually take place at the level shown as *Activities*. The activities interact with the outside world and conduct their processes using the tools provided (shown as the technology infrastructure). The technology infrastructure is constantly upgraded and adapted through the technology design process. Despite this refinement, all these processes are still recognized as implementing the structure, strategy, etc.

Figure 7.8 shows a way of interpreting the EDF which, for the clients concerned, portrayed all that was required to give new insights and provide confidence to proceed to action. As I said before, the principal beneficiaries of these frameworks are the users themselves; the principles are used to construct an insightful model of the issues surrounding them. The illustration of the principles by Figure 7.7 is but a staging post on the journey to clarity; its main aim is to present the principles in a way that is easy to assimilate, and to provide a common language for the participants to express aspects of their situation which they may have previously been unable to discuss, or of which they had previously been unaware.

Links with other learning models

The Argyris[9] double-loop model is seen to be fully harmonious with the EDF, of which it may be seen as a special case. This does not mean that the double-loop model is in any way superseded; indeed, the two models reinforce and enrich each other. The EDF adds to the double loops the recognition of the styles within each loop and how they must be recognized as possible sources of problems which can cloud the issues addressing the balance between efficiency and effectiveness. Moreover, by depicting more than two logical levels of issue within an organization, the EDF can alert us to the fact that one person's double loop may be another's single loop. This highlights the importance of using problem structuring tools to ensure that all relevant levels of focus are distinguished.

On the other hand, the double loop is itself a fine starting point for entry into problematic situations. As mentioned earlier, when concentrating on difficult issues we tend to focus on a single level at a time. When we dc so, any tool which helps us to unlock our perceptions and take a broader perspective will be helpful, and the double-loop model is sufficient to stimulate the recognition of this need. It also has the merit of simplicity while being fully in harmony with the EDF. Essentially, whichever level of perspective we are addressing, the level which shapes its immediate context *is* the second loop. However, the EDF alerts us to the fact that there is not just one double loop but potentially many ways to broaden our perspective and, through the styles component, reminds us that there are also many different ways of discussing each perspective.

Another model with which the EDF aligns is the Garratt[21] egg-timer model, which in any case acknowledges its roots in the Argyris model. The relationships are therefore similar to those with the double loop; however, the EDF might lead us to question the wisdom of associating the two loops with 'Strategy' and 'Operations'. The EDF, backed up by STS, would ask, 'Should we not make explicit the need to see "Structure" in there as well?' After all, how many times have we been told that it is 'the system' that is preventing the adoption of an otherwise acceptable and desirable change? The capacity of organizational structures and procedures to support or impede change is so fundamental that we feel it needs to be made explicit.

Another model in the same family is that of Hawkins.[22] This adds a third loop ('Service') to make explicit the values and ethics issues to which I referred earlier as a potential fifth level for the EDF to portray. In addition, Hawkins specifically features an aspect which the EDF does not address, namely, the precise nature of the process that mediates between the learning levels. In EDF we concern ourselves with the fact of multiple levels of perspective, and have tended to see transitions between them as shifts in awareness which are so rapid as to be outside the scope of the framework. We use other models to address the communication and transduction which actualizes those exchanges and the mechanisms to support them, but the Hawkins perspective seems to offer additional insights into fostering such shifts in awareness.

Finally, it is interesting to see how the EDF interacts with the model of Pedler, Burgoyne and Boydell (PRB).[23] Taking the PBB model as addressing a single logical level of perspective, we might wonder if the sequence of *Ideas, Policy, Operations* and *Action* in their model might be usefully related to the Ideas, Frameworks, Plans and Actions distinctions of the basic learning model discussed earlier and shown in Figure 7.1. It might be used to enable practitioners to be alert to the stylistic and value characteristics that are likely to be exhibited by individuals and groups whose work is localized in one of the PBB categories; and to the possible sources of conflict and misunderstanding that might arise across categories. The multi-level aspect of the EDF framework might also further alert users of the PBB model that 'one person's *Policy* is another person's *Action*'. It may well be necessary to consider a recursive form of the PBB model in order to accommodate the differences in scope of issue, and the consequent interactions, which undoubtedly exist within organizations.

Looking now at the influences of the PBB model upon the EDF, it seems useful to consider the PBB categories of *Policy, Operations* and *Action* to approximate to the design levels of Strategy, Structure and Work within the EDF. The *Ideas* element again suggests the aspect of values and culture that has already been mentioned as a candidate for a fifth level of the EDF to depict the environment within which strategic deliberations take place. This linking leaves the first level of design in the EDF (Technology) without counterpart in the PBB model. As the PBB model in some pictorial presentations has been likened to a lorry, we might suggest that a *Technology* element be incorporated so that the lorry may have an engine!

There are many other models which address organizational learning in some way. The frameworks offered here are not seeking to displace any other model; as mentioned at the start, the value of frameworks lies not in their 'correctness' but in their usefulness. We have found these models useful and easy to communicate, and much of our confidence in offering them for the reader's consideration comes from the attestations we have received from clients.

Conclusions

The framework developed is founded in fundamental models of human learning. These models represent learning as being both cyclic, multi-styled and structured into different logical levels. The features and consequences of these models at the individual level have analogues in the features of an organization as a whole.

Organization are structured into levels, although not always logically, and many processes can be seen to serve similar functions to the process of human learning. There are many insights that emerge from reflection upon this model in the context

Implications

1. No viable organisation can *not* be learning.
2. To support the natural learning processes, we must:
   (a) recognize that different levels of perspective are involved;
   (b) appreciate the need to support the learning processes both within and between levels;
   (c) realize that team-building principles apply just as much to departments as to individuals.
3. Organizational learning depends upon flow of information (opportunity and constrain) upwards as well as downwards:
   'Management must listen as well as brief'.
4. Organizational learning is not a smooth process, is quite likely to necessitate or precipitate step changes in behaviours, structures or beliefs:
   'Impede change and you impede the capacity to learn'.

Figure 7.9   Levels of learning in the organization

of organizations. Figure 7.9 lists just a few that were generated by taking some of the current outstanding questions about learning organizations and relating them to the principles represented in the EDF.

Finally, I am not suggesting that this is the only way to employ the basic learning principles of cycle, style and level to model organizational learning. Indeed, as we have seen in this chapter, the EDF is likely soon to evolve into a five-level framework. Moreover, there are other models derived from these principles[17] which I use regularly and which are equally valuable in their appropriate contexts. There may be no limit to the number of models that may emerge if the principles are applied to organizations. In fact, if these principles are fundamental to the process of learning, and if learning is fundamental to the processes of organization, then they will crop up wherever we look. If we are alert to these principles, they will enrich our understanding of organizational learning in many more ways than are mentioned in this chapter.

References

1. Kolb. D. A. and Fry (1975) 'Towards an applied theory of experiential learning', in C. Cooper (ed.) *Theories of Group Processes*, Wiley, London.
2. Piaget, J. (1954) *The Construction of Reality in the Child*, Basic Books Inc., New York.
3. Lewin, K. (1951) *Field Theory in the Social Sciences*, Harper, New York.
4. Jung, C. G. (1923) *Psychological Types*, Pantheon Books, New York.
5. Kelly, G. A. (1955) *The Psychology of Personal Constructs*, Norton & Co, New York.
6. Ackoff, R. L. and F. E. Emery (1972) *On Purposeful Systems*, Aldin Atherton, New York.
7. Sutton, D. C. (1987) 'Models for developing managers', *R&D Management*, **17**(1).
8. Carlsson, Keane and Martin (1976) 'R&D organisations as learning systems', *Sloane Management Review*, **17**(3).
9. Argyris, C. (1977) 'Double loop learning in organisations', *Harvard Business Review*, **55**(5).
10. Argyris, C. and D. Schon (1978) *Organisational Learning: A Theory of Action Perspective*, Addison-Wesley, Reading, Mass.
11. Bateson, G. (1973) *Steps to an Ecology of Mind*, Paladin, St. Albans.
12. Gagné, R. M. (1970) *The Conditions of Learning*, Holt, Rinehart & Winston, Englewood Cliffs, N.J.
13. Hess, R. A. (1987) 'A qualitative model of human interaction with complex dynamic systems', *IEEE Transactions on Systems, Man and Cybernetics*, 17(1).
14. Beer, S. (1966) *Decision and Control*, Wiley, London.

15. Bruner, J. (1986) *Actual Minds Possible Worlds*, Harvard Press, Cambridge, Mass.
16. Sutton, D. C. (1987) 'Cognitive transactional analysis—towards a calculus of belief?', *The Systemist*, **9**(1).
17. Sutton, D. C. 'Cognitive transactional analysis—a framework to facilitate communication', *Journal of Cybernetics and Systems*, in press.
18. Kuhn, T. S. (1962) *The Structure of Scientific Revolutions*, University of Chicago Press, Chicago.
19. Pask, G. (1975) *The Cybernetics of Human Learning and Performance*, Hutchinson, London.
20. Mumford, E. (1990) *Designing Human Systems*, Manchester Business School, Manchester.
21. Garratt, R. (1987) *The Learning Organization*, Fontana, London.
22. Hawkins, P. (1991) 'The spiritual dimension of the learning organisation', *Management Education and Development*, **22**(3).
23. Pedler, M., J. Burgoyne and T. Boydell (eds) (1991) *The Learning Company*, McGraw-Hill, Maidenhead.

8
Creating space in the learning company
Alan Phillips

I Introduction

When I first began to work in organizations, I was struck by the effect they had on people. In one I worked in, people were often frightened by those 'above' them in the organization, rushing around in pursuit of the most prosaic tasks, anxious of the consequences that might befall them should they fail to complete them as required. This anxiety affected their relationship with others: they would try to dominate those 'below' them and felt jealous and cautious of their peers.

In another organization, I observed that although outright aggression was less in evidence, it was manifested in other ways, such as malicious gossip, rampant careerism and internal politics. People tended to be shut off from one another, closeted in rooms like worker bees in a hive, unable to communicate with one another except in predetermined ways. It seemed that things were deliberately organized this way.

And yet, in those same organizations, I had experiences of a quite different kind—I saw people committed to their work and its meaning, going about it purposefully but without fear and relating to one another in a way that was friendly and sometimes loving. I felt that some kind of potential was not being tapped and that the effect these organizations had on people made them less rather than more effective.

I have two images in my mind which reflect the diversity of these experiences.

One is of a darkened room, windows shuttered and admitting only the tiniest chinks of light. The atmosphere in the room is intensely claustrophobic; it seems that the walls are closing in, slowly but remorselessly. It can support life at only the barest possible level; the human spirit is crushed by such conditions.

The other is of a building constructed entirely of glass, a 'crystal palace', airy and spacious, into which streams light of a pale and piercing quality. A feeling of space replaces that of claustrophobia, a feeling that I could spread my arms wide and take a deep breath. Since the building is made of glass it is entirely transparent and I can see through into other rooms where others live and work. This transparency encourages me to think that there is nowhere in this building that I cannot go and nowhere where I would not be welcomed.

These are just images, of course, but they do give a strong sense of the range of possibilities in organizations. The second image is the one which evokes most powerfully the *possibilities* represented by the Learning Company idea.

Some people may think that I'm being fanciful here, but my image of the Learning Company goes beyond one of an organization which is good at reprocessing information to become better at what it does—that's the dream of a cybernetician. I believe that it should also be a place in which the human spirit is sheltered and refreshed. Indeed, my contention is that the Learning Company cannot exist in a developed form unless it provides the conditions in which the human spirit can flower.

This is what I want to explore in this chapter. I believe that for real learning to come about, thought and dialogue need to take place unconstrained. So freedom and learning go hand in hand, yet 'freedom' is a word we hardly use in organizations. It's a concept we find hard to handle in this context. The right balance between freedom and control seems very difficult to attain: can we let this remain so if we want to create an organization whose primary process is learning?

In the following pages I want to explore the concepts of dialogue, space and rebellion (which seem central to the idea of freedom) and then relate them to a recent experience of a development initiative. I hope that this will help clarify the practicality or otherwise of using these concepts in the organizations in which we work.

We need learning so badly in our organizations, yet we seem to find it difficult to nourish and protect it. How can we change this?

II Dialogue, Space and Rebellion

Dialogue

There is a prior stage to discussing what dialogue means to the Learning Company. It concerns the value of dialogue to people not just as members of organizations but as human beings. Understanding this might help to clarify the extent to which the organizations we work in meet our real needs.

Dialogue is a basic human need. From our earliest days, when we attempt to communicate with our mothers, through to later periods of life, when we establish wider networks of contact, with family, friends, partners, working colleagues, a basic need is expressed. This need for dialogue is about the sharing of what we think and feel, of the experiences that we encounter in life. The more trusting and supportive the relationship between those in dialogue, the more valuable will be the exchange.

But dialogue is also about affirmation. If I am in dialogue with another person, they recognize that I exist and have some value. Dialogue affirms my essential humanity and my membership of a human community.

Dialogue is essential to life, is part of our drive towards actualization, and by the same token, lack of dialogue can be life-threatening. Bereavement, the break-up of relationships, the isolation of loneliness, all represent the breakdown of dialogue and can threaten our well-being. No wonder, therefore, that people will often tolerate dialogue of miserable quality, rather than have none at all.[1]

I have been speaking so far of a person in terms of his or her private existence, of his or her personal relationships with others. Dialogue, however, can also be actualizing in the public realm, where people act and speak together about the world they share. This could be in the organizational world, in the community or in the political world, for example. Hannah Arendt, the political philosopher, wrote:

... in acting and speaking, men show who they are, reveal actively their unique personal identities and thus make their appearance in the human world ... This revelatory quality of speech and action comes to the fore when people are *with* others and neither for nor against them—that is, in sheer human togetherness.[2]

She argued that the fact of speech and action created a *'space of appearance'* between the participants:

It is this space of appearance in the widest sense of the word, namely, the space where I appear to others as others appear to me, where men exist not merely like other living or inanimate things but make their appearance explicitly ... To be deprived of it means to be deprived of reality.[3]

This definition of dialogue has much in common with that outlined earlier, for Arendt was arguing that in this space of appearance, men and women are most vividly alive, in touch with reality and most acutely aware of themselves and others.

Dialogue can also be liberating. Paulo Freire's educational work among Third World peasantry attempted to free them from a 'culture of silence'. He felt that they were trapped within a reality that was 'given' to them and his philosophy of education was based on encouraging them to engage in a process of 'dialogical encounter' with one another, through which they could develop their own consciousness of their realities and deal critically with them, articulating a view of the world which was expressed in their own language, not that of their oppressors:

As this happens, the word takes on new power. It is no longer an abstraction or magic but a means by which man discovers himself and his potential as he gives names to things around him ... each man wins back his right to say his own word, to name the world.[4]

Dialogue can therefore be a means of sharing information, ideas and feelings (vital for collective learning), of becoming richly aware of others and of the world, and of liberation. It is vital to life, or at least to a version of life which is recognizably and vividly human.

This reinforces the notion that learning is not just a process in which we participate as individuals, but one which takes place *between* us. And what enables this to be so is 'space'. Without space, learning is diminished.

If organizations deny their members dialogue, could we argue that they become less than human, even inhuman in some sense? If so, perhaps this is why the lack of 'space' in some organizations is felt as oppressiveness.

Space

I now want to talk about 'space', another concept which is important to the Learning Company idea.

'Space' is a word which has recently been used in a particular way, hence: 'I need some space'. When used in this way the expression signifies a wish to draw a boundary around some area of our existence, one which will protect us from the pressures of the world we live in. Here, space and freedom seem to be intimately connected.

I have used the word recently in thinking about the effects of different learning designs. In working with action learning sets, I found that when they worked well they provided an important space in the life of participants. It gave them:

... an organisational structure for learning: time for reflection, questioning, review; a method of enabling individual and collective learning; permission to be open, to say the unsayable and to voice hopes and fears; and finally, the support people require in terms of comfort, sharing and encouragement.[5]

The structure of the set provided a boundary which protected its members against all the pressures they experienced in their organizations, which at the time were pressure-cookers of change.

In this case, the space is deliberately contrived and organized. Hannah Arendt, in talking about the *space of appearance*, argued that it was transitory and would not outlast the moment of speech or action unless a frame was drawn around the space to maintain it. She saw this in the first political institution (the Greek *polis*), in which the space for public speech and action was formally preserved. What preserved the space, she felt, was not bricks and mortar but *power*, brought into being by people coming together. But it was not just the *fact* of people coming together that created power, but the *way* they came together:

Power is actualized only where word and deed have not parted company, where words are not empty and deeds not brutal, where words are not used to veil intentions but to disclose realities, and deeds are not used to violate and destroy but to establish new relations and create new realities.[6]

Only where people come together in a spirit of openness and constructiveness, therefore, can the space between them be maintained. If the reverse happens, the participants cease to be connected, to communicate—they become isolated and the common space between them disappears.

Again, we see that space is connected with freedom, but now in a rather different way. For while we normally understand freedom in terms of personal sovereignty ('freedom from'), in these two examples, of the action learning set and of political institutions, freedom is intimately connected with togetherness. So to speak of freedom in organizations is not necessarily to speak of separation. Freedom can entail coming together, most powerfully in pursuit of common goals.

Hannah Arendt reminds us of the transformative qualities of space. Harrison Owen[7] also makes this connection. He gives the word 'transformation' a meaning quite distinct from that of 'development', recognizing that in a world of radical discontinuities, organizations have to do things in radically different ways in order to survive. He defines space as the time and place *between* the old and the new, where only the 'essence' or 'spirit' of the organization remains. This *freedom from form* allows the energy which is part of the organizational spirit to seek out new and more appropriate possibilities, new realities and relations.

An organization without form is a bit mind-boggling. It is easier to conceive of one which, in the face of new demands, neither clings to old structures nor jumps straight into new ones, but rather keeps structure loose and fluid, using organizational energy to move forward.

Space in all these examples has a meaning which centres upon maintaining the possibility for movement, for development, for transformation. It can be deliberately contrived and is closely related to freedom; but a freedom which can involve togetherness and not just separation. Space, finally, is where dialogue can occur.

This also raises the question of the relationship between freedom and constraint. When I first presented these ideas it was suggested that freedom and constraint are in fact two sides of the same coin: we cannot conceive of one without the other. What is more, I now realize, constraints can, in a paradoxical way, *provide* freedom and empowerment. The boundary around an action learning set, for example, the ground rules by which behaviour is governed in the set, are constraints. Yet at the same time they provide a set of conditions which enable people to meet together in a spirit of safe and constructive dialogue.

Harrison Owen uses the metaphor of the butterfly to illustrate the process of transformation. Within the cocoon, the caterpillar is reduced to its essence before emerging in a different form. The cocoon is a constraint, a wall around the caterpillar, but it provides the conditions under which transformation can safely take place.

'Absolute freedom' is akin to chaos; in such conditions there can be no peace or safety. Similarly in organizations. For transformation to take place, what is required is *just enough* structure to provide safe conditions in which people can change, but not so much that space, and therefore dialogue and learning, is closed down.

Rebellion

Dialogue and space are words which do not seem out of place in an organizational context, but 'rebellion' is rather different. It is a word which is hardly used in organizations and one which, to be honest, most of us would feel rather cautious about using. Perhaps this is because we feel chary of challenging the structure of authority in our organizations or because we feel that rebellion is essentially destructive, whereas what we seek is something *con*structive.

But if the Learning Company is really to be something different, if it is somehow to institutionalize the process of transformation, then surely it ought to embrace rebellion, which represents the possibility of renewal.

Albert Camus described rebellion as:

... the secular will not to surrender ... Origin of form, source of real life, it keeps us always erect in the savage formless movement of history.[8]

As Owen points out, the rebel is likely to be someone intensely interested in the well-being of the organization of which they are a part and one who sees the current ways of doing things as leading to its demise—rebellion seen in this light is less a destructive force than a

movement towards life ... in the context of the transformative process, the rebel is the emergent edge of a quest for a better way to be.[9]

Conscious of the destructive history of revolution and the cloud which this sometimes casts over the idea of rebellion, Camus introduced the notion of 'limits'. He saw this as a way of being in the world which strove for transformation, but drew back from destruction. In the midst of rebellion should be restraint.

This idea ties in well with the notions of dialogue and space elaborated earlier. I envisage an organization in which people who feel strongly about the need for change and difference are encouraged to speak, but in spaces which enable them to be in dialogue with those speaking from other perspectives. In this way, space is used both to protect rebellion (against better established, conservative forces) and to ensure that it does not destroy what is good in the old ways, so that enduring organizational themes can find expression in a new world. In this space the old and the new are kept in creative, transformative tension.

Camus's notion of rebellion with limits echoes my earlier point about the symbiotic relationship between freedom and constraint. His argument is that to place limits on freedom is to prevent it destroying itself.

III Double-Loop Learning

What I have tried to do here is to give a hint of my vision of the Learning Company, to convey my feeling that the qualities of space, dialogue and rebellion—because they are so essentially human in character—can only enhance the humanity of the organizations we work in. I see that as a valuable goal in itself, but at the same time these qualities have a very pragmatic, 'bottom-line' significance.

The core process of the Learning Company is double-loop learning, the kind of learning which causes it to re-examine as deeply as possible its purpose, values and objectives. This process has to be embraced in order for transformation to occur. It is a difficult process, for one reason because it confronts authority, the most powerful force in any organization generally having the greatest ownership of its prevailing objectives. For double-loop learning to take place, there needs to be *dialogue* between differing perspectives; *space* in which such conversations can take place, and the encouragement of *rebellion*, so that new and challenging viewpoints can emerge and be developed.

All of these qualities are related to *freedom*. Perhaps the most urgent and difficult task for the Learning Company is to reconcile freedom and authority.

I have illustrated these connections in the diagram at Figure 8.1.

IV Action learning

In this section I explore some of these concepts through the medium of recent experiences with an action learning set. By doing this I hope to show how the qualities that I have been speaking about can be supported by development activities and, perhaps, gain insight into how they can be brought to bear in the organizational mainstream.

For seven months in 1991 I worked with an action learning set in the NHS. Its composition was very unusual: four senior managers and four doctors, paired into four doctor—manager learning partnerships. This set was part of a wider, and rather enlightened, initiative to provide opportunities (space) for doctors and managers to learn about and alongside each other, through the medium of real organizational problems; a cross-cultural initiative, designed to encourage dialogue between different perspectives. The backcloth to the work of this group was the most far-reaching changes the NHS had ever experienced.

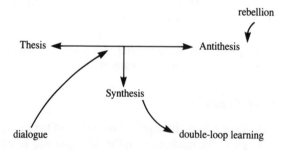

Figure 8.1   The Dialectic

Each person had a time slot in which to talk about the issue they brought to the set. Although the issues were very different, they had in common a concern with how to manage across boundaries, about interdependence and fragmentation.

- One doctor was taking up a managerial role—was this abandoning old loyalties and identities or building new bridges across cultural boundaries?
- Another, working in a new NHS Trust hospital, wondered how she could maintain working relationships with colleagues in other local (and previously integrated) organizations.
- A manager on the other side of this divide needed to find out how he could manage across it without creating bureaucratic structures, recognizing interdependence in the face of organizational fragmentation.
- A doctor/manager pair, trying to get doctors involved in the management of their hospital, wanted to explore how to balance local and corporate interests, challenge the old and build commitment to the new.
- Another doctor/manager pair wanted to look at whether a medical services department could be at the same time a separate business centre and part of its host organization.

The group therefore had some very rich material to deal with, reflecting the important themes being dealt with in their organizations: major personal and organizational change; new roles; new boundaries; the crossing of those boundaries; high levels of ambiguity; loyalties and identities; the old and the new.

What I'd like to do here is to select some of the significant features of this group and its life and look at them in the light of points made earlier in the chapter.

Confrontations

Twice in the life of the set we had major confrontations between people working as learning partners. I took this not as a sign of failure but as one of success.

The first confrontation blew up when a manager brought as an issue his dilemma about making his unit more responsive to a new 'market' environment. Present arrangements, set up mainly to satisfy the medical fraternity (he implied), were simply too slow. His doctor learning partner took him up very strongly on this and blamed managers who didn't have the courage to take decisions.

In the following discussion we spoke about inter-group conflicts, conflicts of interest, differences being managed by procedure or by political means and about whether they could be managed in a more open way. We also talked about who could take leadership and who felt powerful enough to cut a swathe through the real and apparent complexities.

This was an emotional and engaging debate, lasting for about two hours. The group provided a space in which the protagonists could speak to each other about something that had been blocking them both. It also allowed broader issues, of which theirs was a microcosm, to be explored, and for different perspectives to dialogue with one another.

Another manager spoke about developing a vision of the future for his unit. He described a mixture of coercive and participative means of managing change, mirroring the conflicts managers often feel in achieving even the best ends. This generated an animated discussion about the use of power, about change strategy and about valuing the old as well as the new.

Just as the discussion drew to a close, he made a strong statement about the system of care that his unit was moving away from being 'completely unacceptable'. This evoked a sharp response from his doctor learning partner, who reminded him of the personal investment many people had in that approach to care and the damage that could be done to the future by rubbishing the old. We returned to our debate of change strategy with renewed energy.

Again, the group had provided a space for dialogue between perspectives, on issues of critical organizational importance. The old and the new had been kept in play and we were able to have a debate which, in the organizational 'mainstream', might have been closed down much earlier. In particular, things could be said which ran counter to the prevailing orthodoxy—I might call this *rebellion*.

There was nothing 'nice' about this dialogue—it was difficult and emotional. But this was an example of how a particular form of dialogue, which we call conflict, can lead to learning.[10]

Crossing boundaries

At least two of the group members brought issues of transition to the set. One, a manager, was being asked to manage a new organizational unit, in the face of competition from a powerful rival. He was under a lot of pressure, and while I was initially impatient with his inaction I now realize that he needed this space in his life to think through the new demands, to gain relief from pressure and to develop the strength and courage he required to carry out his role.

Another, a doctor, had taken on a managerial role. This is still unusual in the NHS and challenges old-established ideologies and professional identities. He did not bring anything explosive to the group, but used his personal space on each occasion we met to gently explore, with other people's help, the new demands of his role and his own stand on questions of identity.

Structure

Earlier in this chapter I implied that I considered the action learning set an 'enabling structure', one that facilitated learning. This was certainly so in this case. The boundary of the set protected its members from the maelstrom of change which provided its backcloth. Its relative freedom from form internally and lack of oppressive authority made for safe expression of thought and feeling.

But this does highlight one of the difficulties of creating such spaces. After one of the confrontations described above, a strong bid was made for better organization of our time. I saw it then as a straightforward organizational issue in the set—we had been a bit lax in managing time—but on reflection I saw it as more than this, and no coincidence that it followed an emotional session. I now believe that the demand for more structure was a reaction to a surfeit of ambiguity—some brought into the set on the back of the issue, some arising from the structure and organization of the set itself.

People sometimes experience the gift of freedom as threatening, as a harbinger of chaos. When so many of the previously fixed points in their lives were shifting, these people needed the comfort and support of structure. Or at least that is how they felt, for the impact of more structure was to push us towards 'polite conversations' rather than towards challenging dialogue. In the end this may have had the effect of increasing rather than reducing anxiety.

There is a point here about giving and taking freedom. In offering such developmental spaces, there is a subtle balance to be achieved between providing people with freedom and their taking it. Those in authority have to give it away, but not at a pace which exceeds the ability or willingness of people to accept it. By challenging and supporting, this boundary can be extended, so that eventually people take on more than they had thought themselves capable of.

Rebellion

I have talked a good deal about dialogue and space in this part of the chapter, but not much about rebellion, despite my feeling that this possibly the key to the success of the Learning Company idea, for rebellion gives bite to dialogue.

In this action learning set, we did cultivate rebellion, in a number of ways:

- The doctors involved were all, in one way or another, cutting a new path into management. In doing so they not only had to contend with the doubts of career managers, but also those of their own peers, for they were entering new territory, previously the province of 'the enemy'. They were daring to be different, having the courage to be at the leading edge. The set supported them in this.
- Things were said in the set which ran counter to the prevailing orthodoxies in the NHS. It allowed people to develop perspectives which were genuinely their own. This was particularly important for managers, who were naturally under more pressure to conform.
- Lastly, most of our discussions in the set were about organizational change and it seemed to me that what the participants were trying to do was to maintain something good, some independence and humanity perhaps, in the face of a change machine which at times seemed quite remorseless.

It might be argued that the work of this learning set, though powerful for the individuals concerned, would not necessarily have led to significant organizational consequences. I believe otherwise. The participants were relatively powerful people organizationally: mainly chief executives and consultant doctors, influential in the development of their organizations and often deeply involved in the radical changes taking place at that time in the NHS.

The space represented by the learning set gave them the opportunity to withdraw temporarily from the very turbulent stream of organizational life, to look upon it from a different perspective (to reframe it) and to carry that learning back into their work (i.e. leading and reshaping the NHS). Not least it helped them develop the courage required to deal with the pressures of that turbulent stream. And finally, space was provided for real dialogue between two sub-cultures which are among the most powerful in shaping the modern NHS: the managerial and medical. I cannot help feeling, therefore, that in its small way, the space provided by the set will have enabled the participants to wield their power in the NHS in much more productive ways.

V Conclusion

It always seems difficult to contrive a useful ending to a chapter like this. I started off with my vision, my guiding image of the Learning Company, and I have tried to set out my beliefs about the need for freedom, in the form of dialogue, space and rebellion, in order to make this vision a reality. But I do not have any easy answers as to how to 'reach the promised land'. I don't believe there are any, and if anyone tries to tell you otherwise, give them a wide berth!

Chris Argyris[11] elaborated the idea of organizational entropy—the notion that organizations can descend into a cycle of diminishing energy and declining fortunes. The main symptoms of this, he felt, were poor interpersonal relations, apathy, mistrust, inability to deal with conflict openly, and over-control of subordinates—in other words, the opposite of the qualities described in this chapter. The closing down of space, the shutting off of circuits, the drive for control and conformity, lead inevitably towards entropy and, in the end, death.

I'm struck that Hannah Arendt, working in a different field, should arrive at essentially the same conclusion. She pointed out that although many of the great political communities of history may have been finished off by external catastrophe, their decline could almost always be traced back to 'loss of power', to internal decay.

I take it from this that the most 'powerful' organizations are ultimately those which are the most human in character, which do not coerce their members, but rather harness their collective energy.

Organizations in a state of entropy can be kept going—by ever-increasing levels of work and commitment, by tighter and tighter control systems and by the willingness of people to accept such conditions—in other words, by making them less and less human. Is it worth it?

The Learning Company road may be a difficult one to travel, but at least it offers the prospect of organizations which are both human *and* effective.

References

1. Lynch, J. J. (1979) *The Broken Heart,* Harper & Row, Sydney.
2. Arendt, H. (1958) *The Human Condition*, University of Chicago Press, London, p. 180.
3. Ibid., p. 199.
4. Freire, P. (1972) *Pedagogy of the Oppressed*, Penguin, London, p. 12.
5. Alan Phillips (1990) Unpublished evaluation paper.
6. Arendt, H. op. cit., p. 200.
7. Owen, H. (1987) *Spirit: Transformation and Development in Organisations*, Abbott.
8. Camus, A. (1971) *The Rebel*, Penguin, London, p. 265.
9. Owen, H. op. cit., p. 98.
10. Pascale, R. (1991) *Managing on the Edge*, Penguin, London.
11. Argyris, C. (1970) *Intervention Theory and Method*, Addison-Wesley, Reading, Mass.

9
Participation in the learning company
Chris Blantern and John Belcher

'The daily things we do'

The daily things we do
For money or for fun
Can disappear like dew
Or harden and live on.
Strange reciprocity:
The circumstance we cause
In time gives rise to us,
Becomes our memory.

Philip Larkin, February 1979

It seems that the 'dream' of the Learning Company as a practical aspiration is becoming increasingly attractive at a time when the nature of change in the world might well leave us dissatisfied and cynical about the efficacy of the management and organization theories we have subscribed to up to now. Indeed, 95 per cent of the books in the world have been published in the last ten years and one of the largest growth areas for publishers is 'management'. Prescriptions abound, and the thirst for managerial medicine, however bitter, to cure the ill-health of organizations is seemingly insatiable. We have, too, more 'consultants' who diagnose and treat than ever before, and yet the average life expectancy of an organization is getting shorter. What is more, as Pedler, Burgoyne and Boydell[1] acknowledge, the managerial medicine cupboard is cluttered with discarded solutions and tablets of stone:

The history of managing is littered with the remains of yesterday's 'right answers'—scientific management, theories X and Y, Blake's Grid, MbO, Quality Circles, the search for excellence and so on. So where are they now and what did we learn from such experiments?

For an increasing number of people the plethora of discarded 'right answers' has led to a questioning of the conventional and implicit story-line which has framed these parcels of knowledge and thence to the emergence of a different consciousness.[2] This is a consciousness which, rather than receiving such concepts as successive and discrete discoveries of social structure—as progressively revelatory of the scientific 'essence' of organizations—sees the assumption of their objective truth as problematic. Those things which we have taken to be self-evident characteristics of social reality are re-viewed as cultural conventions, the product of social processes, and constructed in the interests of those with the power to establish them. Over time these conventions have developed the appearance of structure inherent in society. Scientific metaphors are being replaced by those of story-telling. Kenneth Gergen[2] describes a consciousness which is bursting out across the spectrum of social science as the information age presents us with a myriad of competing ways of making sense of the world[3]—both currently and historically–and in so doing spells out the inadequacy of a universal scientific truth[4] which has been so prevalent in Western male thought for the last 200 years. This constructionist consciousness has had impact on the field of psychology, which has long been a nursery ground for the epistemology of 'management development':

there has been a generalised falling-out within the academic world with the traditional conception of scientific knowledge. Within the philosophy of science major critiques were launched against the presumption of formal or rational foundations of knowledge. Logical empiricism has largely vanished from serious consideration, critical rationalists are a diminishing breed, and aspirants of a 'new realism' have been unable to articulate an alternative program of science. Since the work of Kuhn and Feyerabend, 'the philosophy of science' has largely been replaced on the intellectual agenda by the history and sociology of knowledge. Both the latter enterprises challenge the view of scientific knowledge as rationally superior, and trace the cultural and historical processes that bring certain conceptions of nature into favor while suppressing others. In effect, it is argued that what we take to be accurate and objective accounts of nature [reality] and self are an outgrowth of social processes. (my parenthesis)

Gergen points, in particular, to widespread developments in literary theory and semiotics in order to further emphasize how that which we take, unreflexively, to be true, right and good has become congealed and embedded in our generalized sense making. In so doing, he draws our attention to one fundamental theme:

our formulations of what is the case are guided by and limited to the systems of language in which we live. What can be said about the world—including self and others—is an outgrowth of shared conventions of discourse.

The 'social constructionists'[3] then are saying that meaning is not inherent either in a transcendent world or even in a transcendent self, but rather arises in relationship and community. Language gains its meaning through the way it is used in any community of relationships. As Gergen[5] quoting Wittgenstein has pointed out:

our words are not pictures of what is the case. Words are not maps of reality. Rather words gain their meaning through their use in social interchange, within the language games of culture

In other words, our interactions or movements in relationship are named by the language which has grown out of the community in which we move and, over time, we come to see ourselves and the world entirely in terms of the constructed repertoire of stories (conventions) into which we have implicitly negotiated our way. Concepts we have taken as things like 'identity', 'being' or 'external reality' for that matter, seen from this frame of consciousness, are names of the stories[6] of self and world which arise from our relationship with any community—whether it be 'partnership', 'family', 'neighbourhood', 'club', 'school', 'childhood', 'adulthood', 'organization', 'team', 'nation', 'religion' or 'world'.

The important distinction that constructionist consciousness enables us to make, which is not available in the scientific or logical empiricist scheme of things, is that the 'names' of our 'stories' are sharable and potentially universal in the abstract, but the 'stories' themselves (meaning) are not. They can only be retold in full in the context of a relationship and community through the kind of 'movement', evocative of all the available human senses, which has led to their original construction. This, of course, can never be fully recaptured, and so each successive telling of the story changes the community and hence, ultimately, the story. We may go so far as to say that at the individual level all stories must, in some way, be different in so much as they are the uniquely constructed product of membership of several and different communities—a unique collection of stories. Our realities as communities may overlap, both historically and contemporaneously, but do not coincide, and our realities as individuals from different such communities coincide even less.

If we can no longer put our full weight behind the certainty of a universal structure, other than that apparent in the convention of 'naming', there cannot be any packaged 'right answers'! For meaning to emerge, these names must be rewoven, through relationship, back into any community or network—wrought, transformed or discarded to suit the purpose of the subscribers. A name without a story is empty and has no meaning—like looking for the inspirational message in a book called *The Learning Company* without ever having moved within the communal convention which is called 'reading', let alone those communities which are called 'company' and 'learning'. Pedler, Burgoyne and Boydell[1] have alluded to something like this, as a main support for the Learning Company idea, when criticizing the 'quick fix' mentality:

... ideas bought and sold as right answers quickly become empty techniques and the life goes out of them. We know in our hearts that there are no easy answers to the complex problems of organising work ...

For the social constructionist then, the advent of the Learning Company offers the opportunity to understand and explore individual and collective learning in the organizational context, not in the scientist/empiricist frame of individual personalities and collective organisms (subject/object), or in terms of rational legitimacy and dysfunctionalism (truth), nor indeed from the benevolent approval of developmental passages[7] (what should be learned), but rather through a concern for the primacy and centrality of relationships and communities of meaning. In short, the seemingly chaotic maelstrom of change, which some have called post-modernism[7,8] can no longer be understood through the story of objective reality, structure and truth, but rather, more usefully for now, through the adjustment we can make in favour of each other's equally valid 'stories'. As Gergen puts it:

And because we have the power to generate agreeable accounts of what is the case, we also have the power of alteration.

Of course, to do so means we must give more focused attention to our relationships and the mutual commitment to alteration, since any reframing not consummated through communal enactment remains 'unrelated' in the senses both of relationship and story-telling. One important realization therefore involves giving up the 'right' to define reality unilaterally, in favour of the promotion of relationships and networks through negotiation and dialogue.[9] Participation, which some have acknowledged as the most formidable challenge facing the aspirant Learning Company, begins to invite mutual definition by the participants.

What follows is a story of the development of participation in one particular context or community. For nearly ten years now the 'social housing sector' has struggled with something which has become known as 'tenant participation'. The 'problem' has largely been defined by the community of professionals whom it engages and, naturally enough, 'right answers' abound—yet the struggle continues. This story says something about how the reflexive shift from imposing the 'right answer' to an acknowledgement of each other's stories is enabling different communities to 'talk' to each other and author-ize some new stories. Although this is a specific context, the 'stories', and not just their names, may indeed be available to the communities of policy makers and operators in other learning companies.

Who defines what tenant participation means—the tenant or the landlord?

Landlord 'programmed' participation
I, like many others, had considered 'tenant participation' to be a good thing—something that no reasonable person could argue with. It does, after all, embody mature social principles of democracy, freedom of expression and choice as well as, seemingly, pragmatic benefits to both landlord and tenant. Then I met Helen, on a one-day workshop for tenants of housing associations. Helen made me think

very fundamentally about the whole basis for my work when, during a discussion on tenant participation, she said, 'Landlords are always asking us for things—and now they want bloody participation as well!'

What Helen did was to challenge the very roots of my approach—whatever she was seeing, it was not, for her, 'self-evidently a good thing'. What do we do in such circumstances? Do we rationalize away this tenant's point of view by saying 'Well, this is only one tenant—she can't be representative!', and in so doing leave our own norms and presuppositions[10] unexamined? Or do we adopt another explanation which similarly leaves our current assumptions undisturbed by introducing yet another—that Helen either hasn't understood, or, worse still, that there must be something wrong with her? Faced with this dilemma, assuming our awareness of it, what does it mean if we adopt any strategy which leaves our own presuppositions unquestioned? What does this say about a way of practising participation as opposed to just espousing it? Perhaps there was another language arising here—one which was 'inclusive' of this tenant's perspective, beliefs and values. I thought this challenge was worth opening up to.

Mine was a view drawn down from a politically correct ideology and, as such, practising tenant participation was largely a matter of borrowing plans and procedures from influential bodies, like the Housing Corporation,[11] whose 'ideologies' in this context seemed broadly consistent with the work I was trying to do. After all, they brought the legitimacy of the establishment to help move this self-evident, 'good thing' in the right direction. My encounter with Helen, though, had helped me to reconsider an intuitive sense that setting up procedures and implementing strategies was not a solution to the problems of tenant participation, but rather part of the problem. Without being more aware of the presuppositions they contained, it was no longer possible to assume that setting up procedures and systems—a 'design for participation', if you like—would be useful to tenants.

This, then, begs the next big question—'What is it that legitimizes what tenant participation should look like if it is not, at least in part, the authentic and diverse view of each tenant?' Putting that question to myself, with a more open spirit, I became increasingly aware that the 'language' being used by tenants I was working with seemed to be different from that of the landlords! By 'language' I am referring less to the words used by tenants to articulate their circumstances than to the underlying and complex web of values, beliefs, assumptions, meanings, knowledge, priorities and ways of relating[12] which emerged through our more open interaction. In other words, paying closer attention to 'how' participation might be achieved begins to change its meaning and redefines 'what' participation looks like!

Perhaps we could look at another real story to add some texture to what I am saying. I was asked to go along to a meeting, called by a small group of tenants' representatives, to discuss some long-standing repairs complaints with the landlord. The landlord was represented by the most senior manager in the Housing

Management Department. The tenants were vigorous and passionate in their frustrated attempts to get the message over to him that, as far as they were concerned, the repairs system didn't work! Trusting in his considerable professional training and experience of repair systems, the Housing Manager responded by meticulously explaining how the repairs system *really worked*. This would make things better. He was very nice about it—he had to be, since at least two of his staff had previously been through the same exercise! *Which is more legitimate—the Housing Manager's professional knowledge of repairs systems or the tenants' experience of it?* What this manager did was to assume, tacitly, that his view of the repairs system, with all its implicit norms, was more legitimate than the tenants' view. Hence this was the *reality* of the situation. Had this manager been able to question his own assumptions and become receptive to the language of the tenants' experience a different awareness and process would have been possible—not because tenants' perspectives must be tolerated for the sake of political correctness, but because they represent the language of a different but equally valid reality.[13]

So, for the landlord to hold a meeting with a group of tenants either to explain how the repair ordering system works or to listen to their complaints and to interpret them in terms of '*how the system is*' is a vastly different exercise from entering into 'dialogue'[14] with tenants to mutually develop and change the system. Each carries a different set of presuppositions[15] about the value, and therefore the influence, of what the tenants have to say and perhaps even their likelihood of being really heard! They make different assumptions about what we take for the reality of the situation and how it should be defined.

In the former case, the reality is always defined by the landlord—from the 'Henry Ford' tradition of 'You can have some changes so long as they are ...'! It is an approach which regards the tenants or users of the system as 'external' to it and assumes the system, which, more honestly, is the landlord's creation and property, to be central to the understanding of the way things work which, in turn, must define the problem as the tenants' failure to understand it. It does not conceive of tenants' experiences, which are likely to be born out of different interests, values, knowledge and priorities, as having equal value to the 'professional know-how' of the landlord. It assumes that the system is 'true' and that problems with it are the product of inadequate individual perception, whether they be those of staff or tenant. Typically, such differences in ways of making sense of the world are denied, devalued or defined as problematic, since they directly threaten the legitimacy of the most powerful to continue making the rules. Seeing a system or *the system* as self-evidently true is a good way of avoiding the need to understand ourselves, others and relationship[5]—and hence community.

But no system stands alone as some benchmark of what is, as some natural underlying law of how things work—it is defined, probably without recognizing its full implications, by those who have the power to define it! As such, it meets the needs of the landlord in preference to those of the tenants. As Ernst Schumacher[10] often said, it is necessary to become aware of the presuppositions of our thought, to understand ourselves, in order to be able to enter into true dialogue with others—dialogue which acknowledges each others' realities as having equal value.

This, then, is the story of a relationship, illustrated through the example of how the landlord controls the perception of reality. The flow of meaning is from landlord to tenant. The example of the repairs system is important enough in itself, but even more significant is the underlying message—a socially reproduced system of thinking which imposes the structure or norms defined by the most powerful upon the reality of others. What is more, this way of defining the relationship with tenants is likely to be applied, because these assumptions are deeply rooted in the organization's psyche, to the introduction of tenant participation procedures themselves (yet another system). Here though, it becomes even more insidious because we actually believe we're doing it for the benefit of the tenants. As such, it becomes falsified and even patronizing ...

Some tenants I was working with were invited by the landlord to submit a bid for some money which the landlord had allocated to a budget heading called 'Tenant Participation'. Naturally enough, they asked what the money might be used for, and they were told—'It's for "Tenant Participation". 'Yes, but is it for repairs?' they asked. 'No, that's what the "repairs" budget is for,' was the reply. 'Well, is it for gardening then, or for the improvements we want to make to the community room or the play area we want for the kids?' 'Well, no, we have "landscaping" and "upgrading" budgets for those things,' said the landlord. 'Well, what is it for?' the tenants again asked. 'It's for "Tenant Participation" and you can spend it on anything you like!'

What is interesting about such a story is that it exposes not only the implicit, abstract concept (presuppositions) with which the landlord is attempting to trade, but also that the meaning was held by the landlord and bore no relation to the grounded experience of the tenants. What was it that the tenants were being invited to participate in? Ironically, in this case, the tenants, who eventually submitted a bid for £500, were sent a cheque for £1000 which, although well intended by the landlord, simply seemed to further obscure what was going on.

Should the tenants reject or question what is being offered, not only can they be accused of 'not understanding' or of 'having something wrong with them', they may be seen as ungrateful too! Yet it goes deeper still.

Wherever 'participation' is seen as the introduction, by the landlord, of a new system or procedure, whether it be local in meetings about repairs or estate management, or where tenants are involved in central—management committee meetings about policy—or, indeed, anything in between, the *system* determines the nature and meaning of 'participation'. In other words, the landlord, whether conscious of it or not, retains the absolute right to determine the conditions of the meeting or process and therefore its meaning. Indeed, in the case of membership of the management committee, the tenant, in any formal or legal sense, becomes the landlord! While as ever it is the landlord's norms which are used to define participation, the landlord is saying, 'We know what's best for you.' In its extreme form it can be seen as a way of 'programming' how tenants are able to express their circumstances, the presuppositions of which are reinforced through a range of activities such as:

- newsletters
- professional expertise and its associated phraseology
- expert-centred training
- structured questionnaires
- invoking the right to 'approve' tenants' groups.

Yet these are the very things which we have come to regard as the essential components of 'participation'. 'Approving' tenants' groups is a blatant example of 'programming', and yet one which is common practice for many landlords. It is typically manifest through the collective views of an emergent tenants' group when they come to believe that their validity and viability as a group depend on the landlord's acceptance.

'Mutually arising' participation

Where this 'approving' is the landlord's practice, and it is likely to extend to a group's activities as well as its right to exist (e.g. expenditure of grant monies), the tenants must employ the landlord's 'language' to express themselves. They must conform to the landlord's image of them, dissent or disband. The agenda, however, remains the landlord's! It follows that it is observably the most energizing and satisfying experience for such groups to realize that they need no-one's reason or approval to exist and organize but their own. Only after a tenants' group has established its own identity and self-worth is there any likelihood of true dialogue which pierces the landlord's interpretation of what's going on. This is the point in the unfolding of a more balanced relationship where tenants are seen to make demands which, viewed from the landlord's undisturbed perspective, may initially be judged as unreasonable or even unacceptable.

But this is not dissent or resistance, it is the tenants' agenda, grounded in their own valuable experience and expressed in their language. It is precisely at this point that the presuppositions in the landlord's language which give rise to judgements of 'unreasonableness' or 'unacceptability' become visible. For many landlords this is the point where tenant participation 'fails', because the outcomes do not conform to previously conceived and projected measures (landlord-defined norms)—there is no room for the tenants' way of relating to things (their language). Right here though, the landlord can begin, reflexively,[7] to learn about itself through taking the risk of genuinely trying to grasp what the tenants are saying, or it can retreat to the habits of old ways, with their attendant comforts. If we take the former case, participation becomes about entering into the mutual commitment, arising out of a more meaningful relationship, to solve problems through negotiation or, better still, dialogue. For the landlord it means letting go of the absolute right to define the problem and the solution. Rather, problem and solution are co-defined by landlord and tenant together in a process which acknowledges each other's values and interpretations. It is a deeper way of relating, and it allows tenants to participate using their own frameworks of meaning, as well as those of the landlord. This is mutually arising participation.

It is important to stress here that although the critique of 'programmed' participation is a strong one, it is by no means suggested that it should be rejected. On the contrary, it is the kind of development of management practice which enables it to be exposed to critical review.[16,17] The argument put forward in this chapter is that such movement towards real dialogue dies where initiatives are employed only as techniques, as mere procedures bolted onto a largely undisturbed collection of organizational norms. For 'mutually arising' participation to emerge, attention must be focused away from professional knowledge of systems and procedures as absolute, and onto grounded ways of problem solving together with the tenants.[18]

Through more authentic and deeper dialogue, systems and structures become flexible, and new ways arising from feedback and exchange with the tenants are tried as experiments. Landlords must take the risk of:

- questioning the validity of existing practice;
- enacting ideas which come from tenants as well as from the establishment;
- allowing the mutual development of solutions to problems and the development of policy in preference to holding onto 'expert' solutions;
- mutually evaluating 'what works' in preference to imposing 'what should happen';
- entering into the spirit of mutual experimentation and learning in preference to the fear of appearing incompetent!

Applied to our example of the repairs system, these different ways of relating to tenants allow them to participate in its redesign and improvement—so long as the landlord and tenant together, not the landlord alone, define the measures of success. In mutually arising participation, landlord and tenant enter into the kind of joint exploration made possible by the dissolving of the hard boundaries between each other's worlds (Figure 9.1).

Some guidelines for action

These, of course, are fine words, but how can we begin to enact their meaning? What does this more grounded way of relating and co-creating look like in practice? The problem is not a new one. Similar debates have taken place over the

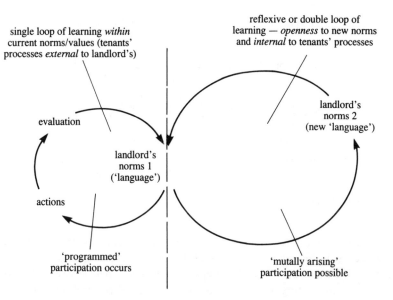

Figure 9.1   Landlord participation in the TP process [19]

last 30 years in other fields, such as education and health. It is an increasing preoccupation too in the activities of organization and management generally, as a rapidly changing world leaves behind those wedded to the past.

For many so engaged, the 'natural and historical' assumption that solutions to such problems will be provided by 'experts' or 'the establishment' is being challenged. For it is this very act, which mostly goes unnoticed, of believing that 'someone must know', that takes us out of relationship and away from giving attention and responsibility to what is going on around us. It is a way of thinking, or perhaps not thinking, which denies us access to other's equally valuable ways of making sense of things because we have given away responsibility for doing so. It is very easy to do, and less threatening too, to invoke 'the facts' or 'the rules', or even to make them up, rather than to acknowledge the 'dissonance'[17] generated by someone's 'awkward' views and ways—ways which, up to now, we have found it more comfortable and convenient to label as wrong, unimportant or even weird. It is suggested here that openness to such 'dissonance' is at the heart of *real dialogue*, self-examination and learning. Without it, participation is limited to compliance or 'programming' (see Fig. 9.2).

So if a formal, or traditional, approach to learning is problematic, how can we begin to think, feel and act beyond its constraints and work with the product of 'dissonance' in order to enter relationship and dialogue? How might we become active rather than passive in the participation process? What will our actions look

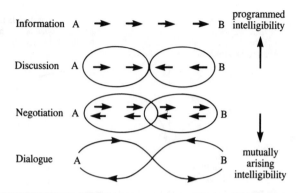

Figure 9.2   Participation in meaning

like? Principally, this involves reconceptualizing relationship and developing dialogue as the conduit of deeper exchange. Real dialogue can come about between the members of small groups who dedicate themselves to the primary importance of relating and describing a shared, local picture[15] of what is going on—in preference to interpreting their experience through assumptions flowing from the rigid allegiance to the idea of some universal truth (as in Helen's story).

In the context of tenant participation real dialogue groups might include tenants or tenants' representatives together with a similar number of 'mandated' representatives from the landlord. It is often helpful to involve a third, independent, party[20] whose role is not to advise, or take sides, but to improve the processes of openness, exchange, challenge, feedback, experimentation and co-learning—that is, real dialogue. The following set of principles, though by no means definitive, has been useful in my experience:

- Participants negotiate and develop their own ground-rules for the way in which they will work, rather than adhering to any external rule-book or policy.
- Learning itself is promoted as the principal process of development rather than any preconceived notion or system of 'participation'.
- Participants are encouraged to acknowledge that others may hold honest and genuine but different views of the same situation which are just as valid as our own.
- Language is expressive of the person's view ('in here') rather than abstract and nominalized/objectified ('out there'). For example, 'I like what you say' is more helpful than 'That's right'; 'I don't see it like that' is more helpful than 'That's/you are wrong'; 'I feel ...' is more helpful than 'That's not fair' etc.
- Participants support each other in experimenting with new ways of doing things.
- Rather than prejudging actions as right or wrong, participants together evaluate their effectiveness.

- Participants try to share their perspectives, values and feelings openly and fully, rather than disclosing only those fragments which might meet with the approval of others or which are anticipated as 'normal' or 'correct'.
- Insightful and intuitive questions, whether awkward or not, are encouraged.
- The experience of the tenants is regarded as equal in importance to the professional know-how of the landlord.
- 'Mistakes' are regretted and used to inform learning, rather than for blaming or scoring.
- Members continually renew their 'mandate' for participating both personally and organizationally. This means that tenants' representatives ensure that the groups they represent are fully informed and that their views are fully represented in real dialogue meetings. Landlords' representatives see it as part of their job to procure resources (usually budgets and decision-making authority) to enable decisions to be made at the local level. At the personal level this means reviewing and honouring the working conventions of the group.
- Participants share their vulnerability and ignorance as well as their certainty and know-how.
- Participants take responsibility for failures as well as successes.
- Groups will benefit from having the assistance, especially in the early stages, of a third party who is skilled in the promotion of dialogical processes.
- Participants, rather than the Housing Association or any other body, determine the criteria for success—that is, success is evaluated locally rather than at an abstracted level.

> The Tao of the Absolute has no name.
> Although infinitesimal in its Simplicity,
> The world cannot master it.
>
> If leaders would hold onto it,
> All things would naturally follow
> Heaven and Earth would unite to rain Sweet Dew
> And people would naturally co-operate without commands.
>
> Names emerge when institutions begin.
> When names emerge, know likewise to stop.
> To know when to stop is to be free of danger.
>
> The presence of the Tao in the world
> Is like the valley stream joining the rivers and the seas.
>
> Lao Tzu

The author would like to thank Helen, the residents of St Elizabeth Close and the residents of Joseph Road Community Group, Sheffield, for helping with this chapter.

References

1. Pedler, M., J. Burgoyne and T. Boydell (1991) *The Learning Company*, McGraw-Hill, Maidenhead.
2. McNamee, S. and K. Gergen (eds) (1992) *Therapy as Social Construction*, Sage, London.
3. Sampson, E. E. (1992) 'The deconstruction of the self', in J. Shotter and K. Gergen, (eds) *Texts of Identity*, Sage, London.
4. Kuhn, T. S. (1970) *The Structure of Scientific Revolutions*, University of Chicago Press, Chicago.
5. Gergen, K. J. (1991) *The Saturated Self*, Basic Books, New York.
6. Glover, K. J. (1988) I: *The Philosophy and Psychology of Personal Identity*, Penguin, London.
7. Hoffman, L. (1992) 'A reflexive stance for family therapy', in S. McNamee and K. Gergen (eds) *Therapy as Social Construction*, Sage, London.
8. Harvey, D. (1990) *The Condition of Postmodernity*, Basil Blackwell, Oxford.
9. Giroux, H. A. (1992) *Border Crossings—Cultural Workers and the Politics of Education*, Routledge, London, pp. 39–88.
10. Shumacher, E. F. (1990) *A Guide For The Perplexed*, Abacus, p. 55.
11. Housing Corporation, East Midlands Regional Office (1992) *Tenant Participation Strategy*.
12. Torbert, W. (1991) *The Power Of Balance*, Sage, London.
13. Revans, R. (1982) 'Worker participation as action learning', in *The Origins and Growth of Action Learning*, Chartwell-Bratt, Bromley, Kent.
14. Anderson, H. and H. Goolishian, (1992) 'The client is the expert: a not-knowing approach to therapy', in S. McNamee, and K. Gergen (eds), *Therapy As Social Construction*, Sage, London.
15. Fairclough, N. (1990) *Language and Power*, Longman, London pp. 77–108.
16. Gergen, K. (1993) 'Organisation theory in the postmodern era', in M. Reed and M. Hughes (eds) *Rethinking Organisations*, Sage, London.
17. Bateson, G. (1973) *Steps to an Ecology of Mind*, Paladin, St Albans.
18. Revans, R. (1983) *The ABC of Action Learning*, Chartwell-Bratt, Bromley, Kent.
19. Argyris, C. and D. A. Schon (1978) *Organisational Learning: A Theory of Action Perspective*, Addison-Wesley, Reading, Mass.
20. Pedler, M. (1991) 'Another look at set advising', in *Action Learning in Practice* (2nd edn), Gower, Aldershot.

10
William Blake's fourfold vision and consciousness in organizations
David Rooke and Jackie Keeley

In 1802, in the full force of the Industrial Revolution, William Blake wrote a poem which offers a vital understanding to individuals, organizations, and thus society nearly two hundred years later. Blake wrote from the perspective of the individual, about levels of consciousness, experience and, perhaps more obliquely, learning. This chapter relates his vision to the contemporary world of the modern organization.

Blake wrote:

> Now a fourfold vision I see
> And a fourfold vision is given to me:
> 'Tis fourfold in my supreme delight
> And threefold in soft Beulah's night
> And twofold always. May God us keep
> From single vision and Newtons sleep![1]

Singlefold vision

What did Newton notice as the apple fell from the tree? Was it the beauty of the bloom, the miraculous merging of greens, russets and reds? Was he moved to poetry by the harmony of nature as it moved through a season of 'mists and mellow fruitfulness'? No. When he saw the apple fall he drew 'scientific' conclusions about what other apples and, by deduction, other objects would do in similar situations in the future. One might say that his vision was at once helpful and limited: he was conscious only of the facts; his experience was fettered. Blake describes this limited relationship with the 'object' world as 'singlefold vision'.

Single vision is associated with a 'scientific' view of the world in which events and objects are viewed as literal. Events and objects have meaning only at one level. An apple is an apple: an object of science to be observed demonstrating its scientific behaviour. Things are thus essentially separate; there is no connection of beauty or meaning beyond what is obviously seen. Nature only exists because of human beings. Thus the entire non-human world is 'dead'; that is, it has no life or spirit of its own. This is a *cold* view of the world, one where the intrinsic value of the other, of non-human life, is missing. This view of the world is reductionist. We do not appreciate the whole, but rather break it down into its sub-parts and in so doing lose all its magic. We try to explain the world in mechanistic ways, always linking cause and effect.

Taylor, in his work on scientific management in 1911,[2] brought singlefold vision to the organizational world. He wished to reduce the operation of organizations to strictly controlled actions based on rigorous analysis, and he and others in this school reduced the human element to a mechanical contribution. At this level relationships are exploitative. Learning is unimportant. The organization, like nature, is essentially dead; it has no spirit or soul. *The organization is a place where labour is organized as efficiently as possible in the pursuit of profit and all else excluded.* There is no place for more, for learning at more than a simple technical level, for contactful relationships between people, and no place for workers to have pride in their work.

Many organizations today are to be found operating at the level of Blake's single vision. This is the economic effective level where concern is always with the 'bottom line'. When a senior manager or director asks 'But what is the bottom line?', you know that the organization is being plunged into, or held in, singlefold vision.

Twofold vision

Twofold vision is described by Blake as a place of 'generation'. Generation arises from the meeting of opposites: man meets woman, night meets day, silence meets noise. When a human being meets nature he or she understands that nature is different from him or herself and is not there as an extension of his or her own being. In twofold vision relationship, and thus deeper dialogue, begins. People become aware of the essential difference between themselves and every other person in the world. Accommodation and resistance rise out of the tension of difference. Human energy is in relationship. In contrast to the coldness of 'Newton's sleep,' there is warmth here, the warmth of engagement, with all its attendant possibilities for conflict *and* resolution. Here we begin to understand something of the poetry and dance of life.

Many organizations spend time in this twofold vision. Here teamwork manifests itself through the genuine joy and challenge of working with others. The sense of abstract separation which defines singlefold vision is replaced by a feeling of connection with others, and the difference between people provides the tension and energy. Complementary and differing skills can be used together, sometimes easily, sometimes not. Customers and suppliers are pulled into the team, though with the caution inherent in tension. The boundaries which emanate from the individual in his or her definition of the world into 'self and other' cause there to be rules and procedures which help to order things into their 'proper', and relatively uncreative, places.

Competition *and* cooperation between individuals and between departments is likely to be the way of working inside the organization. This needs careful management in order to prevent a slide into the cool separateness of singlefold vision.

Threefold vision

Threefold vision for Blake is 'soft Beulah's night'. This is the *marriage of opposites*, a merging into one another. A closeness arises from an inner knowledge, from a deep connection. There is a profound sense of togetherness, between people, and out of this begins to emerge creativity. We glimpse this in those peak experience moments such as falling in love, being closely with someone as they die or being overawed by some beauty in nature. The human relationship with nature is one in which the essential living spirit of nature is recognized and met. This creative meeting may be expressed in poetry, music or art. Life is lived with greater imagination for the possible.

Is it possible that an organization may enter threefold vision? As individuals we are in threefold vision only occasionally. For organizations it is even tougher—there is something in the very act of *organizing* which makes this level of consciousness difficult to hold, and yet we do catch glimpses of it in organizational life.

Great creativity between people is born out of a merging of purpose and action, particularly where the purpose contributes to the larger community. There is an enormous sense of pride and an easy energy in the activity of the organization. The quality of the experience of production as well as of the product is vital, because it is part of the whole connection between the individual, the organization and the world. Learning is deep-seated, and investigates the assumptions upon which the organization operates. There is no separation of learning from activity; there is a passion for both, and both are seen as essential and intertwined. Managers are able to hold multi-perspectives and begin to spot the inevitable paradoxes of organizational life.

Fourfold vision

Fourfold vision is a step beyond. In relationships something emerges from the space between people, almost as if by a mystic third force. The energy of creativity bubbles continuously; genius and inspiration are found. This is the level of mysteries, where events may seem paradoxical to ordinary logic. Individuals are engaged in conscious acts of creation at a higher level. The composer Brahms said, of creating at this higher level:

Then I immediately feel vibrations that thrill my whole being ... in this exalted state I see clearly what is obscure in my ordinary moods ... The term subconscious is a very inadequate appellation for such an extraordinary state of mind ... Superconscious would be a better term.[3]

The ego is no longer absolute and an awareness grows of transpersonal regions where powerful archetypes, the soul, God and great mystery exist.

The self/world duality is seen as illusory. There is a 'surrender' to higher agency. Thus the truly great artist no longer holds the fiction that the ego is the ultimate source of creative power. Mozart, legend has it, once responded when asked how he composed, 'God speaks to me and I write'.[4]

It may only be possible for organizations to have rare and dazzling moments at this ultimate level of consciousness. The creativity is too intense for a community of people to hold, the paradoxes and ironies create too great a humility, the mystery is too vague. An organization may enter into a transformative state, but not for long. The need for 'reality' in a world which is literal beckons people down to a more everyday level of vision. And we must be clear that the task is not to *hold* organizations in the ether of a fourfold vision, but rather to enable them to feel that spiritual lift and soulful depth.

What might we hope for?

We may work in and with organizations to guide them up through the levels of vision, to bring out the potential to live and work in greater creativity, soulfulness and spirit. That the world is cast too much into the deep Newton's sleep there can be little doubt—the task then is to enter and live all of the levels of vision in our lives, and bring this to our organizations too.

References

1. Keynes, G. (ed.) (1979) *The Letters of William Blake*, Harvard University Press, Boston.
2. Taylor, F. W. (1911) *Principles of Scientific Management*, Harper & Row, New York.
3. Shear, J. (1980) 'The universal structures and dynamics of creativity', Paper presented at the Fourth Conference on Mental Imagery, San Francisco.
4. Funk, J. (1983) 'Music and fourfold vision', *Revision*, **6** (1), 59.

11
What is organizational biography?
Mike Pedler

This chapter, and Chapter 12, explore the notion of biography as a way of understanding organizations, especially in the context of the Learning Company. From a Learning Company perspective organizations are in a dynamic process of becoming; and of *being* only in transition. The biographical metaphor with its births and deaths, ages and stages (event), periods and themes, lends itself well to this perspective.

This chapter considers the notion of organizational biography—what do we mean by it? What is the case for it? What are the limitations? Chapter 12 consists of Weldricks—a case study of a retail pharmacy business—together with a commentary which builds upon the case to show how biography can be used to illuminate the development of the company and provide a basis for organizational learning.

Introduction

It is now empirically clear that Darwinian evolutionary theory contained a very real error in its identification of the unit of survival under natural selection. The unit which was believed to be crucial and around which the theory was set up was either the breeding individual or the family line or sub-species or some similar homogeneous set of conspecifics. Now I suggest that the last hundred years have demonstrated empirically that if an organism or aggregate of organisms sets to work with a focus on its own survival and thinks that this is the way to select its adaptive moves, its 'progress' ends up with a destroyed environment. If the organism ends up by destroying its environment, it has in fact destroyed itself. The unit of survival is a flexible organism-in-its-environment.[1]

Organizations are formed from three forces (Pedler, Burgoyne and Boydell[2]):

- *Ideas*—the visions and images which founders seek to realize and which are passed on to succeeding generations to re-create;

- *Phase*—the life-stage of the company, e.g. infant, pioneer, rational, overripe bureaucracy, dying;
- *Era*—the economic, social, political and cultural context.

Approaches to the study of organizations can be seen to favour one or other of these forces. For example, *organizational development* practitioners tend to stress the importance of having the right ideas and values as expressed in 'vision driven by empowering leadership'. *Organizational ecologists* eschew the study of single organizations for studies of population survival rates in particular environments. The agentic assumptions of the former—that organizations control their own destinies and can plot their future course—are confronted here by more deterministic ones which give primacy to environments and contextual forces. For the latter, the actions of individual companies are inconsequential and of little interest. *Organizational biography* focuses on the life of the individual organization over time, and occupies intermediate ground between the agentic and the deterministic. Those who have taken this perspective include Greiner,[3] Lievegoed[4] and Adizes,[5] although a related notion, the 'Life Cycle Model', has been described by Porter[6] as the grandfather of all business models.

What is meant by organizational biography?

Organizational biography builds on the organismic metaphor which sees organizations as living systems, exchanging with a wider environment to satisfy their needs. The concern with the organization as a developing entity draws on other metaphors, including those of organizations as 'cultures', 'brains', 'flux and transformation' (Morgan[7]). The notion of biography takes us beyond an organism to the 'person' or 'living being' with a unique life, a product of inheritance and circumstances, with some free will to make decisions at various times.

Salama[8] goes beyond 'culture' and uses the term personalities to describe the organizations in her sample: 'every company must be understood as an individual with its own idiosyncracies'.

The power of such metaphors, which partly stems from and is, in turn, endorsed by, everyday usage, is open to charges of reification. In speaking about the organization as a collective living being—the company has decided' or 'we are in much better spirits than last year'—it is important to remember, as we are doing it, that we are attributing agency to what is a human construction sustained on a daily basis. Yet, in so far as 'it' behaves as a whole, unique organism, can be said to act, make decisions, be morally responsible and so on, these metaphors are a useful way of thinking about the company.

Life ... and death

If there is life, and a life cycle, then there must also be death. The organizational ecologists have brought to our attention the traumas of organizational conception, gestation, birth and death (Kimberly and Miles[9]). Organizational death does not figure greatly in the theories of organization development, which may account in part for their tendency to 'look on the bright side', but contemporary evidence suggests that the ecologists' assumption is now the likely fate, sooner or later, of all companies.

The infant mortality rates of new companies are as high as 40 per cent in the first year in some samples. But even the largest and most powerful established companies are not immune. Pascale[10] notes that, 'Of the corporations in the Fortune 500 rankings five years ago, 143 are missing today. (By comparison, in the 25 years, 1955 to 1980, only 238 dropped out.)' This appears to be an accelerating trend. Commenting on Peters and Waterman's 1982 sample of 'excellent' companies, he further notes that 'Only five years after the book's publication, two thirds of the companies studied had slipped from the pinnacle'.

Findings like these may partly explain an upsurge of interest in organizational learning—perhaps corporate learning can stave off the inevitable? 'Learning disabilities are tragic in children, but they are fatal to organisations. Because of them few corporations live even half as long as a person—most die before they reach the age of forty' (Senge[11]).

Survival itself is an indicator of learning, albeit a weak one (Burgoyne[12]). The quest for organizational learning may be fuelled by nothing less than the promise of the extension of corporate life. It has been suggested, from a psychoanalytic perspective, that organizations, as larger-than-life structures which can continue for generations, act as a defence against the anxiety of being human and mortal. However, an acknowledgement of the eventual likelihood of organizational death may offer greater maturity and the 'sculpted creativity' of later life (Jaques[13]). The denial of death perhaps constitutes an important aspect of the 'shadow side' of organizational life:

Jung's work shows that the repressed shadow of organisation acts as a reservoir not only of forces that are unwanted and hence repressed but of forces that have been lost or undervalued. By recognising and coming to grips with the resources of this reservoir, Jungian organisation theorists are at one in suggesting that we can tap new sources of energy and creativity and make our institutions much more human, vibrant, and morally responsive and responsible than they are now. (Morgan[14])

Facing up to the need for organizational death and, with care, dignity and proper ceremony, choosing the right time to bring a particular organization to an end, can release new life and energy. Organizations do outlast their useful lives and, in continuing to exist, deny the new. Sheffield's Manor Employment Project, set up in 1980 to create small businesses with local people, voted, after a long struggle, to end itself in 1987, to be replaced by a MaTReC—whose new training and educational aims fitted better the needs of the times (Pedler et al.[15]).

Ages and stages

To the extent that we can see the company as a dynamic being with a life cycle, we can talk about its development over time. Although every organization is unique, meeting particular problems and circumstances, some believe that it is possible to talk about predictable questions which occur at predictable times. Greiner[3], in a seminal theoretical paper, discusses five phases in the company life cycle, from young to mature. The first stage is growth through creativity, followed by growth through direction, delegation, coordination, and collaboration. Growth, however, is not certain. Each phase comprises a period of stability which ends in a crisis. The crisis stems from the current mode of operation–for example, the early creativity phase ends in a crisis of leadership where the young company, full of the founders' drive and vision, struggles when they leave, retire or lose their way.

Lievegoed[4] takes a similar view. Organization development takes place via a progression of phases which are irreversible. It is discontinuous; an old pattern is broken by the crisis and a new one forms over time, and involves qualitative transformation. The new phase is different in quality from the old and is characterized by a different principle, but the latter does not entirely disappear:

The old pattern usually remains in existence in a more or less changed form in the background, as an undercurrent, or in a subordinated or repressed form, or as a historical relic ... (p. 43)

Each phase is more complex than its predecessors because it contains and overlays these earlier forms which may surface anachronistically from time to time. Thus we get a picture of organization as being, in Lievegoed's words, 'always "on the way" from a given past to its own future'. The past is known and influences the present; the future offers some freedom of action to add to this history. This is reminiscent of Marx's dialectical theory of societal development where the struggle over time between old and new ideas leads to an emerging synthesis; and also Kuhn's descriptions of how ideas emerge in the scientific community.

This perspective of development over time offers a dimension which may often be neglected in organizational decision making and direction finding. In this view a balance is required between seeing the organization as similar to others—subject to the same forces, with predictable crises, etc.—and as unique, with different character, purpose and history. The 'core values' of an organization, which are so sought after today as guidance systems in the face of unpredictability, are forged in the sometimes painful process of development.

As a way of understanding our culture

Each person writes down a list of ten words or phrases that he or she feels most aptly describe the organisation ... the whole group combines their lists on a flip chart ... note which words or phrases appear most times, note positives and negatives, and whether one person's positive such as 'busy' is another's negative 'hyperactive' and so on ... the group then discuss why things are done like this around here. (Aspinwall *et al.*[16])

When people engage in explorations of their culture, describing it as 'restless' or 'single-minded', they often have no idea of where these descriptions come from—'they just are'.

In recent times it has become commonplace to talk of 'changing the culture'. Perhaps in part a response to the teachings of academics and writers, this has been powered by a recognition that structural reorganizations alone are insufficient. Aware of the need for something more to engage the hearts, minds and souls of people, we have become familiar with efforts to change the culture via inspiring visions, creative leadership and cascading development programmes. Claims of 'cultural change' have become an important part of new corporate images.

If company cultures are unique entities forged from products, processes, personalities, events and happenings over time, then claims for relatively sudden changes must be examined sceptically. The cultural view suggests that, like people, organizations possess the capacity either to resist or embrace change. It also suggests that although organizational learning is possible there will be limits, with some aspects of the organization being relatively fixed and enduring. Changes in cultures are likely to take years rather than months, even when they are of the 'miraculous' sort. It seems likely that the possibilities for, and the specific directions of, change are influenced by the inner drives, values and fixities of the organization as well as by outer, environmental forces.

The use of stories, myths, legends, case studies and so on is a way of appreciating both uniqueness and pattern, and is a venerable and widespread way of making meaning and understanding amongst. Quoting numerous authors, Torbert[17] notes that 'The notion that story or narrative is the primary manner in which organisational interventionists and people in general make meaning out of their experience has become widely argued in literary studies, philosophy and social science in recent years'. As the narrative of the business, biography can trace the all-pervasive, yet largely invisible, culture which is so crucial to organization development and learning.

Developmental management

An organizational biography perspective implies developmental management. The organization is seen as 'a continuous system over time' (Pettigrew[18]) with a past, a present and a future. There is learning to be gained from the past, perhaps most importantly to do with organizational values and identity. Development requires a present state of readiness to take the next step and an optimistic future orientation to provide vision and courage. To manage developmentally means recognizing where the company is in terms of the developmental sequence, in recognizing the nature of the crisis when it comes, and in seeing the opportunities to develop inherent in that crisis. With this view, the argument goes, managers are likely to judge the timing of changes better and avoid the traps of acting in the wrong direction at the wrong time.

As an aid to business direction finding, biography work may contribute to 'emergent strategy'. Current organizational, research has been criticized as 'static and ahistoric' (Kimberly and Miles in Salama[19], and approaches to strategy making have been similarly castigated as embodying an unproblematic, 'modernist' view of history (Pedler[20]). Mintzberg has pointed to the unmeasurables of ideology and history as the most relevant phenomena in organization research, 'To miss this in research is to miss the very lifeblood of the organisation' (in Salama[21]). In a 1983 study of Chief Executive Officers, El Sawy suggests that there are ways to develop the future perspective and provides some empirical evidence that those with most awareness of past events also looked further into the future (Kouzes and Posner[22])

Problems and limitations of the biographical method

Some of the limitations of the biographical approach have been noted in the above discussion, especially those concerning the assumptions of the metaphor, and the question of 'agency' in the single company versus the environmental determinism of organizational ecology. This latter perspective developed in reaction to the single case study tradition of organizational research, although there are recent signs of common ground:

the premises of ecology are too restrictive to accommodate recent developments in theory, we must have an evolutionary perspective on organisations, one that focuses on change within organisations as well as on turnover of organisational populations. (Meyer[23]).

Beyond this debate there are a number of methodological problems which are similar to those encountered in anthropology, ethnography, participant observation and so on. Aspinwall[24] has usefully summarized these, including problems with managing the data (citing Thomas and Znaneicki's *Polish Peasant* in five volumes); the emotional commitment to the method, 'perhaps in reaction to more positivist approaches (again Thomas and Znaneicki—*The Perfect Method*); and the difficulty of maintaining sufficient distance from the data -'going native' or 'sympathetic identification').

I experienced these problems most acutely on the Manor Employment Project in Sheffield (Pedler *et al.*[25]), where, as a member and 'participant observer' over five years, I became so strongly identified with the original aims of the project and with the other people involved that I felt estranged from my academic colleagues—who came in only at the final evaluation phase—seeing their judgements as superficial and simply wrong. Only at several years' distance can I write the 'balanced' description of the MEP's death above. A case like Weldricks, based on a few visits plus time at the word processor, does not create such 'sympathetic identification' problems, although other issues of data management and method remain.

Then there is the question of the validity of cases owing to their incomparability—they are individual and unique, and therefore hard to compare and contrast, so how can we generalize? Is it possible to acknowledge things to be unique but not atypical? The positivist's method of triangulation vies with the constructionist's preference for creating meaning. Following Becker's 'problems of inference and proof', perhaps you can infer, but not prove, on the basis of biographical cases? And what does proof mean in these circumstances?

Against these limitations must be weighed the 'inside' view which biography can offer, and also the contribution to 'generative theory' (Gergen[26])—the importance of the construction of new meaning perhaps especially through a 'learning conversation' with 'the Biographical Partner' (Aspinwall[27]). There are many opportunities for further research, especially in longitudinal studies which map development paths and patterns in organizations. There are also specific topics which would lend themselves to larger empirical studies, for example, linking the individual biographies of long-serving leaders with their company biographies. Finally, there is the question of appropriate methodologies. In the Weldrick case, only the owner was interviewed—it is his account. In another study I tried to assemble the stories of a 'representative sample' of the organization.[28] In terms of development work, where this is different from research, I have a lot of sympathy for Weisbord's view that we have to 'get the whole system in the room' even if, as he suggests, we don't know how to do this yet.[29]

References

1. Bateson, C. (1973) *Steps to an Ecology of Mind*, Paladin, St Albans, pp. 425–6.
2. Pedler, M. I., J. G. Burgoyne and T. H. Boydell (1991) *The Learning Company: A Strategy for Sustainable Development*, McGraw-Hill, Maidenhead, pp. 3–4.
3. Greiner, L. E. (1972) 'Evolution and revolution as organisations grow', *Harvard Business Review*, **50** (4), 37–46.
4. Lievegoed, B. C. J. (1973) *The Developing Organisation*, Celestial Arts, Millbrae, Ca.
5. Adizes, I. (1988) *Corporate Lifecycles*, Prentice-Hall, New Jersey.
6. Porter, M. E. (1980) *Competitive Strategy*, The Free Press, New York, p. 157.
7. Morgan, G. (1986) *Images of Organisation*, Sage, London.
8. Salama, A. (1992) 'The use of an organisation's biography as a research method for investigating organisation development', *Management Education and Development*, **23** (3), 225–33.

9. Kimberly, J. R. and R. H. Miles (1980) *The Organisational Life Cycle*, Jossey Bass, San Francisco.

10. Pascale, R. (1991) *Managing on the Edge*, Penguin, Harmondsworth, pp. 11–17.

11. Senge, P. (1991) 'The learning organisation made plain', *Training and Development* October 43.

12. Burgoyne, J. G. (1992) 'Creating a learning organisation', *Royal Society of Arts Journal*, CLX (5428) 321–32.

13. Jaques, E. (1970) 'Death and the mid-life crisis', in *Work, Creativity and Social Justice,* Heinemann, London, pp. 38–63.

14. Morgan, G., ibid., p. 225.

15. Pedler, M. J. *et al.* (1990) *The Community Development Initiative*, Avebury, Gower, Aldershot, p. 47.

16. Aspinwall, K. A. *et al.* (1992) *Managing Evaluation in Education*, Routledge, London, pp. 35–6.

17. Torbert, W. and D. Fisher (1992) 'Autobiographical awareness as a catalyst for managerial and organisational development', *Management Education and Development*, **23** (3) 195.

18. Pettigrew, A. M. (1979) 'On studying organisational cultures', *Administrative Science Quarterly*, **24**, December, 570–81.

19. Salama, ibid., p. 225.

20. Pedler, M. J. (1992) 'Strategy or destiny? Biography work for organisational learning', *Management Education and Development*, **23** (3), 260.

21. Salama, ibid., p. 225.

22. Kouzes, J. M., and B. Z. Posner (1987) *The Leadership Challenge: How to get Extraordinary Things done in Organisations*, Jossey Bass, San Francisco, p. 95.

23. Meyer, M. W. (1990) 'Notes of a skeptic: From organizational ecology to organizational evolution', in J. V. Singh (ed.) *Organisational Evolution: New Directions,* Sage, Ca., pp. 298–314.

24. Aspinwall, K. A. (1992) 'Biographical research: searching for meaning', *Management Education and Development*, **23** (3), 248–57.

25. Pedler, *et al.*, op. cit.

26. Gergen, K. J. (1991) *The Saturated Self: Dilemmas of Identity in Contemporary Life*, Basic Books, New York.

27. Aspinwall, *et al.*, op. cit.

28. Pedler, *et al.* (1992) op. cit.

29. Weisbord, M. R. (1987) *Productive Workplaces: Organizing and Managing for Dignity, Meaning and Community*, Jossey Bass, San Francisco, p. 273.

Part II: Applications

12
Organizational biography and organizational learning: Weldrick: a case study and commentary
Mike Pedler

Overview

Through employing a case study and commentary, this chapter demonstrates the biographical perspective on organization and links this with ideas about organizational learning. The case begins with a brief introduction, followed by history, current performance and future prospects.

Introduction

Weldrick is a retail pharmacy chain of 22 shops, a warehouse and a 1993 turnover of 12m. It is the creation of owner Ron Alcock, who opened his first shop in 1967. Business is in his family background, and his grandmother, an entrepreneur and shopkeeper was an important influence in his life. In partnership with a pharmacist who died leaving debts, she took control, employing another pharmacist until the debts were repaid. Ron Alcock worked in her shop from the age of 12, and she advised him to become a pharmacist.

Weldrick's mission statement now begins 'to dominate retail pharmacy in South Yorkshire', and Mr Alcock has a strong entrepreneurial drive, which he believes is unusual—'it's rare to get a pharmacist with first-hand business experience'. Mr Alcock is dominant within the business and displays an impressive grasp of both strategy and detail. To question after question he reaches for a file, an in-tray, a ledger, to demonstrate evidence for his answers. His watchword is 'monitoring', he says, displaying a list of 41 items on which he keeps a close eye.

History and growth

On the purpose of the business, Mr Alcock comments that originally:

The idea behind the company was to provide a living for me and it has escalated into what you see now. I was trained as a pharmacist and I stick to what I know ... I have diversified into a number of other things ... with having seven children, not all could be pharmacists ... I suppose I do have a reasonable amount of business acumen because the family have always been in business, but I chose pharmacy rather than general retailing, market trading or manufacturing—manufacturing I don't know anything about. I qualified in '64, my first business opened in '67, and on November 29th 1973, I bought H I Weldrick, 28 Hallgate. At the time I had about six branches ... RAW Alcock Group ... I started with one at Hatfield, and then the second was at Dunscroft, the third in Askern, the fourth was in Barnby Dun and the fifth was in Maltby. I opened my first business April Fool's Day 1967, the takings were £16 and 4 pence and I dispensed 22 scripts.

He describes the growth and development of the business as being rapid and smooth. Turnover has risen year on year and continues to do so. From 1967 he bought new shops at a rate of about one a year which operated under their own names. With the acquisition of Weldricks in 1973 he took the opportunity of its existing limited company status and good reputation to take that name for all the shops. 'The bank was happier dealing with a limited company', says the ever-pragmatic Mr Alcock.

Weldricks continued to grow in a positive situation until 1986/7 when a legislative change meant that NHS contracts were only awarded to pharmacies more than a mile apart. This slowed growth and dramatically put up the price of pharmacies because it created guaranteed markets. During the period of steady growth prior to 1986:

I expanded on my own money, I never borrowed money—it's only recently I've borrowed money to expand ... further did all the work myself ... signed all the cheques, dealt with every invoice, even did the shop fitting ... Diversification only started in '84 when I opened a computer company, an office equipment company and the following year, a training company ... but only the computer company was a natural outgrowth from pharmacy ... I'm the major or only shareholder in all these ... but keeping to pharmacy as the core business.

During the two years 1984–86 Mr Alcock had a general manager to oversee the business while he turned his attention to these new interests. Once the new businesses were up and running, he returned his full energies to Weldricks. This seems to mark another turning point; perhaps these two years served as a refresher and a break from the mainstream business, as well as a chance to prove his abilities outside pharmacy. Certainly Weldricks took a different direction after his return:

... after 1986/7, I decided that the business had got big enough that we actually needed some stronger management ... there were certain grants available and I approached David Hall in 1988 for marketing and Wingfield Slater for a business plan ... and ... due to the advice given by those two consultants, we decided to go for it and expand as fast as we could and change banks in the meantime ... changing banks was a step forward, we negotiated far better terms and facilities from the one we're with now ...

... this was after showing them the consultant's 5-year business plan ... and at that time I decided to employ what I was advised were highly efficient and well-trained people to take some weight off my shoulders so I could, specialise in certain areas and they would specialise—one in buying, one in training and one in general management. It didn't quite work and we had several shots at it, now it's settled down into a nice little team of three people—the retail director we have at present, the training manager and me. We had reached a stage where I couldn't do everything ... the business would have been out of control had we not done something—formally training people, getting better calibre people and being better organised. After saying all this I must say that I made more profit in 1975 than I do now—it all goes on staff—and central office overheads.

Was it difficult to give up these functions? No, says Mr Alcock, not to the right people and not given close continuous monitoring of performance. The handing over of responsibility was 'relatively painless'. A few mistakes were made. Two of the people appointed did not meet expectations. The first training and personnel manager was a promoted shop manager who moved things on but also caused a few problems, for example with pay, by making decisions without consultation. Marshall Glyn, who only joined Weldricks in 1987 but who immediately showed business acumen, was promoted from shop manager to retail director in May 1991.

This period marks a clear developmental change with delegation of some management functions, a five-year strategic plan and a more ambitious vision. However, the shift from the 'pioneer' organization to the bigger, more profession-ally managed one has a down side—funding well-paid, professional staff means a bigger turnover. The process of reorganization and change over about five years has cost money and reduced profit. However, life is now easier than it was for Mr Alcock, and there is a structure in place for growth:

A key change was the creating of a strategic plan which we did for the first time a couple of years ago ... sticking to the strategic plan has had quite an impact on the direction and helped everyone in the company to focus on what they're doing ... we review it every three months, but the people who formed it meet weekly and discuss parts of it all the time.

Over the years the idea behind the business has also developed. Providing a living for himself and his large family has remained a primary consideration together with an early ambition to improve the image of pharmacy. 'I've been very, very ethical and most of the pharmacies I've bought have been in need of improvement.' What does he mean by 'ethical'? 'Good housekeeping, well-trained staff, good range of merchandise, prompt dispensing, communicating, helping old people, clean windows, more clinical looking place, so its different from the shop that sells a can of beans.'

As the business grew, and presumably as pressures to earn a living lessened, Mr Alcock admits to getting a 'buzz' from building a business, from opening new branches, from seeing profits rise. At this point in the late 1980s he had the choice of sitting back on a successful business or, following the advice of the consultants, going forwards and aggressively. He chose the latter course. However, the word 'dominate' in the new mission statement is Marshall Glyn's. 'He's heading the group on the retail side, he's totally responsible for profitability and it seemed to be very much in character ... and ... it's not a bad idea to dominate a certain sector of the market, is it?'

This shows some willingness to allow new people to influence the purpose and direction of the business; however, Mr Alcock retains a firm grip. As well as managing strategically, he goes on more professional refresher courses than anyone else and still works in the branches dispensing once a week:

to keep in touch and to keep my hand in for my own satisfaction ... I do like pharmacy and I do like meeting my customers, and the only way of getting the marketing right and to monitor the situation is to be there. And monitor with a capital M ... that was a New Year's Resolution about two years ago and it's still top of the list.

Current operation

Monitoring on the inside
Weldricks is managed by monthly returns from branches which are turned into a central computer report. Each manager has jointly arranged targets to meet, set on a yearly basis. Managers get a detailed report on their branch performance each month, with 'league tables' showing their position on key indicators such as turnover, prescriptions, retail sales, staff costs and stock of all 22 branches. If targets are met, a bonus on salary for managers and staff is payable. The plan is to link bonuses to profitability in branches, which has not been possible partly due to lack of computerization in branches.

How does Mr Alcock use this performance data?

If they don't respond to memos or their paperwork isn't in on time or they don't attend managers' meetings or whatever, everything goes on their file, so when it's appraisal time and they're wanting a 10% increase the file is used for negotiating a realistic revision of salary.

There is a six-weekly meeting of all managers chaired by Mr Alcock, at which performance figures are discussed. What effect does this feedback have on managers?

They certainly don't like to be in the minus section ... they certainly don't ... you'll never be able to quantify the effects, but we just have a feeling that the ones in the middle have quite a positive attitude to get up to here and there is a fair amount of swopping of ideas because they have a session for brainstorming for half an hour afterwards ... we bring them drinks up from the bar ... they're all exchanging ideas—what they've taken on and sold well and why don't you try it at your branch, talking about any dead stock and can you take this off me and what have you ... I need something and I can't get it from the wholesaler and can you supply it ... it is very productive. We do have ... other than one manager ... a very good team spirit.

All stock must be ordered from the warehouse to maximize control and bulk buying. Because branches are not geographically close there is not much competition between them; however, a 'branch of the month' award recognizes special achievements. The managers' meetings have become livelier of late with the consultant's help, and Mr Alcock contrasts them with earlier occasions when he did all the talking.

Is learning measured in any way—the speed at which ideas are picked up or practices changed?

We have two profit and quality managers introduced 12 months ago who look after 11 branches each and are responsible for being out of their own branch once a week to go and look at other branches. They swop with the managers sometimes and that one manager goes and works in the profit and quality manager's branch for the day. So there are ways of ideas being brought from branch to branch ... so we have two of the better people in the group taking some responsibility for the better running of the branches in the business. They report in to Marshall Glyn, the Retail Director.

Feedback of information is on a need-to-know basis and is limited to branch operations. Mr Alcock maintains an overview on the performance of the company by monitoring year-to-date figures monthly and gives an annual update on profit/loss and trading account to managers. He runs a tight ship. Given the managers' apparently enthusiastic involvement in brainstorming on each other's problems, is there a case for involving managers more in thinking about the company as a whole?

They are a super team and they do try to benefit the company as a whole, they realise what's going on in the outside world—that the Government is cutting down on the cost of drugs, etc. etc.—but you must remember that a pharmacist is an academic and there are very few business-aware pharmacists. We have all on to make them business-minded in the shop never mind make them business-minded as a group ... I think really ... they'd drown if we tried to make them too involved.

Managers do make suggestions for new services; one example, monitored by Mr Alcock during the interview, is the recent installation of a Polaroid camera at the Maltby branch to take passport photographs. With driving licences likely to require photographs in the near future, this development may spread to all branches.

Monitoring on the outside
Two of Mr Alcock's key roles in the restructured business are developing new businesses and keeping in touch with the outside world. To one side of his desk are several piles of cuttings from trade journals in which he has searched and noted changes and developments in products, national and international trends,

legislative changes and so on. This is his way of keeping up-to-date, and all these items are for discussion with Marshall Glyn for possible action. Would he consider delegating this job?

If I delegated it I would always fear something was missed ... and it keeps me in touch at the same time ... it keeps me in touch more than anybody else. I just prefer to do it. I study all planning applications to every council where we have branches and go through them for doctor's surgeries opening or moving, changes of use, nursing homes, etc. ... I just sleep better doing it personally.

To keep in touch with customers, Weldricks carries out surveys, where questionnaires are handed out at branches. Has the company changed as a result of information from customers? Mr Alcock is readily able to reel off three such changes: using radio advertising and changing shopfronts to make 'Weldrick' stand out (after having discovered that the company name was not well known); rejigging staffing at branches to get them there at the best times for dispensing; and introducing new items to stock.

Does the company learn from what other companies do? Mr Alcock does not think other chains have much to offer, but cites learning from Boots. When Boots set up a controlled unit dispensing system of drugs for nursing homes this was seen as a threat, and all Weldricks' nursing homes were offered a similar, free system:

Obviously the Boots' idea has spurred us into doing it, and nursing homes, as a result, get a far better product and service ... and I suppose it has improved things—had Boots not done it, then we wouldn't have to the same degree ...

Similarly, Boots offered a free collection and delivery service for prescriptions, and Weldricks responded quickly to do the same for their area to 'nip them in the bud' before Boots could take any business. This is a benefit of competition to the customer, but a 'nuisance' to Weldricks with a clear impact on profits 'because the new service is being abused by certain members of the public'.

Are Weldricks experimenting with any new ideas? Indeed they are—a lockable display shelving system for items whose sale must be supervised by the pharmacist has been patented. As a result, several articles have appeared in national magazines featuring Weldricks. A second innovation is postal dispensing: 'if you post us your scripts, we'll post them back to you'. They can even be faxed in. While this service is aimed at current customers, it appears to offer many future possibilities and is still being researched.

Mr Alcock also sits on a pharmaceutical sub-committee of the local FHSA (Family Heath Service Association) which coordinates local primary health care. This keeps him in touch with all new, local health care developments, and one example of the effect of this is that Weldricks' shop displays are coordinated with the FHSA's 'theme of the month'. This month it is 'keeping warm', next month it will be 'breast feeding', then 'stopping smoking'.

Recruitment, training, development and learning in the business

Recruitment is delegated almost entirely to Marshall Glyn and Christine, the personnel and training manager. Under the current 'Investors in People' initiative, shop managers will be trained to recruit their own staff. Mr Alcock's criteria for manager recruitment include good professional appearance, ability to communicate, knowing their pharmacy, and 'trainability'—able and willing to update, learn and develop themselves.

On the training front, there are induction programmes and operations manuals for both managers and shop staff. Pharmacists, and sometimes other staff, are encouraged to update their product knowledge by attending seminars put on by pharmaceutical firms. There are distance learning opportunities—for example, Apothecaries Hall which involves a residential course of two weeks at University—and all counter staff are encouraged to do the Medical Counter Assistants Course. In addition, Weldricks has an in-house training facility and has carried out management training using the consultants who have been involved under the various grant schemes.

How does Weldricks evaluate this training effort? First, in reduced turnover of staff which has gone down almost to zero; and secondly, in staff response, for example to the Medical Counter Assistants Course which is popular and where staff seem to retain the knowledge afterwards, giving them greater job satisfaction and taking pressure off the pharmacists.

Counter staff can develop through four grades from trainee to dispensing assistant, but opportunities for managers are very limited to innovations such as the new role of profit and quality managers. Most, says Mr Alcock, are not ambitious and focus on community care. With this and low turnover, keeping good people in the business is not a pressing issue:

We pay reasonably well—not the best ... they can earn more by attaining targets ... but I think because of the training, the regular meetings, the way they feel the company thinks of them ... and it is sincere, the way the company thinks of them ... they feel part of the company and the team and they're one big happy crowd ... you must sit in on one of the managers' meetings as an observer ... . We've had to have terrific team spirit ... for example, a new warehouse computer has been letting us down on the software side, and they've really helped in every way, we've asked them to fill in yellow cards to report any faults and they've done it religiously, they've helped us enormously. All the managers, and that has been a team effort ... the Christmas party, all ... all of them attended ... we make them feel valued.

The influence of the owner

The extent and nature of the owner's learning experiences are often a guide to the attitude to learning within the company. What are the key learning experiences in Mr Alcock's career? Most recently he cites the Institute of Directors Diploma Course which he attended in 1992:

I learned a lot from the course ... . I was aware of a lot but it sharpened my awareness and made me use it ... and the workshops were fantastic. All these courses are now official, but I've been going on them ever since I qualified, so going on post-graduate courses has been an on-going thing for the past 20 years. The Trent Regional Health Authority are very good at organising advanced courses.

So formal continuing professional education, and latterly management and director development, have been important. What or who else has been important?

I read a lot ... *The Director, Management Today* ... . I've not really had a mentor. I suppose I've mentored myself through reading. I talk now with Marshall and I've always talked a lot with my wife about the business. And going right back, my grandmother ... she was a very organised person and I think I learned a lot from her about being organised, having things in the right places and being tidy ... and I suppose I've learned from Ian (consultant) as well ... he's come up with some ideas and his reports have made me ... the report on marketing—we've put most of that into practice. Listening to Ian and reading his reports has helped a great deal!

1987 marked the beginning of the use of outside consultants. Mr Alcock had always felt a need for outside knowledge, but had never thought it cost-effective until he was able to get a grant. Now he would do it without a grant because of the benefits he has experienced—a good advertisement for pump-priming.

Finally, how does he think he is seen within the business? He is uncomfortable with this question, suggesting that others need to be asked this, and giving the impression that he isn't used to thinking like this. On asking the reason for the question and receiving the answer that, because he is so central to the business it is likely to reflect his character, he agrees:

The character of the business, in my own mind, is supposed to represent a good, solid family business rather than a monster out of control or an empire where we have ways of making you, or you must, do ... and I think we get people to respond far better that way, and I suppose in a strange sort of way I think of the staff as my family. In other words, I regard the company as a family business.

The future

So what is the vision of the future—more of the same? The aim is to continue expansion via the buying of new branches, but staying tight-knit within 25 miles of Doncaster. The company is currently in a consolidation phase, having acquired its last four shops only in November 1992—although if a good opportunity came along Mr Alcock would not ignore it.

Internally, major changes will take place, especially via EPOS (Electronic Point Of Sale) capability being installed in the branches which will enable better control of stock and inventory, merchandising, security and accounting, and will help the company to respond more rapidly to changes. In addition, a complete audit of office systems is being carried out. Both these projects are being undertaken by Leeds University graduates under a Teaching Company scheme with a 75 per cent DTI grant. Other developments include an expansion of own label products, the establishment of a health shop, and the employment of a marketing person and a representative to visit nursing homes and factories.

With the help of consultants, Weldricks is also aiming to become an 'Investor in People' and a 'centre of excellence'. This will happen by defining what excellence means for Weldricks and setting out to attain it's and especially through passing responsibility for training and development down into the shops. In future, the people employed by Weldricks will be more highly qualified and of a higher standard. Post-graduate education is becoming compulsory.

Changes on the outside, to which the company will respond, include government aims to take the pressure off the NHS and doctors by increasing services from pharmacies. A new payment system will reward performance on specific services as well as for just dispensing scripts. Increments will be given for installing Health Education Leaflet stands and establishing private consultation areas in pharmacies. Further rewards will come from each pharmacy handling patient medical records, from offering house deliveries, for staff going on refresher courses and for other services. For example, courses 'are' or 'will be' increasingly offered on areas of work hitherto part of the GP's preserve, such as initial diagnosis of diabetes, cholesterol testing, pregnancy testing and dietary advice. Mr Alcock sees this as the shape of the future—more and more branches will be offering these services.

On succession, he is ready to step back and become chairman if, and when, Marshall Glyn is ready to take over as managing director:

Now I've got to this stage in life, and having seven children who need my attention, I would gladly be paid to keep out of the way as long as I had all the facts and figures presented to me once a week in a nice folder, so I could still monitor the situation! When the information that I can get from the computer is exactly what I want, then I will be content to step back.

Beyond becoming chairman Mr Alcock does not intend to retire—it is not a word in his vocabulary. He is quite happy for one of his seven children to come into the business, but only on the same terms as anyone else. If they wanted to be managing director, that would be fine as long as they were better than Marshall. At the moment, however, though one is a hospital pharmacist, none of them show signs of wanting this.

Commentary

What can the Weldrick case study tell us about organizational learning and development? First of all, the limitations of the case, especially that what we are examining here is the account of the founder and owner, need to be borne in mind. It does not represent the voice of anyone else in the business. Because of the centrality of Mr Alcock—founder, owner, manager, director and ex-shopfitter—it is not possible or sensible to separate him from the business. The owner's career biography and the organization's biography are part of the same story.

Some companies are fiefdoms, extensions of the personalities of their owners and founders. The influence and dominance of particular individuals is often marked, especially in small firms, but even in much larger, even multinational, companies. The academic literature may underestimate the influence of personality on organizations, preferring to focus on the 'rational' managerial arts of finance, marketing strategy and so on. To explain and justify their acts managers may articulate this rational script and the 'laws' of business—many of which are well displayed in the Weldrick story—but it is more difficult to articulate and trace the force of personal values and beliefs which may more fundamentally guide the development of the business.

Are all living companies learning companies?

Weldricks qualifies as a Learning Company on the following grounds:

1.   It is alive and well after 25 years, continuing to expand and grow in terms of shops, turnover, employment and the sophistication of business management.

Burgoyne[1] has suggested that if learning is defined as what any entity, individual or institution does to change, adapt and survive, then it is possible to argue that any organization which survives for a reasonable period must, to some degree, be a learning organization. Twenty-five years is perhaps more than a reasonable period for a small business, given the mortality rates discussed earlier.

Looking in and looking out

2   Weldricks shows impressive commitment to looking in and looking out and acting quickly in response to data—it is adaptable, flexible and thriving.

The evidence of internal monitoring (via performance data, managers' meetings, manager swops via the profit and quality managers, the managing director continuing to dispense on a weekly basis and so on) and external searching (via trade journal scrutiny, customer questionnaires, responding quickly to competitors, experimentation and innovation of new products and services, etc.) shows a vigilant and adaptable company which looks to the future. There is evidence of productive use of data from inside and outside.

This is an indication of another level of Learning Company functioning beyond the first one of survival over time. Burgoyne[2] suggests that learning organizations may be described as weak or strong:

It is useful to sort out weak and strong learning organisations by thinking in terms of three levels or a three-step hierarchy of degrees of learningfulness the first level (is) a kind of *memory*. It learns processes, then puts them into procedures and keeps them going. ... The second level is of organisations which can be described as *adapting systems*. ... Such organisations manage to change and adapt to meet the changing demands of markets. These are primarily self-interested organisations and the outcome of learning is their survival. ... Third level organisations develop their contexts, make their own world better for them to live in and to contribute to ... (my italics)

Weldricks clearly exists beyond the *memory* level and models many of the desirable characteristics of the *adapting system*. From a market economy perspective the adaptive system may be seen as the acme of the Learning Company, so the level three 'strong' learning organization needs more explanation. Why change a winning team?

Double-loop Learning

3. Transformation: 1987 to 1992 is a period of change for Weldricks, which has altered some of its basic operating assumptions, i.e. it has achieved some double-loop learning.

This is a more difficult assertion. It depends how we interpret 'double-loop learning'—a term linked to many definitions of organizational learning and to cognate ideas such as 'reframing' and 'transformation' (Argyris and Schon,[3] Garratt;[4] Watzlawick, Weakland and Fisch[5]). Core to the argument is whether these changes constitute a fundamental change in operating assumptions or whether the learning took place within the current business perspective.

Most of our learning is 'single-loop'. Someone who sees him or herself primarily as an engineer, and his or her business as a factory for making things, will learn mainly about new engineering ideas and ways of making production systems more effective. If the person is a good learner, he or she will examine critically his her methods to see if they can be improved and will scan the world outside for new ideas about engineering and production systems. This model follows the cycle described by Kolb,[6] building upon Dewey and others, of learning from our experience of the world through observation, reflection, forming new ideas and trying them out.

Argyris and Schon[7] define single-loop learning as 'error detection and correction'. The analogy given is the thermostat, monitoring temperature and, depending on the data feedback, turning the heat either up or down. This learning model is about maximizing effectiveness—ensuring that we achieve a set target. It is limited in that it gives you 'more of' or 'less of' the same; it allows adjustments to the current way of doing things, but it cannot change the fundamentals.

But let us suppose that our engineer is supplier to a large manufacturer who goes out of business. Will new engineering skills or production ideas help here? Possibly, but more likely the need is to look *outside* the current frame of

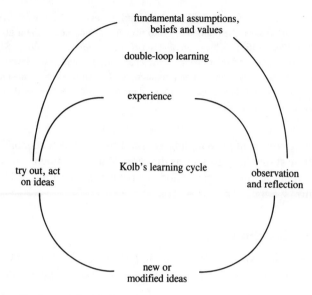

Figure 12.1   Single- and double-loop learning

reference—perhaps to selling or to finding new markets. But the engineer is no salesperson, doesn't have the 'gift of the gab', doesn't know anyone who knows how to carry out market research, and so on. In their world, this sort of information, skill and learning are not present. 'Double-loop learning' often starts from this sort of crisis.

The single-loop 'error detection and correction' model is appropriate most of the time and there are plenty of examples in the Weldrick case (the responses to customers, competitors, trade journals, consultants' ideas and so on). It is only necessary to double-loop or reframe when the basic assumptions on which we are working are no longer valid—either because the outside world says 'We don't want this any more' or because those inside say 'We don't want to do this any more'. While single-loop learning is always about 'How can we do this thing better?' double-loop learning starts with 'Why are we doing this thing?'

We are usually well defended against these fundamental 'Why?' questions which are threatening to what we do and who we are. As Pascale points out, commenting on the fall from grace of many of the *In Search of Excellence* sample, individuals and companies often carry on doing certain things long after they have ceased to be functional:

While it is by no means true that all of these companies foundered for the same reason, the foible most common to them all was that they took a good thing too far.[8]

To avoid this—no easy matter—we have to stop what we are doing well in order to consider the options and change in a fundamental way: in the case of a person, perhaps give up a job and start a new career; or in the case of a business, stop thinking about ourselves as a bus company and become a travel firm. This sort of transformation is not achieved without pain and disruption. When it occurs it is an occasional rather than a continuous happening, and we can only achieve this kind of change periodically. In these terms the 'continuous improvement' of the quality movement refers to single-loop learning.

Problems with single- and double-loop learning

There are two problems with this distinction between single-loop and double-loop learning. First, how do you distinguish between the two? When is learning radical enough to classify as reframing? Is there not a continuum between single- and double-loop learning rather than a bi-polar split? How can the 1987 to 1992 changes in Weldricks be classified? (And who cares, as long as the company is surviving, growing, prospering, etc.?)

The distinction is important because everybody knows that you stick with the winning team ... until you need to do something different. We fail when we continue with single-loop learning, i.e. doing what we know how to do but better, when what is really required is a more fundamental questioning. Persisting with continuous improvement on the basis of operating assumptions which have become inappropriate may make things worse by entrenching our commitment to these assumptions and by using up energy and awareness which should be directed elsewhere.

Secondly, how do you perform double-loop learning? Can you choose to do it when desired or is it more usually a response forced upon us by crisis? And having chosen or been pushed into double-loop learning, how does it work or happen? This second problem represents the nub of the organizational learning quest. To consider this from a different angle, we can look at Weldricks in terms of a developmental theory of organizations.

From pioneer to rational to integrated organization

One way of describing what happened to Weldricks in these years is in biographical terms: to see it as moving from the small, fast-growing pioneer driven by a strong central figure to a more rational organization which has outgrown the abilities of one person to become bigger, more independent, more complex. Successful completion of such life-cycle transitions are key to survival and learning.

In this model (Lievegoed[9]) the pioneer organization, built around one individual or small group, gives way to the rational as scientific principles replace personal ones in work systems, structures and processes. Weldricks moved from one person doing everything, including the shopfitting, to employing managers who special

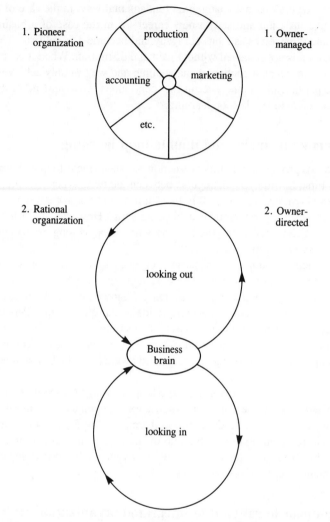

Figure 12.2   The pioneer/owner-managed and the rational/owner-directed organizations

ize, and setting up systems to ensure consistency, order and fairness. Skill and professionalism replace energetic amateurism.

From owner-managed to owner-directed

One striking aspect of this shift is the transition for the person at the centre of Weldricks. Moving from pioneer to rational means control shifting from the managing to the directing function. This can be seen clearly at Weldricks with Mr Alcock's shift from manager to director. In Figure 12.2 opposite, the owner as manager in the pioneer organization does everything. In the rational organization functions and roles have become more differentiated (Lievegoed;[10] Garratt[11]).

Garratt suggests that in the rational, owner-directed model, three things—operational planning and action, external monitoring, and integration and direction giving—are required for effective performance and should be linked in a learning system[12]. The lower, 'looking-in' loop is the operational one where plans are put into action, performance is monitored and appropriate changes are made. The 'looking-out' loop is the policy one where the external environment is scanned for changes and direction is altered accordingly. The role of the director is to integrate the operation of these two loops and to provide direction.

Garratt suggests that it is in the upper policy loop that double-loop learning occurs: 'Reframing, by getting a better perspective through monitoring the external environment, rising above the immediate organisational problems, and identifying the wider issues, allows second-order change and, therefore, learning.'[13] He also equates the operations loop with single-loop learning.

However, this poses similar problems to those discussed earlier of how we may distinguish single-loop from double-loop learning. The Weldrick case appears to show that the impetus to reframe came as much from within the operations loop, as the business grew too big to be managed in the current way, as from the outer policy loop. It seems more likely that single- or double-loop learning can be triggered in either the policy or the operations loop, but that the learning process involves a reciprocal passing through and an integration of both.

Garratt recognizes this 'action learning' process and sees integration as the director's job; the director is the 'business brain'.[14] However, there are other problems here: should the directors be the only 'business brains'? And can they be relied upon to generate double-loop learning when this process requires a challenge to existing operating assumptions, i.e. policy—of which they are the guardians? In Weldricks, Mr Alcock has made the move from manager to director, but has maintained a strong degree of control—through directing and monitoring rather than the typical hands-on, face-to-face relationships of the owner manager. Although he challenges others in the business, and keeps himself up to the mark in various ways, he is not challenged from within. In this context it is significant that Pascale places much emphasis on the need for internal conflict in organizations, if they are to be learning organizations.[15]

From the sensible to the super-sensible: the self-transforming learning company?

How can we improve on the current satisfactory and sensible operation of Weldricks? The owner is directing affairs while, to some extent, keeping hands-off operations which are now delegated. When the company is doing as well as Weldricks, why on earth would you want to change a winning team?

Four possibilities suggest themselves:

1. The problem of succession.
2. The probability of continuing rapid growth.
3. The possibility of environmental change.
4. The possibility of inner changes.

Succession

Many small and some larger companies founder on the rocks of replacing the central person. Family members may be 'groomed' to succeed but when they do not have the same drive or qualities as the founder, this course of action may fail.

A recent, poignant example is that of Wang Computers, built up by a Korean immigrant to the USA into a major multinational over 30 years, which then collapsed in just three years. An unsuccessful father-son succession, followed by the import of a 'company doctor' from a different industry, proved ineffective. This danger was recognized in the male-dominated Sheffield steel companies of the 1950s, where it was a good thing when the owner was blessed with daughters rather than sons. The daughters could be married to the best young prospects in the firm.

Mr Alcock does not appear to be falling into the family trap, but Weldricks has not yet met the succession crisis proper. Although he has stepped back from the position of manager to that of director, he is still very much the dominant presence.

Growth: more of the same

A second possibility is that of Weldricks growing rapidly and 'dominating pharmacy' over a much wider area than South Yorkshire. Mr Alcock envisages a leap forward which, in part, he sees as necessary to pay for the increased costs of the rational organization. In such circumstances there is a possibility of indebtedness as costs and systems increasingly burden the business. In addition, there might be a loss of vitality and energy in the extended company as the founder draws back, his initial vision long exceeded. Growth may make a currently adequate operating system and structure ineffective—something which Weldricks has already experienced once. Growth, which can be blind, is not the same as development, which involves consciously taking the next step.

Mr Alcock seems aware of the possible 'bureaucratic crisis' in his unease over 'expensive' professionals, financial borrowings and the like. One way of acting to prevent this happening might be to develop further the people in the company through delegation, training and development, and the general encouragement to take more initiative and responsibility. Counter-indications which might limit such a move include the tight central control and the perception of shop managers as unambitious and not particularly interested in development opportunities.

Change in the environment

Again, a threat of which Mr Alcock is well aware; the company's track record of environmental monitoring, together with experimentation and innovation in new products and services, is impressive. An obvious potential threat is that of takeover, which could only happen if Mr Alcock—as 100 per cent shareholder with his wife—wanted it. Indebtedness or loss of interest, which seem unlikely at present, could be factors in this threat.

However, there are plenty of examples to show that it can be difficult to anticipate environmental changes, however good your flexibility and adaptability. People's Express, which grew at a rapid rate to become a major threat to the established major airlines, failed because it got everything right except a misjudgement of the impact of computer reservations systems. The majors controlled these and strangled the dynamic upstart.[16] Another example concerns a large part of the Finnish engineering sector which was for years closely tied to the Soviet Union. With the collapse of the customer in 1989, many of the firms lost their orders. When they tried to sell elsewhere, people laughed at the low quality of the 30-year-old designs. They had fallen so far behind that most were unable to respond quickly enough to find the capital, new skills and new markets, etc. Many companies closed down and unemployment shot up contributing to the deep crisis in the Finnish economy in the early 1990s.

Change from within

While business strategists have tended to focus on change that comes from outside, the learning organization is interested to know how it can come from within. One obvious block is the extent to which directors and managers are concerned to keep a tight grip.

Managers in Weldricks are tightly controlled. Current training opportunities could equip people to become more proactive and begin to question and challenge more, but the evidence suggests that this will only happen if those in power encourage this change. Not surprisingly perhaps, managers are often wary and fearful of the consequences of doing this. The issue is often seen in adversarial terms, and there are a few examples where trade union actions have brought changes in companies. However, there are many more where this is not so; a celebrated case in the 1970s saw Lucas Aerospace reject the 'alternative corporate plan' for new product ideas and alternative markets put forward by the trade unions.[17] Employees pressing for change in non-unionized, private companies must be very rare indeed.

Ideally, in a learning organization the challenge from within is a vital potential source of strength and new ideas, if only the threat can be managed. In Lucas Aerospace, potentially useful ideas were lost to the company; whereas in Honda today, the development of new products and prototypes is encouraged and celebrated annually. How can companies tap and release the creative energy and ideas of all the members of the organization?

In limiting the 'business brain' to the directors, organizations may be trading tight control for creativity. Recent, unpublished research by myself and my colleagues in the Learning Company Project suggests that senior people have a much more favourable view of the company as a learning organization than do junior people; and also that the demand for learning and development opportunities at lower levels is much higher than estimated by those nearer the top. Such differences in perspective are commonplace, but do we make use of them?

The owner as developer

In this section the case study of the development of Weldricks is taken on beyond that which can as yet be justified on the basis of empirical data, for the purpose of illuminating the idea of the Learning Company. This is not, however, an attempt to suggest a direction for that company.

A biographical perspective requires that we live with the notion of the company as dynamic even when it is 'consolidating'. Equally, all environments are dynamic. The company does not and cannot stand still. This fourth possibility of change from within takes us beyond the empirical in this commentary on the Weldrick case to an even more speculative link to our model of the Learning Company—as an organization which actively seeks to give voice to all its people and to involve them in the direction of the enterprise as well as in its operations. This involves a different conception of management from those we have been discussing. It raises the notion of managers as facilitators or developers of learning in individuals and organizations.

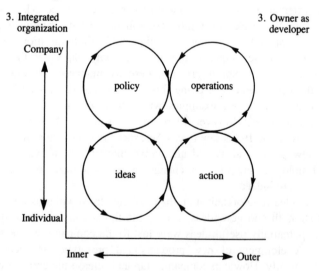

Figure 12.3   The learning organization

In this model of the Learning Company,[18] the organization creates learning opportunities for all members and also seeks to harness the fruits of all this learning and personal direction finding so that the company as a whole may learn and appropriately find collective direction. This goes beyond the rational to the integrated stage, where the company is seen as a set of flows of energy, activity or consciousness which need to be harmonized, balanced and integrated.

Beyond the rational stage is the bureaucratic (or overripe rational) stage where differentiation of knowledge and roles becomes too rigid, energy drops and entropy accelerates. To escape this, there is a need for shake-up where attempts are made to loosen the organization and breathe life into it. Large companies are disaggregated; individuals are urged to take initiatives and become leaders rather than managers. The integrated phase is the realization of these changes.

This goes beyond 'the director as business brain' to using the brains of all company members. The need for learning in the organization outstrips the ability of any one person or small group. The director becomes a facilitator or developer, and a 'co-creator' in partnership with other company members.

Drucker[19] uses the term 'orchestrator' for the 'CEO-conductor' of the organization as symphony orchestra:

We are entering a period of change: a shift from the command-and-control organisation, the organisation of departments and divisions, to the information-based organisation, the organisation of knowledge specialists.

But from the complex world of hospitals, three key strategic roles have been suggested for managers which takes us away from maestros towards facilitation and development.[20]

• Providing a 'sense of direction', rather than detailed plans or prescriptions;
• Helping people and groups come to agreements about directions rather than relying on coercion, managing a process of continually negotiated meanings and decisions;
• Working with the endemic conflict between the values and aspirations of the various professional and other groupings.

The development of the learning company

The case and the commentary illustrate an idealized path of organizational biography. Four double-loops or 'figure eights' can be discerned in Figure 12.3, each of which involves a reciprocal flow of energy from one part to the other. By adding 'Infant' to Lievegoed's three-stage model of organization development we can hypothesize that energy is differentially focused at these stages in the company's life, and that each stage requires a different role from the owner.

The lower two spheres of Ideas and Action comprise the Learning cycle which the *infant* company must pass through to survive in the first place; by the time the company has reached the *pioneer* stage, the focus has shifted to the managing cycle of Operations and Action; in the *rational* stage the focus now moves to the Directing cycle of Policy and Operations; and in the *integrated* phase the focus shifts to the facilitating cycle of Policy and Ideas where individual ideas are incorporated into collective Policy and vice versa. This fourth cycle of Facilitation is the critical one for the realization of the Learning Company. Although these ideas are presented here as a linear or historical development, they can also be seen as four complementary foci to which a company needs to direct its attention and energy appropriately. Loss of energy in any of the foci can lead to imbalance in development or neglect of particular spheres.

References

1. Burgoyne, J. G. (1992) 'Creating a learning organisation', *Royal Society of Arts Journal* CLX (5428) 321–32.
2. Ibid. p. 323.
3. Argyris, C. and D. A. Schon (1978) *Organizational Learning: A Theory in Action Perspective*, Addison-Wesley, Reading, Mass., pp. 20–9.
4. Garratt, R. (1987) *The Learning Organisation*, Fontana, London, pp. 58–61.
5. Watzlawick P., J. Weakland and R. Fisch (1974) *Change: Problem Formulation and Problem Resolution*, W. W. Norton & Co., New York.
6. Kolb, D. A. (1984) *Experiential Learning*, Prentice-Hall, New Jersey.
7. Argyris and Schon (1978), op. cit., pp. 18–20.
8. Pascale, R. (1991) *Managing on the Edge*, Penguin, Harmondsworth, p. 11.
9. Lievegoed, B. C. J. (1973) *The Developing Organisation*, Celestial Arts, Millbrae, Ca.
10. Ibid, p. 76.
11. Garratt, R. (1987) *The Learning Organisation*, Fontana, London, p. 81.
12. Ibid. p. 33.
13. Ibid. p. 77.
14. Ibid. p. 78.
15. Garratt (1987), op. cit.
16. Hampden-Turner, C. (1990) *Charting the Corporate Mind*, Blackwell, Oxford.
17. Elliot, D. (1977) *The Lucas Aerospace Workers' Campaign*, Young Fabian Pamphlet 46, November.
18. Pedler, M. J., J. G. Burgoyne and T. Boydell (1991) *The Learning Company: A Strategy for Sustainable Development*, McGraw-Hill, Maidenhead, pp. 33–4.
19. Drucker, P. (1988) 'The coming of the new organisation', *Harvard Business Review*, January–February.

20. Barrett, S. and L. McMahon (1990), Public management in uncertainty: a micro-political perspective of the health service in the UK', *Policy and Practice*, **18**(4), 257–68.

13
Learning to achieve transformation in health
Hilary Lines and Bob Ricketts

The problem is to create organisations that are stable enough to persist, but flexible enough to adapt to pressures for change

(Huczynski and Buchanan[1])

The true objective is to take the chaos as given and learn to thrive on it

(Tom Peters[2])

Why learning organizations in the health sector?

The National Health Service (NHS) has witnessed, and been responsible for bringing about, unprecedented strategic and operational change during the last ten years. This has been particularly noticeable in the establishment of general management in the mid-1980s and the more recent development of an 'internal market', in which the functions of assessing health needs and planning to meet needs (health purchasing) are separated from those responsible for delivering high-quality health care services (health providing).

Both of these major strategic changes have involved a redistribution of power and authority and, particularly recently, a devolution of management and control functions closer to the point of service delivery, promoting greater flexibility and responsiveness to client need. This has been matched by a recognition of the need for new approaches to people resourcing and development which not only help to embrace and manage current changes, but which promote the organizational resilience to adapt in a continually dynamic environment.

The concept of learning is not new to the NHS: education, training and development have been cornerstones of personnel practice for many decades, as would be expected in an organization whose strength lies in the specialist application of knowledge. Action learning and action research had a significant influence on change management practices in the 1970s and 1980s, and the plethora of programmes under the total quality and culture change banner have addressed the issue of cultural adaptation and change and the establishment of new management systems and procedures to support change. The growing popularity of the learning organization concept in the late 1980s/early 1990s in some areas of the NHS has seemed to derive from four interrelated factors:

1. Since the future methods of operation of NHS organizations cannot be precisely defined, success will be dependent on the innovation and courage of individuals and their ability to learn and develop new ways of working and thus to create the future organization in which they work.

2. Change in the NHS is inevitable, but successful change management will lie not in reacting reluctantly to future changes, nor in minimizing their impact, but in building organizations which are flexible and responsive to the needs of the population they serve: whether expressed through policy, through strategic plans, through general practitioner referrals or through patient choice. Thus there is a critical need to move from bureaucratic to a more integrated or organized way of working.

3. Organization change, as well as threatening individual need for control and security, can also provide opportunity for individual learning and development. Thus, given the inevitability of change, organizations should, wherever possible, seek opportunities for personal development through the process of organization change. This interrelationship between organization and individual change is illustrated in Figure 13.1.

4. The continued future success of health service organizations will be dependent on the collection, transfer and assimilation of knowledge and expertise—in assessing health needs, determining the impact of health interventions, identifying and sharing best practice, and promoting technical excellence—and this means working across boundaries of work group, profession, hospital, health authority and nation to promote learning and skill development.

Despite the apparent attractiveness of the concept, there are a number of characteristics inherent in the current culture of the NHS which make it a difficult and complex theme to take root: the barriers to communication and openness brought about by functional and professional specialization; the procedural rigidity still in existence in many areas; the often witnessed tendency of certain management levels to undermine or ignore the potential and desire for development among lower graded staff; the inevitable scepticism over new change concepts in a world dominated by policy initiatives and novel programmes for strategic change.

In this chapter we aim to illustrate in more detail some of the issues involved in applying the learning organization concept in the UK NHS, and the lessons learned to date. We will derive our learning predominantly from a case study of two health authorities (a) going through a process of merger; and (b) establishing a new health purchaser organization. This relates to work undertaken during the period April 1991 to April 1992.

Figure 13.1

Merging health authorities and the learning organization concept

On 1 April 1992 the two health authorities concerned in this study merged to become one, after a culmination of 18 months' change management activity. The rationale for the merger was that the combined management and resources of the new authority would have substantially greater purchaser leverage and a public health function strong enough to ensure the effective health-needs-based purchasing of health services.

The process of change involved in the merger comprised a substantial task—it involved not only the bringing together of two geographically separate organizations, but the creation of a new type of organization, with a focus on health strategy and planning rather than the management and control of hospital services. It also entailed the management of a complex and frequently fluctuating political agenda in order to ensure that the new authority had the support and commitment of key relevant stakeholders—MPs, Community Health Councils, general practitioners, local population, the Regional Health Authority—to name but a few.

The concept of the learning organization was considered valuable to the change process for two main reasons:

1. The purchaser organization is essentially information and knowledge-based. Its effectiveness will depend on its seeking out and listening to the views and needs of its population, drawing on best practice, challenging the status quo and keeping an open mind on the best interventions to meet health needs. Being outwardly focused and highly competitive in marketing are therefore

key priorities, and a learning mentality is critical at all levels of the new authority.

2. A merger involves bringing together two organizations, two cultures, two 'sets of people'. Its success involves learning the best from each other and allowing the development of new options and choices for action. A climate which encourages openness, trust, tolerance of mistakes and the sharing of alternative views is critical to making this work.

In introducing and developing the concept of a learning organization we were guided by a number of key principles:

*   that, by definition, the exact criteria for a learning organization should not be imposed, but should evolve and be defined by the managers and staff concerned;
*   that the approach should build on work already undertaken by managers and professionals in defining the characteristics and criteria for success of the health authority, and therefore should represent values which, while being challenging and exciting, are commensurate with the evolving value system;
*   that any models used to assist the process should be simple and transferrable to real-life situations and therefore able to promote and guide learning at all levels;
*   that the approach should ensure a holistic approach to organization development, in which all aspects of the working of the authority—its structures, systems, people, culture, environment—are addressed. That attention should focus on how these organizational elements support and hinder learning and the creation of trust and openness between individuals and groups.

Elements in building a learning organization—what we did

Below we describe some of the key steps that were taken to help develop the new health authority along the lines of a learning organization. They are not intended to be totally comprehensive, but to provide insights into those elements which we found helpful and why. We conclude the chapter by summarizing some of the lessons learned.

The key elements are addressed under the following headings:

*   Creating a vision
*   Building teamwork from the top
*   Developing and applying models of learning
*   Understanding the process of learning and change
*   Instilling learning and feedback mechanisms

Creating a vision
A key problem in developing a learning organization lies in the essential

vagueness of the concept—by definition, there is no definite endpoint to its development since success means that the organization is still learning. And while the attractiveness of the concept is indisputable (who could deny that learning is a good thing?) it is difficult to convey with it a sense of urgency in order to generate commitment to bring about real change. Indeed, if it is seen purely as a `good thing to do', nothing much will actually change. Thus creating a vision of what the learning organization would mean for the purchaser and demonstrating commitment from the top that this concept was vital to success was a critical part of the process of change in this case study.

The vision was developed and shared with a range of different stakeholders and built up over a period of time to promote understanding of what it would mean for the new organization and how it would be reflected in practice. Activities included workshops for the merger project team and parallel seminars for other staff with a strong focus on envisioning corporate roles and values. Emphasis was placed on taking the 'best from both' health authorities, rather than transplanting an established culture from one or other of the constituent health authorities.

These activities were underpinned by the development of critical success factors for the merger process and for the merger project team to enable progress to be monitored and evaluated. But for most people, a vision is not enough until they see the implications for how they will work. Creating roles which promoted flexibility and processes which enabled information flow, learning and feedback were also critical aspects of the change. The second of these is examined below.

Building teamwork from the top

Merger has been described as the 'most emotionally charged of all organisation (change) situations' (Hastings *et al.*).[3] It often brings together two parties with a history of accentuating differences rather than similarities of identity and culture. The insecurities and anxieties caused by the merger, if not addressed carefully, may only serve to reinforce differences and thus prevent learning, even where few tangible examples exist in reality. Integrated teamwork at the earliest possible stage of the process is critical to establishing and demonstrating common understanding and trust and to recognizing the value rather than the threat of learning from people of different backgrounds and experience.

The object must be to create an integrated team from the two parties that are able to achieve more than either partner could individually.

A merger project group was therefore formed to serve the following purposes:

- to bring together key people from each constituent health authority in a joint endeavour, recognizing the specific contribution of each member and building confidence in a new management arena;

- to project manage the merger process in order to ensure that key objectives were fulfilled by required deadlines;
- to involve the two sides in the formulation of a joint vision aimed at transcending potential differences in approach and procedure and thus providing a sense of direction and optimism for staff;
- to establish an understanding of the learning process at an organizational and individual level and the impact of individual style on teamworking and effectiveness, thus aiming to build a process which could be cascaded through the organization;
- to provide a forum for sharing concerns and misgivings about the implications of the changes for individuals and therefore generating an understanding of, and sensitivity to, the issues of personal loss and their impact on the process of change.

This process was facilitated by the application of a behaviour-style inventory to help managers share individual styles, and to encourage disclosure and feedback on the impact of style on group learning. It was further aided by an in-depth examination of the personal experiences of loss and transition felt by team members and their staff in the past year, and the generation of a sense of common identity among members from both sides—a process which was aided materially by the disclosure and openness of the chief executive.

Developing and applying models of learning
We have already referred to the difficulties posed by the essential vagueness of the learning organization concept and the problems of making it 'live' for individuals. For this reason we placed significant emphasis on the development and application of simple models to help demonstrate and underpin the learning process.

Figure 13.2 was developed to represent the process of organization change and learning and holds that:

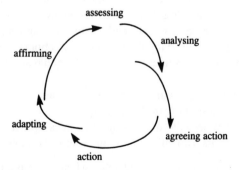

Figure 13.2 A change process model

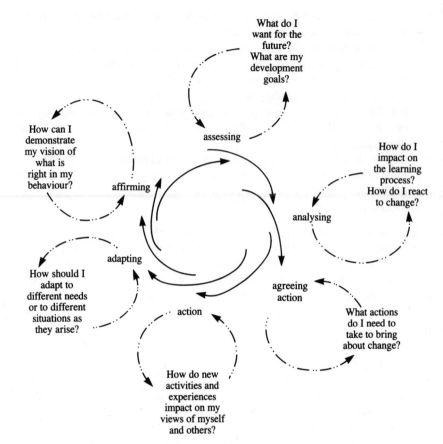

Figure 13.3   Integrating organization and individual learning

- organization development and growth occur through an ongoing process of learning, involving assessing the need for change; analysing its consequences for the organization, its staff and customers; agreeing a plan of action; implementing and observing the effect of our actions; adapting as appropriate; affirming our decisions in everything we do; and reassessing with reference to where we started;
- this cycle of learning should occur continually and entail an ongoing review of progress and questioning of the status quo;
- an organization needs to draw on all resources available—from the environment and from its own employees—in order to promote effective learning.

The power of the model is demonstrated when we examine how often we miss phases out, and the impact of this. Too often, change programmes fail because we ignore the potential for resistance to change (analysing) or fail to assess progress against initial objectives and to adapt our actions as we learn from our mistakes (assessing and adapting).

The merger project group was able to relate its process of organization change to the phases of the model and to plan its activities accordingly.

Figure 13.3 shows how individual learning can be linked to this process of organizational learning and thereby provide opportunity for individual development at each phase of the process. This dual model of organizational and individual learning can provide a powerful support to the activities of project teams or learning goups at any level of the organization.

Understanding the process of learning and change

All organization change involves loss of some kind to the individuals employed within—loss of old ways of working, loss of security and familiarity, sometimes loss of status, earnings and employment. The perception and reality of loss can be particularly acute during mergers. The merger project group recognized the need to understand the effect of the changes on motivation, morale, emotional stability and performance so that it could gear its actions both to respect individual needs and to help staff contribute constructively to the new agenda.

The process of loss and transition is variously represented in the literature as the change or transition curve or coping cycle, in which individuals go through a process of shock, denial or minimalization, defence, guilt, depression and gradually move on to adaptation, reflection and internalization. The severity and duration of these phases will vary according to the personal circumstances and personality of, and perceived and actual threat to, individuals and the background of change in the organization as a whole. The phases are seldom discrete—individuals may appear to 'regress' and express feelings of hopelessness even after things have ostensibly changed for the better. Understanding of these change processes was critical to the building of a learning climate within the top team, to spreading an understanding of the issues of change within the two authorities and to developing insight into how to handle them.

A factor which is often overlooked is that learning itself involves similar (if sometimes less severe) feelings of loss and consequent resistance. Figure 13.4 illustrates a typical reactions sequence experienced when an individual suggests to a colleague, subordinate or manager better ways of going about things.

Learning entails giving up old perceptions, comfortable assumptions and states of knowledge or ignorance and draws into question the past approaches, habits and mind-sets of individuals and groups. The achievement of a learning climate which will tolerate and support difference, openness, challenge of the status quo, tolerance of failure, requires a flexibility and resilience of behaviour and perspective which may be alien to a functionally specialized organization, and particularly to two organizations merging. The process of getting there will therefore be a

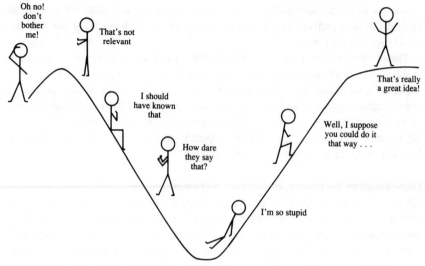

Figure 13.4   Learning and loss

threatening and fearful one for many people. Time spent on understanding this process at all levels of the organization and providing support for personal transition is critical to getting a learning organization started.

Instilling learning and feedback mechanisms
We said above that a vision of the new is only a first step in putting the learning organization concept to work: an early priority must be to demonstrate, at a practical level, the benefits of joint learning to the future of the organization. This was done in this case by looking for opportunities for joint problem solving which would speed up the development of effective purchasing and the integration of the two units. These included project teams to address issues of critical and joint concern, joint seminars, monthly learning events for all staff, journal clubs and development of a joint marketing plan.

Two integrated issues which need to be addressed are the competences that are needed to make teams and networks effective and, concisely, the way in which such processes can help in individual skill development, for example in team leadership, project management and problem solving. A step in the right direction was the identification of the competences necessary to enable the characteristics of the learning organization to be fulfilled. In addition, a process of maintaining individual learning logs was started to help individuals to record their learning goals and monitor learning experiences and attainments on a day-to-day basis.

One set of critical issues that senior management must address prior to the establishment of learning or project groups is the exact nature of the authority being delegated, the scope for discretion in their actions, and the way in which recommendations, and indeed failure to succeed, will be handled. One of the key barriers to achieving a learning climate derives from a failure to listen to the views of those at lower levels of the organization and from a tendency to apportion blame or punishment for mistakes rather than seeing them as opportunities to learn from experience. Of course, the very nature of a public sector organization makes the issue of mistake tolerance a difficult one to tackle, especially during the heightened political sensitivity surrounding major changes or elections. At such a time, the organization's capacity to risk-take and to face potential failure is very limited, and invites controlling rather than enabling behaviour from management.

Lessons

The work outlined above forms only the beginning of a process of building a learning organization. From these initial steps we summarize the key learning points of this early work and thus hope to point the way for others attempting to make progress in this area.

• *The concept must be seen to be critical to successful change*, not just a 'nice thing to do' issue. Only with full commitment and a thorough examination of the barriers to learning presented by current structures, systems, practices and styles will any true progress be made. Investment of time with senior management early on to build a true team commitment to the concept, and an understanding–at a rational and emotional level—of the implications for personal role, action and style, is a prerequisite to achieving real change.

• *The purpose of the learning organization must be brought to life* and put in a language which has real meaning for individuals at all levels. This means making it an integral part of the vision and purpose of the organization and a catalyst for learning processes at strategic and operational levels.

• *Understanding of the process of learning* its impact on personal security and the relationship between individual style and people's ability and scope to learn is vital to success. The potential conflict between established management styles and those required to perform effectively as a learning organization must be addressed early on. Middle management's ability to adopt a more open, questioning and developmental approach is dependent on the demonstration by senior management of a learning mentality and a willingness to adapt their behaviour to encourage learning. This presents particular challenge in organizations such as the NHS which are publicly accountable.

• *The inherent vagueness of the concept must be tackled* through the use of simple and tangible models, the establishment of processes and tools to facilitate teamworking and information exchange across functions and disciplines and the regular monitoring and review of developmental processes against agreed criteria for success.

- *The threat of moving to a more fluid, questioning and open working environment needs to be recognized*, and participative, developmental and counselling mechanisms put in place to support people through the transition and to help them develop skills in personal development and learning. Management's skill and resilience in helping individuals to confidently move to a new style of working is key here.
- *The time required to move towards a learning organization must be recognized upfront.* This not only means that time and space must be made available—which always presents difficulties at a time of change—but that checkpoints need to be built in to help people recognize progress and the benefits achieved and celebrate success as key milestones are reached.

References

1. Huczynski, A. and D. Buchanan (1991) *Organisation Behaviour: an Introductory Text*, Prentice-Hall, New Jersey.
2. Peters, T. (1989) *Thriving on Chaos: Handbook for a Management Revolution*, Pan Books, London.
3. Hastings, C., P. Bixby and P. Chaudry-Lawton (1986) *Superteams: A Blueprint for Organisational Success*, Fontana, London.

14
The never-ending journey
Margaret Attwood and
Chris Minett

or

How, with the help of organization
development, a little bit of the NHS
in Essex has started to change by
putting consumers before
professions and bureaucracy

Author's note

This is the story of how one quite small part of the National Health Service (NHS)
transformed itself through learning (throughout the story reference is made to
organization development (OD)).

In our story OD is *both* an institutional presence—a small process consultancy
which provides services through contracts with a range of NHS clients in Mid
Essex—*and* a process which aims to assist clients to develop their staff and
change their organizations to deliver more efficient and effective health services.

We first presented the story as a drama called 'The Never-Ending Journey',
which was performed for the Learning Company Conference in March 1992. The
original drama had two acts: the first, entitled 'Through the eyes of the novice',
told the basic story of how change was achieved from the viewpoint of the organization's chief executive; the second, entitled 'Through the eyes of the sage', was
a commentary on the events by the organization's OD adviser.

For the purposes of this book, the format has been adapted—the comments and
analysis of the sage are now interpolated into the novice's text. They appear in
boxes at appropriate points in the story.

The setting

Mid Essex Hospitals is a group of six NHS hospitals which provide a wide range of general hospital services for the 301 000 people living in and around the Essex towns of Braintree, Maldon and Chelmsford.

It was formed in April 1990, has a turnover in excess of 60 million and employs more than 3000 people to deliver care. It became a 'second wave' NHS Trust in April 1992.

Scene 1   *The prelude*

At the start of our journey, in mid-1989, there were two medium-sized management units in Mid Essex, an Acute Unit and a Community Unit. Each unit's general manager was directly and closely managed by the Authority's general manager. Power and status gravitated to the top of the organization, at district level, with the most powerful, highest paid people being functional directors, such as finance and estates and the heads of professional hierarchies.

The role of the unit general manager was largely to try to coordinate the different hierarchies and look after the fabric of the hospitals. The Community Unit was better managed than the Acute Unit. In reality, as in most of the NHS, although general management had happened in name, it was not really put into practice.

Enough of the gloom. The district's general manager was an able, caring and enlightened man who was easily influenced by assertive women.

ENTER OUR SAGE

Back in 1986 he had the vision to appoint a Director of Organization Development and empower her to influence and shape the organization. Although still operating in a largely 'top down' hierachy, she was a bright, creative beacon in a grey sea of careful administration and tight financial control.

Box 1   'Times gone by'—a view from the sage

Inevitably, I interpret history slightly differently. During the late 1980s we undertook a range of activities concerned with both developing individual managers *and* developing managing by providing a framework within which individuals and groups could ask and answer questions such as:

Personal development	*Organization development*
Who am I?	What kind of organization is this?
What stage have I reached in	What are its current characteristics/
my life so far?	the issues it faces?

Where do I want to go in the future?	What needs to change?
How am I going to get there?	How can change take place?
How will I know if I have arrived?	How will we know if change has occurred?

By using this framework and a range of activities including:

- a structured organizational debate about mission, vision and values;
- a great many 'core' management development workshops to enable managers to take stock of their competence in the light of the demands of general management;
- optional development activities to enable these same people to develop new and needed skills;
- a structured and continuing dialogue between these middle and junior managers and the board to ensure that corporate decision making took account of views from beyond the top team on the state of the organization and the best way of moving it forward.

we were attempting to develop a management sub-culture alongside professional sub-cultures to increase service effectiveness.

When the government issued its White Paper, 'Working for Patients' in 1989, the District Management Board reflected on these initiatives and decided to react early. Some of our attempts to change the culture had been successful; other things had not changed. The organization was still too divided into professional and occupational groups, who sometimes worked more in their own interests rather than those of patients, clients, carers and the public at large. The medical staff still seemed very separate from the organization and, while there had been an early understanding that doctors should not be brainwashed to think like general managers or, indeed, to take on general management roles, insufficient progress had been made in developing joint approaches to organizational issues with doctors. The Board saw the reforms as the logical extension of its attempts to make general management work by enhancing organizational and individual managerial capability through devolved responsibility for decision making.

The District Authority's response to the government's reforms, especially the split of the NHS into those who purchase health care and those who provide it, was radical. In many respects it was well ahead of the rest of the service. It decided, very early on, that it would make a clear division between itself as a purchaser of services and the units as providers.

It also decided to regroup the units to form one very large 'superunit', comprising all the district's hospitals, and three very much smaller units. Thus the new unit which became Mid Essex Hospitals was a 'shotgun' marriage between the whole of the former Acute Unit, which comprised three large hospitals, and three smaller hospitals from the Community Unit. The balance of the Community Unit was split up to form the three smaller units.

The three large Acute hospitals had not really felt the benign influence of the sage and her disciples. Communications had improved and many managers had volunteered for development but, at root, the culture had not changed—management responded to bureaucratic dictats from above. The professions saw management largely as an irrelevance and continued to deal with patients as they had always done. The three smaller community-based hospitals showed beneficial and promising signs of having been influenced by our sage.

The Authority decided it needed a new manager to create the new 'superunit' and take responsibility for the provision of services:

ENTER OUR NOVICE WHO HAD HEARD ABOUT
THE SAGE AND WANTED TO LEARN MORE

The Authority's General Manager, who went off to start his new life as a purchaser, gave the novice some advice: 'Stay within budget and follow the word of the sage as enshrined within the "Management Guidelines" which I bequeath to you.'

Box 2   The sage's renunciation

It is time to tell you that I am not and never have been a sage and the novice is not a novice. How could he be? He has many years of experience in health care. It is true that he did not understand my role when he came to Mid Essex, but I think he quickly knew *what* he wanted to do to improve services; he came to understand that I could help him to work out *how* to do it.

However, that does not make me a sage. I find it more apt to describe myself as a travel agent. As such, I resist the temptation to sell cheap, though glossy, package tours to the unwary traveller; on the other hand, I am not in the business of peddling castles in the air. I insist that those who wish to make a journey are clear about the paths that they have trodden so far and the kind of person they have become as a result. I consider it to be my role to help them to think about the destination for their next journey.

My clients are not concerned with short-haul destinations; ours is very much the long-haul business. Sometimes they think that they would prefer a couple of weeks in the sun. I press them to explain how this will help them to achieve the longer journey which they usually say they want to make one day. If, through my questioning, they convince themselves that this trip is useful preparation, then I go ahead in helping them to make a booking.

Once they have decided where to go, I then get them to think about what it will feel like when they have arrived and how they will judge whether the journey has been a success for them. I also insist that they not only think about this for themselves, but equally for other people whom they seek to take with them.

Some of them get very frustrated with this process, insisting that I sell them a quick and easy package, which gets them to the destination with the minimum of aggravation. Sometimes to help with this I tell them travellers' tales in the hope that this will help them to plan their journey. Others, once they have started to travel, send me word that, although answering my questions seemed an unnecessarily long-drawn-out preparation at the time, on reflection it was worth the trouble. They explain that, having made the decision themselves, they feel that they are on a road which they are now more hopeful will lead to the right destination. Moreover, they are beginning to learn something about travelling, which should mean that it will be easier to decide how to go about this on other occasions. Those who involved their fellow travellers in the planning of the journey seem to be most content and to be learning the most. It is always interesting that, when they meet the inevitable problems of unfamiliar or unexpected terrain, those who travel as teams or groups often describe themselves as 'comrades in adversity', and seem most successful in finding a way forward. After or during their journeys I ask my clients to reflect on their experiences to clarify their learning. Those who are the most competent seem to have developed a more flexible view of the world, are relaxed with its complexity, can 'play it cool' even in the most difficult circumstances and have become skilled in making judgements about the most appropriate next steps for them.

Scene 2   *Demolition*

The novice sought the advice of the sage and decided on a strategy for action. He knew that the institutions and structures of the unit had to be destroyed before he could build a new organization which would succeed in the reformed NHS. He needed a clean canvas on which to work. The novice, who knew about demolition, got on with it. The sage warned him: 'Honour the past and build a new future.'

The novice understood that real power in the organization lay with the senior doctors—the 40+ consultant staff were the people who actually controlled the services which the unit existed to provide. So he wrote to them all, listened to them, took their advice and helped them to trust him.

The problem lay with the hospital managers and district managers of specialist professional services—there were too many of them, too many layers, and they were ineffective. It wasn't their fault, but there was not enough time for them to change or be changed.

The novice agreed new management arrangements with consultant staff which would introduce a single line of general management and fewer layers of management. In future, services rather than hospitals would be managed.

He appointed his top team quickly, seeking the advice of the sage and the consultants. All except one came from within the organization, but most were new to top management and the sage helped them to knit together, gain confidence, agree priorities and decide immediate action.

The new team, not the novice, completed the rest of the management arrangements quickly. There were more than 40 'at risk' managers for only 16 jobs. Twelve were filled; the balance either took redundancy or were made redundant.

Box 3 The sage reflects on the novice's demolition phase

'Demolition' was a painful time for me, as you might imagine. As a member of the District Management Board I had recognized with my colleagues that strong visionary leadership was required for the big provider units. Therefore, we sought to recruit a new general manager.

We never faced one of the ambiguities in our decision—we wanted someone strong, but we equally wanted someone who, like us, would value the work that we had done. We had come to take our world for granted; perhaps we were losing the will to tackle resistances to change other than in a very (too) 'softly softly' fashion. Maybe the novice failed to understand our ambivalence or perhaps he deliberately misread it, but we quickly came to understand that some demolition was necessary and that he was adept at it. The whole organization experienced pain as our espoused statements about flatter hierarchies and less bureaucracy quickly became the order of the day. These initial traumas, and the establishment of a new management team, soon led to the beginning of a vision of the way ahead in the development of a strong provider unit within the internal marketplace of the reformed NHS.

My first job for this new group of clients who quickly named themselves 'the interim government' was to help to establish them as a team. Fortunately, the value of effective teams had been recognized for some time and the individuals concerned worked hard and effectively to establish their roles and relationships. The newly appointed novice decided on a new structure based on services rather than institutions (hospitals) as the means of achieving key improvements to services.

From his arrival it was clear that he wanted help to develop appropriate processes for the management of the necessary changes. Team building and other activities were supported by myself and my fellow 'travel agents'.

Nevertheless, this period continued somewhat uncertainly so far as I was concerned. I think I would summarize this as the need to be sure, when you are trying to change something, that you are are clear both about what you want to hold onto and what you want to change. At times I felt that the novice failed to recognize any achievements made before his arrival.

Scene 3   *Laying the foundations*

While the old management structures were being demolished, the novice and his new top team were working together to lay the foundations for the future, helped and guided by the sage and her team. The sage helped them by asking questions:

'What would success look like?'
'What is your shared vision?'
'What are your first steps on the path?'

She also advised: 'Be aware of what you want to hold on to as well as what you want to change.'

The first step was for the team to decide why they existed, what success would look like in the future and to agree on what principles and values were important. This was tough and took time, but the guiding hand of the sage was there throughout. (The organization's purpose, principles and values are set out in the appendix.)

With the 'middle managers' of the organization in turmoil, the novice and his team decided to tackle the roots of the organization—the 82 ward sisters and charge nurses who actually managed the direct delivery of services.

The sisters from hospitals in the former Community Unit were superb; those from the Acute Unit, demoralized and cynical—all had potential. The major problem was that the old management arrangements had stifled them—Nursing Officers had made decisions for them and controlled their lives. Now they saw the Nursing Officers being removed and were excited as well as being a bit apprehensive—who was going to tell them what to do in the future? The novice told them that nobody would, but he realized that they had to be helped to change themselves.

He called upon the sage for help, and together they created a development programme to enable ward sisters and charge nurses to shape and succeed in their new 'liberated' role. The sage's apostle worked with the sisters to understand their learning needs and expectations, and the result was a 16-week 'day release' programme for each ward sister and charge nurse.

The framework was created by OD, but the content was controlled by the participants and consisted of a continuing dialogue between them and the top management team. The dialogue both helped the sisters to learn and helped shape and build the future organization. The top management team also learned, changed and improved.

Because of the large numbers the programme was run in four tranches, each of about 20 sisters/charge nurses. The initial phase of the programme lasted from October 1990 to March 1991. It represented a massive investment by the organization, with senior management spending between 20 and 30 per cent of their time on the programme for the six months.

The investment was justified—it laid strong foundations for outstanding managerial performance throughout the organization.

Box 4   The sage comments on the development of the ward sisters and charge nurses

So we designed a programme which an external evaluator later described as based around the organization's goal of becoming a 'learning organization'. The objectives of the programme were to equip ward sisters to:

- describe Mid Essex Hospital Services' plans for change;
- discuss their work in the light of 'Working for Patients';
- describe the core purpose, values and objectives of Mid Essex Hospital Services and analyse the ward sister role in relation to these;
- evaluate their individual experience and competence in the light of the changing role of the ward sister;
- analyse their personal training and development needs;
- negotiate with advisers who provide them with support in their management of people, money, capital assets and the use of information;
- demonstrate enhanced competencies in the delivery of high-quality patient care;
- assess the degree to which they had achieved personal development goals.

Participants could attend only Phase 1 of the programme or could also undertake Phase 2 involving the development and fulfilment of a personal learning contract leading to the award of a Certificate in Management Studies.

My team and I are competent developers and could have designed, managed and delivered this programme. But would this have been the best way to proceed if Mid Essex Hospital Services was to be better equipped to responding to the demands of its stakeholders? Debates with the senior management team led to the conclusion that the most effective role was 'backstage', assisting in programme design and the development of managers and management advisers as developers. This should ensure that individual and organizational development could be integrated to optimum effect. This enabled the ward sister development programme to become the focus for corporate thinking on strategy and tactics in the short to medium term.

Scene 4   *Building the middle and reaching new parts*

Thus, while the sisters and charge nurses were enjoying their development programme, chatting to top managers and shaping the future, their future managers were being traumatized by the storm of demolition.

The twelve people who were appointed as service managers felt good and possibly guilty about surviving, but some of them were anxious about the future and their role in it. They also felt 'left out' by all the attention and time which had been lavished on the people they were supposed to be managing—some of them felt that the sisters and charge nurses knew more than they did.

Their new role as enablers, helping their staff to succeed, was very different from the role most of them had been used to—that of the Nursing Officer. These were figures of authority who told rather than helped, controlled rather than empowered. Most nurses, because of the way they have been trained, are comfortable in and respond to a structural hierarchy—nurse management is typically very 'top down'.

We had started to liberate the managers at the bottom of the hierarchy (the sisters), had raised their expectations, and they were starting to challenge the way things were done. The novice wasn't very good at appreciating this situation; he hoped that once they had been appointed, the twelve service managers would get on with their jobs. The sage helped him to see how wrong he was; there was still a lot of development work to do.

The novice recognized that the service managers would have to develop new skills and competencies, but he totally underestimated the need for them to understand and value their new role. He also expected to be directly involved in their development—so he was quite surprised when the sage suggested individual development programmes based on 'learning sets', and external facilitation.

Box 5 'Getting out of a cupboard' — the development issues

The most telling comments for me came from a senior manager during the service managers development process. He said, 'They have gone into a cupboard and I don't know what they are doing in there.' This demonstrated the distance felt by the senior managers from this development process. There had been a sense of euphoria at the success of the ward sister programme. Our aim in this case had been with the assistance of a management consultancy to design and deliver a self-managed learning programme with the aim of enabling service managers to clarify their roles, analyse their associated development needs and begin to work together as a group to meet those needs. The quotation is indicative of the initial reluctance of the service managers to share their learning contracts and emerging learning needs with their senior managers which resulted in frustration and feelings of exclusion by the latter.

The novice's interpretation of the past is correct and yet unhelpful in trying to understand what was happening at this time. Here are my perceptions. Although the service managers understood the reasons for the novice's 'demolition' activities, they had feelings of insecurity, both as a result of the structural changes and from the transition which they were required to make from nurse manager to general manager. Most of the senior management team had quickly become part of the 'interim government' referred to earlier, hence their period of personal insecurity had been short; most were occupying functional roles based on their professional training; those that were general managers had a nursing background, but had made the transition from nurse to general manager many years earlier. There was a tendency, therefore, to fail to appreciate the personal change process through which the service managers were going.

However, from the appointment of the novice a pattern of frequent 'away days' has become central to the *modus operandi* of the senior management team. These have provided a vehicle for reflection on the management of change. These issues about the development of the service managers and their role formed part of the agenda of one of these 'away days'. Discussion ranged over the need to assist the service managers to manage their personal transitions, to resist the temptation to 'train' them or even to put them through a mini version of the ward sister development programme. It was also important for me to understand the sense of frustration felt by senior managers about their exclusion from the development process. We approached the whole issue by thinking about the style which we wished service managers to adopt if Mid Essex Hospitals was to change in the desired ways. This was described as 'a transition from managing to enabling'. Wondering whether this was clear to the service managers raised questions about the extent to which the senior management team had succeeded in sharing its vision.

The senior management team therefore decided to continue to support the service manager development programme by emphasizing willingness to assist with the furtherance of the learning contracts. A workshop was held with the aim of encouraging the senior management team and the service managers to share their visions of the future. The significance of this activity was demonstrated by the divergence of views between the two groups, particularly in respect of their optimism about the capability of the rest of the organization to thrive in the internal marketplace created by the reforms. As a team the senior managers had developed a very optimistic ethos, which percolated most areas of their individual and collective work. While in many ways it was proving helpful to culture change, this workshop demonstrated the danger that senior management might become divorced from the realities of life in the rest of the organization. The service managers felt it likely that they would have to emulate the novice's demolition period to put this right. Senior management was shocked and some painful confrontation occurred. Subsequent reflection by all parties led to some new structural arrangements to improve communications between the groups, better recognition by the senior managers of the difficult transition which service managers were slowly but successfully making, and further plans for focused individual and organizational development work in three specific areas central to service manager roles. These were:

- negotiating predominantly in relation to contracting with purchasers of health care services;
- improving the organization's approach to quality;
- influencing skills.

Initiatives developed to meet each of these not only focused on individual development needs, but also on organizational requirements. In the case of the first two issues, the processes established enabled the issue itself to be taken forward organizationally as part of the development activity. For example, the service managers have taken the lead in establishing a quality coordinating group for the organization with other major stakeholders. Again, individual and corporate development are integrated. A further benefit of this approach is that through the service managers' and others' efforts in this area different aspects of the management of change—for example, the overall quality initiative, the Patients' Charter, resource management and business planning—are beginning to be connected in meaningful ways. This should help us to avoid the tendency (currently prevalent in the NHS) to adopt a step-by-step approach to change whereby huge strategic issues are reduced to disconnected items which can be 'ticked off' on organizational agendas.

The sage was right: the service managers were very positive about the programme, they felt 'special' and thrived on the freedom to develop in a 'protected' environment with peer support. The novice still felt a bit excluded, but he could see that it was working and he was content.

While all this was going on, huge demands were placed on the top team and the service managers—they were magnificent—the organization was brought under control, costs were driven down and the quality and volume of services provided both increased. Consultant medical staff started saying positive things about management and actually helped managers to succeed.

The whole organization was starting to pull together, optimism was breaking out in unexpected places, and cynics, although by no means extinct, were less vocal.

Box 6   The forgotten people

Managerial capability cannot lie only with line managers. Before the novice came on the scene, Mid Essex had committed itself in its 'Guidelines for Management Practice' to the development of all its managers. Though those in advisory roles had taken an active part in the running of the ward sister programme, there had been no specific attempt to meet their development needs. One important facet of organizational culture now is the recognition that 'we do things through development'. The down side of this is that those who receive little development attention may also feel that they have no role in the development of the organization. The advisers had been expressing their need for attention in this respect for some months when, in the autumn of last year, we began development counselling interviews with each of them. The aim was both to assist individuals to think about their needs and ways to meet them and to enable the resultant data to be shared with their managers in ways which protected individuals but supported thinking about appropriate changes both to ways of working within directorates and in the development of individuals.

Scene 5   *The never-ending journey*

Unlike Heineken, the new, devolved, management culture hasn't yet reached all the parts of the organization reached by 'old style' management—there are still large groups of support services staff who, as yet, have not been refreshed. General managers and their advisers (finance, personnel, information, public relations, marketing and business planning) are all 'on board'. The staff providing all the 'hotel' services have yet to join.

Managers now seek OD advice and support directly, without reference to the sage or the novice—nobody would think about undertaking significant change without applying OD principles or facilitation. Change will be radical, but nobody thinks that it won't happen.

Over the next few months, all the 'hotel' services (portering, catering, transport, site management, laundry, estates, etc.) will be reorganized into a new, internal 'facilities organization' which will be known as Fast Forward. Its clients will be the direct service providers and it will have a distinct 'customer-driven' culture. Even though external managers are being leased from the commercial sector to share the leadership and development of Fast Forward, our principles and values will continue to be non-negotiable.

The clinical support services (therapy services, radiography, pathology, dietetics, etc.) will be managed as an integral part of the general management process and will form consultant practices. These are the novice's next 'big idea' for the development of the organization—they are the logical progression of the devolved management culture which has been implemented so far. The organization's business will be grouped into approximately 17 units called practices. Each practice will be responsible for a single 'product line' of care based on the speciality of the consultant medical staff working in the practice.

Thus there will be practices for orthopaedic services, accident and emergency services, medicine for the elderly services, general surgical services, maternity services, etc. Each practice will have its own manager who will work in partnership with the consultants of that speciality. Each practice will be autonomous, working within a corporate framework of rules, systems, principles and values, and each will be responsible for the marketing, contracting, business planning and actual delivery of their particular service.

Box 7   The never-ending journey

I continue to tell the novice that the real 'trick' is to manage paradox. This is the case in point. Consultant practices must both conform to, and be controlled by, corporate decision making and act autonomously, creatively and entrepreneurially within this framework. One of the problems of the organization thus far has been that the parameters of devolved decision making must become clearer. The development of the strategy for the establishment of consultant practices is again being achieved through a number of senior management team 'away days'. At one of these the absence of a 'corporate framework' was identified as one of the inhibitors to the successful development of the practices. Work is in hand to achieve a draft or 'green paper' to be worked through in a developmental way with major stakeholders in readiness for the preparation of a 'white paper' for early presentation to the Trust Board.

Principles underpinning consultant practices also include several which bring consultants 'centre stage' as key figures from their former position in the wings. For example, there is a clarity that consultant practices are not the same as the clinical directorates many of which have been established elsewhere. In a consultant practice the key general management role will normally be occupied by a service manager, not consultants, whose roles will be to manage services and to exert clinical leadership. By contrast, in clinical directorates consultants are the key general managers.

Our current agenda centres on the implementation of a strategy to get consultant practices up and running. In designing and agreeing the strategy we have been keen to learn from our experiences of developing the organization to date. Hence key elements of the strategy are:

- development of clear principles underpinning consultant practices;
- sharing of the vision with key players;

- establishment of a development group which will manage the transition to consultant practices and which is distinct from the management of the 'here and now';
- integration of individual development processes with the development of the consultant practices themselves. For example, a team of 'helpers' will be established to get each consultant practice off the ground. These will comprise management advisers as 'expert' consultants and one of my fellow 'travel agents';
- clear phasing of the work to establish the practices in an attempt to avoid the development agenda becoming overloaded;
- further thinking through by the most senior managers of the necessary linkages between values and action such that development is handled in ways congruent with principles of autonomy for practices within a clear corporate framework;
- following on from this, a refusal by more senior managers to prescribe service manager roles within practices, and the operation of a process whereby service managers following an introductory workshop conduct a role-set analysis within the organization to ascertain the expectations and needs of those with whom they will interact;
- clarity that while many things will change, others will not. There will be no repetition of the novice's 'demolition' period, and service managers will be able to influence the choice of the consultant practice which they will manage;
- determination that all involved in the establishment of practices will have the opportunity to learn in order to think through, and develop into, the roles that they will occupy as a result;
- a requirement that consultant practices demonstrate that service improve-ment will emerge as a result of their establishment.

Although practices will be an extension of the organization's present approach, they represent massive change. Yet another layer of management will be removed and new business planning and marketing skills will have to be developed within each practice. A network of support and management advisers/helpers will also have to be developed.

To achieve this change, the novice decided that each practice should actually do their learning and preparation before the change was implemented rather than, as in the past, after or during the event—a novel approach for him! The sage agreed and a new phase of development commenced.

The organization will also have to learn new skills in response to the wider reforms of the NHS, to understand the concept of a 'consumer-led market and how that will shape the organization's priorities and the way it does things.

Scene 6   *Finale*

At the end of two, very short, years the novice reflected on what had happened. He realized how much had changed and that change would never stop—it had a life of its own. Now was the time to put his feet up and relax.

He was also starting to understand that people create their own change and that all he had to do was help and support them. They would do the work; he had to learn to empower, help and look for ways for further improvement. What made his organization different from the other bits of the NHS that he had visited and stayed at before? It was the sage.

She and her OD disciples, although not part of the organization, had insinuated their way into the very fabric of the way it works. The relationship felt good, not threatening: now nobody contemplated change without using OD; even the doctors were starting to use it.

The irony is that, at the beginning of the journey, the novice didn't really know what OD was and, at the end of this first stage, he still doesn't. He can't describe it, but he can use it and he's certain that it works. The sage and her disciples make it all look very easy, but the novice suspects that, like all seemingly effortless processes, it's really quite difficult to do well.

Box 8   The future

I have news for the novice! He won't ever be able to put his feet up. The environment of NHS organizations becomes ever more complex. No longer are there straightforward hierarchical bureaucratic reporting mechanisms. Provider organizations must be responsive to District Health Authorities and GP fundholders as purchasers, to the new zonal monitoring offices of the Department of Health and to the Department itself as well as to Regional Health Authorities whose role in respect of service provision is increasingly ambiguous. This is all in addition to the everyday needs and demands of patients, their relatives and the local community. This turbulent environment creates the need to respond both to the 'here and now' and to the long term by building an organization able to continually reposition itself in its environment.

Postscript: A final comment from the sage

Just as I ask my clients to reflect on their learning, so I must now ask myself what I have learned after two years of this life as a travel agent.

I've learned that helping people to travel well is enormously time- and energy-consuming. At times I have felt totally sapped by the traumas experienced by clients. It can be a lonely life sitting in this office while they discover the diversity and challenges of the globe. Keeping in touch with them can be harder, and knowing when to suggest that they might need further help is difficult—after all, we all need to be needed and to earn our living; equally, turning away requests for help in planning some further journeys, or, worse still, requests to accompany people, is demanding.

Do I know whether my clients together might become a learning organization? To answer this question I need to be sure that this would lead to them providing better services to their residents. My intuition—and as I get older I work more with this—tells me that this would be an outcome. How can you continually improve what you do unless you continually learn how to do so? To me this is an increasingly obvious truth.

Appendix   Programme notes from the original production

Cast

THE SAGE   Margaret Attwood—Director of OD, Mid Essex Health Authority

THE NOVICE   Chris Minett—Chief Executive, Mid Essex Hospitals

THE TRAVEL AGENT Margaret Attwood—Director of OD, Mid Essex Health Authority.

Other parts in this drama were and still are being played by the staff of Mid Essex Hospitals and their OD consultants.

The purpose of Mid Essex Hospitals:

'to provide better hospital based care
for the benefit of people in Mid Essex'

The principles and values which underpin the management of Mid Essex Hospitals:

- If you can't demonstrate that what you are doing contributes to the overall purpose of Mid Essex Hospitals then you shouldn't be doing it.
- Nothing, other than patient care and safety, is sacred.
- Be generous—find ways of working together as a team.
- Politics matter—you must work at creating the right environment for change.
- Clinicians must be helped to influence and shape the general management process.
- 'Growing our own' people, principles, practices.
- Devolve power—those closest to the delivery of care are best placed to make decisions.
- Help people to manage, don't tell them how to do it—enabling and empowering make their task easier.
- It's acceptable to make mistakes (the only sure way of never making mistakes is never to do anything).
- Place the emphasis on getting things done rather than talking about getting them done.
- You don't have to have line management authority in order to influence others.
- It's all right to say you don't know and ask for help.
- We all share responsibility for our services, some directly and some in support/helping roles.

15
Becoming a learning organization: how to as well as why

Michael Pearn, Robert Wood, Johanna Fullerton and Ceri Roderick

Introduction

Compelling reasons

Not so long ago, the notion that an organization could learn would have been greeted with something approaching derision. Learning is something you do at school; adults grow out of it. But perceptions are changing thanks to a major insight—the capacity to learn, individually and therefore organizationally, is an asset with a value which may turn out to be priceless.

The insight is formulated in various ways. According to Ray Stata, 'The rate at which an organisation learns may become the only sustainable source of competitive advantage'.[1] Reg Revans proposed that 'For an organisation to survive, its rate of learning must be equal to or greater than the rate of change in its external environment'.[2] Peter Senge notes that, as the world becomes more accessible and even the smallest companies can obtain whatever skills and technologies they require at a reasonable cost, the only source of competitive advantage is an organization's ability to learn and react more quickly to a fluid market than its competitors.[3]

Today, the average lifetime of the largest industrial enterprises is probably *less than half* the average lifetime of a person in an industrialized society. A study by Shell showed that one-third of the 'Fortune 500' industrialists listed in 1970 had vanished by 1983. By contrast, a small number of companies had survived for 75 years or longer.[4] Was it luck, or did they know something the others did not?

In a world of rapid change, industrial giants like Eastman Kodak, IBM, DEC, and General Motors are finding new ways to cope and transform themselves. The challenge of the 1990s is to 'produce more with less'.[5] Greater output of higher quality must be achieved with significantly reduced utilization of resources and/or people. To fail to do so will inevitably mean the demise of the enterprise caused by increased competition in global markets. It is not being melodramatic to say that it is a case of 'adapt or die'. There are many published accounts of major enterprises making dramatic and often painful transitions as a result of external threats or a crisis caused by dramatic loss of competitiveness.[6]

Not one definition

The learning organization is in the news, much talked about but seldom spotted. Like intelligence it is a tough concept to pin down in one definition. A useful approach is to employ Wittgenstein's notion of the family-resemblance concept, for which his classic example was the concept of games. Not all games share the same conceptual features; some are competitive, others are not. Some are team events, others are not. But they share enough constellations or families of features to enable us to call them games.

Applying the same reasoning to the learning organization, we can say that it is more likely than not to display certain features. These include:

- taking every opportunity to learn both from experience and in general at individual, group and corporate level;
- experimenting with new ways of organizing work and new ways of learning both within and outside the organization;
- establishing a climate in which learning in general and from each other is supported and actively encouraged;
- using the training function to support and facilitate the development and learning of all employees;
- seeing a primary role of management as facilitating workers to manage themselves in groups and to acquire a greater degree of autonomy;
- developing a structure which encourages two-way communication as a vehicle for learning and development;
- encouraging questioning, experimentation and exploration of new ideas and opportunities at all levels in the organization;
- removing barriers and blockages to learning in both the individual and the environment;
- encouraging and fostering continuous learning and self-development in all employees, not just managers;
- recognizing that individuals often learn effectively in groups and encouraging project-based learning and action learning;

- developing coaching skills in managers and supervisors;
- developing learning skills in all employees.

By contrast, a learning organization would tend *not* to exhibit certain other features. These include:

- 'command-and-control' as the dominant method of management;
- almost exclusive reliance on formal conventional training as the primary source of learning and development within the organization;
- the assumption that past success is the key to future success;
- the view that the workforce is essentially passive and therefore incapable of autonomy and self-regulation;
- the view that 'new blood' is essential in order to produce adaptive change within the organization, in the belief that the established workforce is 'too old to learn';
- the belief that advanced information and manufacturing technologies are sufficient in themselves to guarantee desired quality and output levels.

The big idea in all this is to do what most organizations do not do—release individual and group talents. As has been said, 'with every pair of hands you get a free brain'. We know there are brains working out there because people talk about the existence of tacit knowledge and skills and how those can be shared.[7,8]

The hot-air balloon as an analogue of the learning organization

If the objective of the learning organization is to maximize opportunities for learning at all levels and to exploit the potential for learning and adaptation of all the people who make up the organization, then this can be likened to the air within a hot-air balloon. In order for the balloon to rise, it is necessary to expand the volume of this air. This is done by means of the flame which can be likened to individual or organizational enhancers to learning. The implication is that nothing at all will happen if enhancers are not put in place at individual, group or organizational level. See Figure 15.1.

That is not the end of it. Even if the enhancers are put in place, it is possible that the balloon will not lift because of the individual inhibitors represented by the sandbags. The sandbags have to be removed in order for the enhancers to have the maximum effect. Even then it is still possible that the balloon will not lift because of organizational or structural inhibitors, which are represented by the ropes. Therefore, it may be necessary to put enabling structures in place to provide support for sustained learning and development at individual and organizational level, represented by the temporary scaffolding to hold the balloon until it is ready to lift.

The value of the analogy of the hot-air balloon is the way it makes plain that all contributing forces need to be taken into account in order to optimize the learning opportunities within the organization. In order to become a learning-oriented

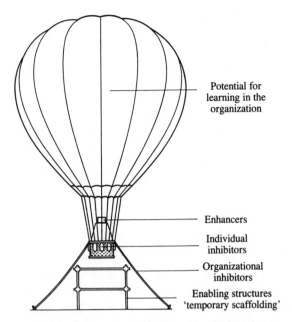

Potential for
learning in the
organization

Enhancers

Individual
inhibitors

Organizational
inhibitors

Enabling structures
'temporary scaffolding'

Figure 15.1   The hot-air balloon as an analogue of the learning organization (from Carré and Pearn, 1992)

organization it is necessary to identify and remove, over a period of time, the unjustifiable organizational inhibitors or constraints and also to remove individual or group constraints.

One disadvantage of the balloon analogy is that the balloonist has little control over the direction of travel and eventual destination of the balloon—the balloon is very dependent on the prevailing winds at any time. By contrast, an organization which regards itself as learning-oriented needs to have a very clear idea of its overall objectives, what it is trying to achieve, and how it will know when it is succeeding. Senge, Lessem[9] and others have placed great emphasis on the 'visioning' process. There is, of course, a great danger in having a too clear, too confident and unchallenged view of the future. In this sense the hot-air balloon is not inappropriate, as an organization must be prepared and able to change and transform itself to reflect not wholly predictable changes in markets, technologies, socio-economic, political and environmental conditions. The hot-air balloon is a useful reminder that if you can see the destination too clearly you may be looking in the wrong direction.

Another useful viewpoint is that an organization may not be equally successful in capitalizing on the learning potential available to it in all its activities and functions. The organization can move from small areas of exploited learning potential within it towards the almost limitless possibilities that lie within the area of unexploited learning potential. If, at the same time, the organization identifies and puts in place support mechanisms for continuous individual and group learning, this eventually becomes part of the self-sustaining and dynamic culture of the organization.

We cannot stress strongly enough that the learning organization is not achieved overnight, nor is it an end-state. The whole point is that you never get there. That is why it should never be regarded as 'flavour of the month'. It is evolutionary or it is nothing. Karen Ross is right when she says that 'the learning company is about changing something more than just its appearance'.[10] The goal of the learning organization is a process of continuous change and self-transformation generated from within the organization.

A practical approach to making learning organizations happen

Paradoxically, it is not possible to teach an organization to become a learning organization; it must learn to become one and it must want to become one.

Our approach to helping organizations help themselves is shaped by years of developing practical tools and methods for improving learning at work. Much of the early work on 'learning to learn' was funded by the then Training Agency and was carried out by Sylvia Downs and Patricia Perry of the Occupational Research Unit at UWIST and, more recently, while Sylvia Downs was with Pearn Kandola.[11] In 1989 Pearn Kandola entered into collaboration with Interface in Paris to design an implementation model for the learning organization and to compile a compendium or toolbox of tried and tested practical tools.[12]

The British side of the project has been enriched by the involvement and sponsorship of eight organizations who, with Pearn Kandola and Interface, represent the ten partners working on this project. They are: Glaxo Manufacturing Services, Shell Oils, Marks & Spencer, the BBC, the National Health Service Training Directorate, National Westminster Bank, Courage and Colgate-Palmolive.

For two years the project was an approved member of the Eurotecnet network of innovative training and development projects across the European Community. Eurotecnet is coordinated, but not funded, by the Eurotecnet Technical Assistance Unit in Brussels. The Unit is itself active in this area, notably Nyhan's study of 'self-learning competency'[13] and the more recent account of the learning organization from an EC perspective by Stahl, Nyhan and D'Aloja.[14]

The ten actions

To help an organization become learning-oriented, the model proposes ten actions, shown in Figure 15.2. For each action there are associated tools which together build into a toolkit. The tools and actions cross-reference as shown in Figure 15.3.

Ten key actions

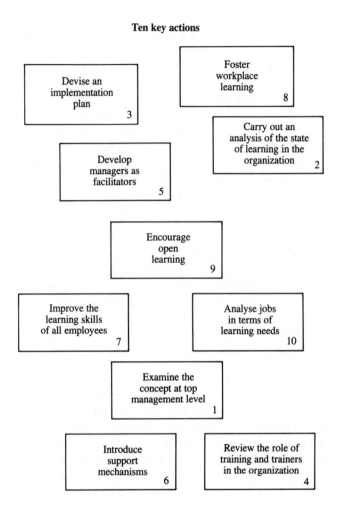

Figure 15.2   Ten key actions for organization wanting to learn

The tools consist of workshop plans, modular exercises, questionnaires, checklists and other aids to learning. They have been tested over a two-year period and incorporate tools developed in the earlier 'learning to learn' research. Where appropriate, reference to other relevant tools or instruments and other advice is given. It is without doubt a real toolkit, not a concept touted as a toolkit, about which Karen Ross complains.[10]

It is important to realize that not every organization will need all the actions, nor need actions be carried out in any particular order.

1.   Examine the concept at top management level
The learning organization is a big idea reaching into almost all aspects of organizational behaviour and thinking. Workshops for senior or top management are necessary to develop an understanding of the learning organization and the links to corporate objectives and values. If the characteristic culture of the organization is not addressed, there will be less chance for optimum learning to occur at all levels throughout the organization, and the risk of isolated 'pockets' of learning will increase. The organization needs to check that its current vision, if it has one, is compatible with a newly developed understanding of the significance of learning. Its current vision may be its Achilles heel, narrow and inflexible, not open to genuine challenge, and propped up by what Argyris has called 'organisational defence routines'.[15] The creation of a new vision, in many cases, will be the first step towards becoming a learning organization.

2.   Carry out an analysis of the state of learning in the organization
A key step towards becoming a learning organization is a survey of the current situation and the identification of areas that require change. An audit of employees at all levels which identifies inhibitors and enhancers of learning, at both individual and organizational level, is essential for detailed planning. Alternatively, a quantitative survey of 'learning climate' of the kind developed by the Employment Service[16] is useful, both as a diagnostic instrument and also as a 'before and after' measure to evaluate degree of change on selected parameters.

3.   Devise an implementation plan
An essential prerequisite of an effective implementation plan is a workshop process for a project team designed to develop further their understanding of organizational learning with a view to detailed action planning. It is essential to identify and put in place performance indicators which will function as barometers and will show changes in behaviour (e.g. increased level of asking questions and challenging), outputs (e.g. quality and customer service measures), and other indicators.

4.   Review the role of training and trainers in the organization
The learning organization is likely to move away from heavy reliance on formal training, which often satisfies the short-term needs of the workforce, to a training function which supports, facilitates and sustains learning and self-development at all levels. It follows that the role of training and trainers and the boundaries between work and training will change. The critical interrelatedness of work and learning will be a subject of continuous scrutiny and monitoring.

5.   Develop managers as facilitators
A 'command-and-control' style of management can inhibit individual learning. For a variety of reasons, many organizations are developing coaching and facili-

tating skills in managers and team leaders as part of a more open and consultative style of management and as a key ingredient in empowerment. Making the processes of learning clearer to managers (how they themselves learn and also fail to learn, how they can inadvertently block others from learning, and what they can do to facilitate learning in others) leads to them increasing their competence as learners and also their effectiveness in facilitating an empowered workforce. Managers can also learn simple but effective practical techniques for encouraging and facilitating self-learning and autonomy in the workplace.

6. *Introduce support mechanisms for continuous learning*
A primary role of management in a learning organization is to provide support for a culture of continuous learning. Some of the ways in which support can be provided are coaching, mentoring, networking and support groups, learning contracts, learning logs and personal development plans. Many organizations already use such mechanisms, but a company wishing to become a learning organization will need to integrate the support activities within an overall strategy.

7. *Improve the learning skills of all employees*
The learning skills of all employees can be developed by means of self-completion inventories, practical guides and special exercises. 'Learning to learn' sessions can be built into induction processes, personal development, basic training courses, or offered as options whether through open learning or some other arrangement. The link to learning styles and the work of Honey and Mumford[17] is important here. Overcoming fear of learning, or lack of confidence to learn, should be balanced by activities which actually increase competence to learn, especially in terms of understanding.

8. *Foster workplace learning*
The development of skills at learning as well as the confidence and desire to learn, both for individuals and teams, is crucial to the achievement of autonomy in self-directed or autonomous teams, and for the achievement of world-class manufacturing and other organizational goals. Team or group learning, as well as team-based problem solving and decision making, will play an increasingly important part in everyday working life at all levels in the learning organization.

9. *Encourage and provide access to open learning*
Helping employees to get the most out of open learning material and distance learning resources is critical to the success of open learning strategies. Too many open learning materials are not used, or not used properly. The toolkit contains some stand-alone tools which can help the learner to get the most out of open learning and to choose judiciously between different open learning packs, not all of which are equal in quality or their suitability for particular learners.

10.   Analyse jobs in terms of learning needs

Work-related learning needs can be identified, for individuals or groups, through the use of a structured job learning analysis questionnaire. Most job-analysis instruments focus on the outputs or objectives required of a job or the behaviours and competences that are necessary to achieve them, but the job learning analysis is different in that it places considerable emphasis on the range of learning (types)

Tools	Actions									
	1	2	3	4	5	6	7	8	9	10
Exercise 1A. Understanding total learning	x			x	x		x	x		
Exercise 1B. Learning from others	x									
Exercise 1C. How good are we at learning?	x									
Exercise 1D. Are we a 9/9 learning organization?	x			x						
Exercise 1E. Review exercise	x			x	x			x		
Learning audit	x	x		x						
Exercise 3A. What blocks learning?			x	x	x		x			
Exercise 3B. Review of learning			x		x			x		
Exercise 3C. SWOT analysis			x					x		
Exercise 4A. Identifying different types of learning				x	x		x	x		
Exercise 4B. Improving memorizing				x			x	x		
Exercise 4C. Encouraging a questioning attitude				x	x		x	x		
Exercise 4D. The keys to understanding				x	x		x	x		
Exercise 4E. SWOT analysis of the training function				x						
Exercise 4F. A new role for trainers				x						
Exercise 5A. Case studies					x					
Exercise 5B. Coach(er) enabler self-assessment profile					x					
Learning logs						x				
Checklist on mentoring						x				
How to develop your own personal development plan						x				
Self-assessment questionnaire						x				
Action planning						x				
Development activities						x				
Everyday learning							x	x		
Learning blockages questionnaire			x		x		x	x		
Exercise 8A. Using the keys to understanding				x				x		
Exercise 8B (8C, 8D). Learning in teams							x	x		
Selecting and using open learning material									x	
Job learning analysis										x

that are required in order to become proficient at a job or role.[18]
Figure 15.3   Learning organization: tools and actions

What people say about learning (and not learning)

In the past year the authors have run a number of workshops on the learning organization, or on aspects of it, for the project sponsors and other companies. There are also ongoing evaluative case studies, with new ones expected to materialize as the toolkit is taken up and used.[19]

The workshop exercises, which are some of the tools in the kit, have elicited from participants a wealth of material. Here are some of the responses senior managers of a large brewing company gave to the question:

What are the possible benefits of encouraging learning in *all* employees?

Competitive edge	Less use of status and
Profit/efficiency/quality	position
Savings	Changing culture
Productivity	Ownership
Job enrichment	Flexibility
Quality of working life	Better cross-functional
Changes in behaviour	working
Ideas/innovation	Improved customer service
Attract and retain best	
people	

To the question: What are the consequences of *not* succeeding in encouraging learning in all employees? Managers of a major insurance company in South Africa came up with these answers:

Lack of awareness of problems
Increased competition
Increased pressure from competition (smarter!)
Time-warped organization (stuck!)
Build inflexible systems
Inability to attract/retain good people
Inefficient use of resources

How can we tell if we are succeeding? is another key question. Senior training managers from one of the big five banks produced these responses:

Increased participation in training programmes
Increase in morale
Flatter organization
Better profits
Customer satisfaction
Fewer misfits
Jobs become more attractive
Lower turnover
New ideas/practices
Staff initiate self-development
Increased risk taking
Multi-skilled staff
People ask questions (and get answers!)
Favourable press
Fewer mistakes
Willingness to make mistakes (in order to learn and improve)
Fewer complaints
Reduction in negative industrial relation issues
Learning actually becomes part of the culture
People wanting to be involved and having opportunities
Team performance will improve
Seen as quality organization

We posed the question 'What blocks learning?' to members of the training function of a large pharmaceutical company. These were their answers:

Lack of understanding of what is required
Lack of confidence
Lack of money/facilities
Boss feels it is not relevant
Lack of time
Environment, e.g. unsuitable room, etc.
Personal history—find learning difficult
Do not see the point
Low status of learning
No connection between learning and work
'No mistakes' culture
Learning is something you do at school
No tradition of learning
Training by numbers

Learning not for real people, soft option
Lack of interest
No encouragement to learn
Fear of failure
Culture wrong, discourages learning
Lack of opportunity
Wrong method of delivery
Too complex too early
Jargon
Distractions
More pressing demands on time
Lack of knowledge
Learning a cost, not an investment

To define or not to define?

There is always a great danger in prematurely defining a new idea or concept. There is a risk that a premature definition can close down possibilities, resulting in a narrow or inappropriate conceptualization. Thinking becomes comfortable and then defensive positions are taken in relation to competing definitions which become the focus of intellectual energy, thus distracting from the continued examination and expansion of the original set of ideas. Thinkers and exponents of the learning organization concept are no less prone to adopting mind-sets than anyone else.

However, without some form of pointer it would be difficult to focus and engage in debate, let alone take action of a form which would not otherwise have occurred. Prescriptive definitions may not be very helpful, other than to offer the organization something it can react to, but indicative definitions can be helpful because of the lack of a 'this-and-only-this' interpretation. It is in the spirit of an indicative definition that the authors propose the following, which has developed out of an earlier definition which underlies the toolkit referred to above.

A working definition of the learning organization

- A learning organization places high value on individual and organizational learning as a prime asset.
- It is working towards full utilization of all individual and group potential for learning and adapting, in the interests of meeting and eventually setting organizational objectives.
- It does this in a way which also satisfies the needs and aspirations of all the people involved.

- Inhibitors and blocks to learning are being identified and removed, and strong enhancers and support for sustained continuous learning are being put in place.
- A climate of continuous learning and improvement is being created.

There are two important points to note about this approach. First, it is non-exclusive. Other approaches which, for example, lay great emphasis on systems thinking are compatible with it, and the working approach can easily be modified to fit with other organizational objectives, however defined. Secondly, the 'definition' is expressed in the present tense. If the learning organization concept has any meaning it is as a process rather than as an end-state.

Conclusion

However, it is really the responses to the key questions posed to managers in diverse organizations which amplify in a very real way our earlier moves towards a definition of a learning organization in terms of what it will be like and what it will not be like. They also provide strong clues as to what can be done to build learning as a core component of organizational success.

The learning organization toolkit described above offers ways of working on inhibitors and blocks to learning. It is relatively straightforward for an organization to undertake the improvement of individual learning skills as there are well established 'learning to learn' techniques at both operator and managerial level. It is also not difficult to create learning 'havens' or learning environments within more or less self-contained sections of the organization, especially when associated with the introduction of advanced manufacturing and information technologies. It is quite a different matter, however, to commit to becoming a learning organization, for that involves major shifts in organzational culture, structure and behaviour.

Ultimately, the approach to becoming a learning organization must be coherent, organization-wide and must stem from a vision created at the top, a vision that the optimization of learning and the readiness to respond and adapt associated with everyone learning is crucial to the achievement of competitive edge and thus to longer-term survival and organizational success.

References

1. Stata, R. (1990) 'Organizational learning—the key to management innovation', *Sloan Management Review*, **30**(3), 63–74.
2. Quoted in Garratt, R. (1987) *The Learning Organisation*, Gower, Aldershot.
3. Senge, P. (1990) *The Fifth Discipline*, Doubleday, New York.
4. de Geus, A. P. (1988) 'Planning as Learning', *Harvard Business Review*, March–April, **66**(2), p. 70–74.

5. Kanter, R. M. (1989) *When Giants Learn to Dance*, Simon & Schuster, New York and London.

6. Belasco, J. A. (1990) *Teaching the Elephant to Dance*, Hutchinson, London.

7. Myers, C. and K. Davids (1992) 'Knowing and doing: tacit skill at work', *Personnel Management*, 24(2), 45–47.

8. Nonaka, I. (1991) 'The knowledge-creating company', *Harvard Business Review*, **69**(6), pp. 96–104.

9. Lessem, R. (1991) *Total Quality Learning: Building a Learning Organisation*, Blackwell, Oxford.

10. Ross, K. (1992) 'The learning company', *Training and Development*, **10**(7), 19–22.

11. Pearn, M. A. and S. Downs 'Developing skilled learners: The experience of UK companies', in Nyhan (1991).

12. Carré, P. and M. Pearn (1992) *L'Autoformation dans l'Entreprise*, Editions Entente, Paris.

13. Nyhan, B. (1991) *Developing People's Ability to Learn*, Eurotecnet.

14. Stahl, T., B. Nyhan and P. D'Aloja (1993) *The Learning Organisation: A vision for human resource development*, Eurotecnet Technical Assistance Unit, Commission for the European Communities.

15. Argyris, C. (1990) *Overcoming Defences: Facilitating Organisational Learning*, Allyn and Bacon.

16. The Learning Climate Questionnaire (1993) The Employment Service,

17. Honey, P. and A. Mumford (1986) 'The Manual of Learning Styles', 2nd ed., McGraw-Hill, Maidenhead.

18. Pearn, M. A. and R. S. Kandola (1993) *Job Analysis*, IPM.

19. The case studies will be featured in our book *The Learning Company in Practice*, to be published by McGraw-Hill in 1995.

16
Engaging and confronting the personal responsibility of the learning company perspective–adding new skills to old

Jim Butler

Introduction

There is probably nothing really new about the learning company or organization concept—it has been in the literature for many years now. Argyris and Schon[1] have been writing and continously updating their ideas about the subject for the past 20 years or more. What does appear to be new, however, is that the concept is now having greater impact on managers and employees who make up public service and business organizations in the UK—or is it? To have a meaningful impact, the concept must lead to new and improved ways of doing things. In this sense, learning to change will take both will and skill. Will in this context is taken to mean motivation of individuals to learn, and skill is the capability of those same individuals to carry out the change. In my experience both must be present in very large quantities to really ensure organizational learning.

Learning to change and changing to learn[2] or perish in the attempt seems to be the message in today's turbulent business and service environments, but has it not been so for many years now? When Argyris and Schon wrote of their experiences in the USA in the late 1970s:

There has probably never been a time in our history where members, managers and students of organisations were so united on the importance of organisational learning. Costs of health care, sanitation, police, housing, education and welfare have risen precipitously and we urge agencies concerned with these services to learn to increase their productivity and efficiency.[3]

This was, I believe, similarly the case in the UK and other parts of Western Europe.

Many of the clichés borne out of this period and since are supported by the fact that few companies survive to their fiftieth birthday. Some, for example, although household names that we all remember in retail and manufacturing during the 1960s and 1970s, seem to have disappeared altogether. (Whatever happened to the 'fifty-bob tailors' and my favourite motorbike manufacturers, Norton BSA and Triumph?) Such change has taken place not only in the private sector—public service organizations in Britain seem to change their structure and mode of operation, if not their ownership, almost as frequently as private sector businesses. Hospitals, schools, railways and even prisons are under constant pressure to improve their performance and service to the public. Assuming that the majority of doctors, teachers, managers/employees and prison officers in these organizations have always striven to do the best they can in difficult circumstances, and always with limited resources, it is difficult to see how the aspirations of 'customers' can be met without significant and perceptible changes in effectiveness and efficiencies and that such changes can only come about via some form of new and continuous learning. Hence the current level of interest in the concept of the learning company and the learning organization.

The challenge to individuals

For companies and organizations to learn, individuals must learn first, or at least simultaneously as they work in their teams and groups which make up the organization. Perhaps this is where the difficulty lies. In what sense can we talk about organizational learning without referring to the responsibility and need for individuals within to change in the way they go about their work?

Allocating real accountability for new learning in any organization can, in my experience, be extremely difficult. Top and senior managers in most organizations will readily admit that new learning and learning to change is important and relates directly to their plans and objectives, but then 'hand down', so to speak, the responsibility for making it happen, through the hierarchy, for others to deal with. And of course it is not just senior people who distance themselves from the need to learn/change—many others similarly either pass the responsibility down or up, depending on where they themselves are located in the organization. At whatever level, the personal responsibility seems to get passed to the proverbial 'them', not 'us'.

But why and how does this buck-passing continue when, in the face of all the evidence, the one thing which we can all be sure of is that change in the environment will require commensurate change and learning in individuals? I believe it is both the 'way' and the 'what' we have learned in the past that causes the difficulty. The 'way' is the 'conventional' educational learning method. The 'what' is the concrete substance of experience which we internalize and use again and again to solve other problems. Both the 'way' and the 'what' need to change, therefore, before an organization actually begins to learn. In other words, at an individual level we all need to learn new learning and action implementation skills.

As a simplistic illustration of the omnipresence of the conventional method let us consider how we normally go about learning to successfully achieve or complete a task—any task which involves other human beings (i.e. an 'organization setting'). We acquire the requisite knowledge of carrying out the task, we then experiment with applying it and observe the result. If, as far as we can tell, we successfully achieve our intentions, then the 'feedback loop' is positive and reinforces our actions to be stored, recalled and used again. If, however, there is some *clear* signal in the 'feedback loop' (usually but not always provided by other people) that we do not in fact achieve what we had planned or set out to do, then the negative effect causes us to modify, adjust or refine our action in some way and then to try again and again. In most cases, of course, the repeated attempts continue until we approximate a directly observable link between intention and actuality. The process described here is what Argyris[4] has called 'single-loop learning' and is the method by which we learn a great deal of our organizational behaviour. Any errors that occur are corrected on-line as we actually interact with others, and for the most routine learning requirements this process is both successful and adequate. The errors referred to here are, of course, 'Type one', so described by Handy[5], and account for a great deal of our problem solving and learning in everyday life.

But it is the 'Type 2' errors (also so described by Handy) which cause us the most problems in organizational learning, when what we have to learn is non-trivial, non-routine. This is a genuine change in the way we go about our work. For solving Type 2 problems we require Argyris's double-loop learning process. Type 2 errors are those which we either do not recognize at all, or, if we do recognize them, only partially solve them, and therefore they continue or even escalate in their impact over time. The old adage 'I never make the same mistake twice' is, in my experience, not true—in fact, we make the same mistakes over and over again. In this sense Type 2 errors are guaranteed to be repeated, and the perpetrators are seemingly unaware of their own responsibility in first producing the error and then perpetuating it over time.

The causes of error and learning difficulties: some limitations of conventional organizational learning—real examples

Let us now turn to some practical examples of learning difficulties within organizations. In working with managers and employees of large companies over the past 25 years, it has become very clear to me that intelligent people, both young and older, seem to demonstrate similar difficulties when attempting to implement major or radical change, even when they apparently have a clear mandate and agreed objectives to do so.

Consider the following vignettes:

While working with real management teams in a multinational company, it became apparent to me that human beings, of whatever national culture, seem to experience similar problems in implementing change programmes. The teams to which I refer came from very different businesses: from the retail, insurance, tobacco, pulp and paper, and packaging industries, and each was led by a managing director or director with organizational authority to effect the change that the team were about to implement. It is also important to mention that members and individuals of these teams were in no way novices in the sense of organizational life and managerial competence; they were mostly well educated individuals, qualified to a recognized professional standard, and each had, albeit perhaps not in the job and teams in which they were currently working, considerable business experience.

Case 1[6]
Team A, the top management team of a manufacturing and distribution company operating in Europe, had debated the merits of applying a particular technique of competitor analysis, the outcome of which could result in them changing their pricing policy, which indeed could have a major impact upon their competitive advantage and competitive positioning. This company was in great difficulty, and there was a pressing need to do something about its current strategy although the company enjoyed market leadership in its product range in Germany and France it was losing market share in both, while at the same time trying to expand in Spain). There seemed to be a shared understanding of the technical features of the approach, and certainly consensus on the advantages of applying it to the job in hand, and yet a marked reluctance to commit to implementing the strategy by some or the majority of the team. But how could this be so? Team A certainly understood the concept and they were agreed as to what they should do to implement the new policy. Interestingly, whatever was 'blocking' them was obviously not due to an ignorance or lack of skill in the sense of not knowing what technical devices were available and how to implement them; it seemed to have more to do with the very 'skilful' way in which some team members managed the potential 'embarrassment' and 'threatening prospect' of changing current practice. 'Status quo rules OK!' seemed to be the unuttered sentiment. The high level of skilfulness in avoiding potential threat and embarrassment was resulting in the maintenance of existing ways of doing things and constituted a block not only to learning new ways of solving a strategic problem (i.e. a technical problem) but also to learning new learning skills (i.e. a human behavioural problem) which would reduce the potential embarrassment to individuals personally and the threats to the organizational norms and values. Those team managers 'covering up' in this example did so very competently; it was difficult to detect the cover-up and

certainly almost impossible to discuss it in the group, hence the need for some sort of new learning intervention. In this example, it turned out that team members were very adept at protecting their manager from any embarrassment that they attributed to him (without, incidentally, any enquiry or testing of such an attribution) because he was the original perpetrator of the current pricing policy and, as a member of the team had later explained, had been overheard on many occasions confirming his commitment to this policy. In this case, the team did eventually confront the issue (with some help from a tutor who was helping to run the session), and when they did so they were able to test, by making genuine and open enquiry, the validity of their attribution. They found that the managing director was anything but embarrassed or hurt by their suggestion that they should consider fundamentally changing the policy, especially given the dire straits the company was in. A good deal of genuine surprise was shared by members of this group when they actually 'levelled' with one another. The important point here is that they levelled with one another when they eventually understood that the blockage to actually implementing a technical change was being caused by something to do with their 'usual' approach of doing things that might cause embarrassment or threat to others. They had learned the new technique, and, indeed, shared its merit through the usual single-loop process, but it was in actually applying the tool that they required a double-loop perspective. Thus in practical terms they needed to examine and challenge the ways they normally dealt with such problems as a management team.

Some of the defensiveness and resistance to change described in this case may be attributed to the age, experience, seniority of the individuals involved or even so-called organizational politics. In fact, I can hear the reader saying that 'seasoned' professionals are bound to be cautious and careful in a business like this. Their organizational experience (i.e. norms, values and 'how we do things around here') has taught them to be so. Therefore, there is nothing new or surprising about the episode described in this case.

So now let us consider another example, this time involving younger managers on a young managers' programme.

Case 2[7]
This episode occurred during a management education event which brings together in the UK recognized 'high flyers' from different parts of the world for their first formal general management programme. Intelligent young people on this programme have all enjoyed the fruits of higher education and are quick to learn concepts, techniques and systems in management functions. They can usually display their new learning through quite sophisticated presentation skills, which may have been learned or at least honed on the programme itself, and produce intricate and fascinating diagrams and other visual aids to explain how the business world can be changed and 'set to rights'. They are able to do this confidently and

with conviction, and on this particular programme in front of senior directors, each of whom could have a direct influence on their career prospects with the company. Not surprisingly, when these presentations go well and are evaluated and commended by senior directors and tutors present, the young trainee managers are reinforced in their belief that they have really learnt something important.

The fact is that what they have 'actually learnt' is 'more of the same' in the sense of concepts and 'ways of explaining', similar, if not identical to, what they have already experienced in their various conventional education courses before joining the programme.

But now contrast this apparent capability to espouse the remedies and solutions to business and organizational problems with the personal competence of the same individuals to deliver and produce the actions that will render the improvements/ changes which they can now seemingly so effectively explain.

During a four-week period the young managers participating are exposed to a variety of formal learning/educative inputs. They also have the option of attending short modular seminars (usually of 2–21/2 days' duration) within the overall framework of the programme. During almost all formal sessions, individuals have the opportunity to take front stage and lead explanation/discussion sessions on the findings of their analysis in various problem-solving exercises, all of which are designed to extend their knowledge and skill to the task of 'general management' in running business units and/or eventually even complete companies. The standard of presentation and quality of problem solving is usually very high, with groups and individuals within groups competing for the highest recognition.

The contrast between participants' performance on the formal subject area exercises in the main programme, and their ability/competence in dealing with the real-life problems which they bring for examination on one of the optional choice seminars offered, called 'Implementing Change Skills'[8] (two days' duration) is very marked indeed. This seminar is designed to provide for those who choose it an opportunity to examine and progress a real problem with which they are currently engaged back in their company workplace. Prior to attending the programme those who opt for this seminar are asked to prepare a short piece which explains the organizational context of the problem, those involved and their objectives in implementing some form of change. Participants on this programme are junior managers; the focus and breadth of the problem to be solved is therefore limited to their specific area of responsibility/accountability, i.e. each participant has or believes that he or she has the organizational authority to change whatever it is that is causing the problem (with the help and consent of others).

Participants are also asked to write up a short personal case which illustrates a real episode that has already taken place involving all significant protagonists and with which the participant was not entirely, if at all, satisfied with the outcome. This 'personal case' material is usually 'rich' in both explanation of the problem (i.e. what went wrong and why) and who is to blame. The case is written in a format which records, in two columns, the thoughts and feelings of the participant at the time he or she was actually interacting with other parties involved, and what he or she actually said to such parties in 'conversational forum' (i.e. the words and prose actually uttered as accurately as they can remember). The separation of thoughts/feelings not uttered at the time (for whatever reason) and what was actually said by the participant is a powerful heuristic for exposing participants' mode of reasoning when dealing with potentially difficult problems involving other managers and employees.[9]

In a very large majority of these personal cases the mode of reasoning could be described as 'defensive' to 'very defensive', and this is readily acknowledged by those who have prepared the case (albeit not presumably to themselves at the time of preparation) during the formal session of this seminar. The effects of such defensive reasoning leads to a similar, almost identical, set of data for dealing with such problems submitted from very different participants. Interestingly, all who work on these cases recognize this fact very quickly indeed, and their awareness that they are each dealing with what they believed to be their own peculiar problem in different functional areas of management, and in different national and company settings, leads to real examination of their own performance.

Consider the example of Mal's (not real name) personal case:

Profile: Thirty years old, first class degree in economics, an MBA and qualified accountant currently working in internal audit for international company. Five years' experience in the company. (NB: This is a fairly typical profile for participants on this programme.)

Situation and context: As a travelling internal auditor I am expected to 'add value' to how businesses are run, in particular on financial matters but not exclusively so, by submitting a report to managing directors and finance directors on the overall current state of their financial controls. (NB: Providing advice and reports on all aspects of the business, including organizational details, is now readily accepted by the whole company, i.e. it is officially part of company policy for the internal audit process.)

Problem: The audit of Company X had gone well—no real surprises for anyone and no real disaster, either. The principal report had been supportive of most of the company's own control systems and already discussed with the chief accountant (CA) before meeting with the finance director (FD) and managing director (MD). This was the normal procedure and usually worked well in practice.

Only one real area of concern had been uncovered, that of treasury management. This was an area very important to this particular company and, I believed, an area where we could make substantial improvements.

Solution: Mal then went on in his 'solution report' to explain the technical details of treasury management and foreign currency transactions. (He was recognized by the company as something of a specialist in this area of expertise.)

His solution to the problem then followed a logical sequence of actions. He would meet the FD (who, incidentally, he believed would easily understand the technical features of his solution, but who had some 'hang-up' (Mal's words) about 'increasing paperwork'), *explain* a, b, c; *suggest* e, f, g; *offer* to help with h, i, j, and benefits would accrue all around.

Mal's plan of action, as explained and discussed with others present, seemed perfectly feasible. He obviously had both the responsibility and authority to not only report on the problem, but to help with implementing a solution. Moreover, he had the expertise to 'change what presently existed'.

Let me summarize what was happening at this point of the seminar. All participants had prepared interesting and real cases illustrating clearly an area in their work where they believed that they had the authority to make changes. Each had prepared the case in the required two-column form and, like Mal, had offered fairly lengthy explanatory paragraphs outlining the context of the problem and his or her perceived solutions. Without exception, all present at the seminar, including Mal, agreed with the solutions offered to each of their prepared cases, perhaps adding fairly minor advice to help with implementation. However, all also agreed that the personal 'conversational' data presented in Mal's case would not or did not represent competent behaviour/action in implementing what he had espoused in his plans and objectives and what they had supported previously in real-time conversation.

Consider this extract from Mal's case [Figure 16.1]:

Implementing Change Seminar
(Mal's case)

Thoughts and feelings (Not made known to finance director)	*Conversation* (What Mal actually uttered and what significant others said in reply)
I don't reckon he will agree this because of his obsession with reducing paperwork, but I would like to talk it through anyway. Keep it tactful.	Mal: Everything is on schedule. In fact, I wanted to discuss one particular point with you. I have been looking at the treasury management (TM) function in some detail with the chief accountant. *The level of FX dealing has increased considerably over the last year, both in terms of value and number of transactions.* I think we have reached the stage where we should formalize TM by introducing a

I'm sure he'll agree this point.

Can I ship this one past him too?
Yes or no?
Yes, I bet he came running as soon as I left him.

The paperwork obsession again. I knew it!

You've got to agree on this at least. Let's bring in the HQ factor to make sure.

How can he expect to remember movements in five currencies—he's a busy man. We could argue all day and he still wouldn't agree. I should cut my losses here. OK, he has agreed to the first part, but it's hardly the right attitude.

At least I tried, and there's no point in falling out over this one. Let's try to be more positive about the benefits of a policy.

Cynical to the end.

policy statement to establish our objectives and the methods of operation. I also feel we should draft monthly cashflow forecasts to promote a basis for the buying and selling decisions. I would be interested in your thoughts on the matter.

Finance Director (FD): Yes, the chief accountant told me you were thinking along those lines. However, I don't really think this is necessary. After all, we are trying to reduce the amount of paperwork, not increase it.

Mal: HO sent a request last month asking all Operating Companies to prepare a TM policy statement. I think it would be a good opportunity to define exactly what we are trying to achieve in our FX dealing. The chief accountant who makes all the deals doesn't seem to have any specific objectives in mind. Also, all transactions take place in the third week of the month since this is the only time the chief accountant can spare for TM. I think we could achieve better results with currency cashflow (CF) forecasts.

FD: The chief accountant is aware when the foreign currency is coming in. I don't see any point in producing the CF forecasts. However, I did see the request from HQ about a policy statement. I will draft something to keep them happy by the end of the year.

Mal: OK, we shall have to agree to disagree on the cashflows. I think you will gain some benefits from formalizing the policy and methods of operation.

FD: I don't think so, but we shall see.

From this extract of Mal's case it can be seen that his responsibility for the problems is clearly central and that his understanding and intention for the need to introduce change is not commensurate with his skills to implement it. Mal seems to have forecast his own unsatisfactory outcomes of this episode in his very first 'censored thought' in the left-hand column (something of a self-fulfilling prophecy). And note that his last censored thought/feeling seems to confirm his worst prediction. It's as if he had 'designed' his own predicted failure. This is not, of course, to say that the finance director, etc. in this episode bears no responsibility for the outcomes, but simply to emphasize the fact that Mal is unable to produce in 'action terms' what he can competently explain in conceptual terms. Moreover, he was not aware of this fact before his personal case was examined at this seminar.

Mal, having convinced everyone present of the validity of his findings and recommendations to a finance director on how to improve business results, and then having been criticized by his seminar colleagues on what he had ultimately produced in his conversation with the finance director, was invited to role-play with others present the action skills required to implement his recommendation.

As this seminar progresses, participants like Mal and his colleagues practise through role-play and discussion the action of first *inventing* and then *producing* actions/behaviours which more accurately represent what they are already able to explain. A two-day seminar is just about long enough to get started, but much more practice is required in real-life situations to ensure that the new skills stick.

Mal was, incidentally, a very good example of a young manager able to demonstrate during many other formal sessions that he had indeed learned a lot (outside his own discipline/profession) about general management and what needed to be done to run effective and efficient businesses. In other words, he was almost the perfect student. He had wholeheartedly participated in the entire programme and he demonstrated his ability to learn, in the conventional sense. However, in his own area of expertise, let alone the new areas to which he had been exposed on the programme, he was unable to make his knowledge 'actionable' so as to ensure that he was able to implement what he could explain, and, most importantly, he was genuinely unaware of this until experiencing the inventions of his peers and tutors on the 'Implementing Change Skills' seminar.

The difficulties experienced here by younger managers are the same in nature as those experienced by the more senior protagonists working in teams in Case 1 above. The ability we all seem to have, in varying degrees, to discover something new through what I have called the conventional learning method, and then to explain it in an espoused and prescriptive way, affects young people as much as it does older, more experienced operators and, indeed, seemingly across different national cultures too. It is, I believe, a fundamental error in how and what we think we learn. Learning to implement something new in any organizational setting requires new learning skills which produce new skills of action. So many human

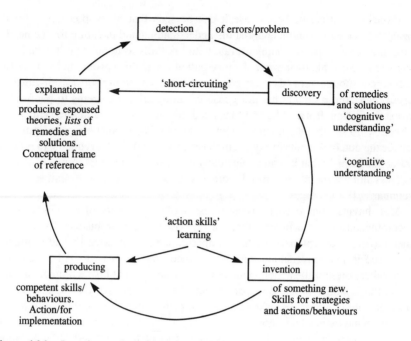

Figure 16.1   Learning cycle and learning new action skills

beings perpetuate the error of 'I understand', 'I can explain', therefore 'I can implement', particularly the well educated. They seem to 'short circuit' the critically important empirical learning cycle (see Figure 16.2) by moving directly and quickly from discovery to explanation and prescriptive lists of solutions (i.e. the 'producing' of explanation in conceptual terms is done at great speed and without noticeably stopping to think, a behaviour that Argyris has called 'skilled incompetence') [10] missing out completely the all-important change of behaviour phase of mastering personal competency in first inventing new strategies and then actually producing behaviours that will ensure their espoused theories (i.e. what ought to be done) correlate with what they are personally able to deliver and implement.

The above learning cycle illustrates what Argyris [11] has said about the difference between 'knowing' and 'doing', 'espoused theories and theories in use', 'knowledge and concepts for explaining and actional knowledge' (i.e. actually producing something new and/or different), and, of course, the difference between 'single- and double-loop learning'. The former explains how we get from *discovering* something new to being able to *explain* it, and this, of course, is a very important piece of learning. It does not, however, take us from discovery to being able to implement the change/remedies/solutions we described. In this sense we need both single- and double-loop learning in organizational life, but the latter requires new skills to be added to our existing repertoire (not to replace it). Single-loop skills are so indelibly ingrained in how we go about maintaining the status quo of organizational life that it is doubtful whether we could completely replace them even if we wanted to do so. The fact is these existing skills help us in our day-to-day competence in dealing with routine (albeit perhaps very important) tasks. They also ensure that in an organization context we are able to 'refreeze' Lewin [12], and consolidate new frames of reference and action after the turmoil of unfreezing and changing norms of status quo. Indeed, we must add new skills to old if we are to be able to manage current and future change.

The adding of new skills to old takes on a practical meaning if we consider that the most important 'learning change' takes place when we are able to use Argyris's 'double-loop' learning skills[13] to understand how bad 'single-loop' learning approaches can be for solving certain problems (i.e. those that require real challenge 'existing ways/methods of doing things'. I believe this is illustrated above both in the example of our management team members (Case 1) struggling with introducing new practices and new ways of running their business, and the younger manager, Mal (in Case 2) desperately trying to implement what he 'knew' to be important to the company he is responsible for advising.

Conclusion

In approaching the challenge of the Learning Company I do not believe that anyone working within organizations can avoid the personal responsibility of learning to change. As I have tried to illustrate in this chapter, intelligent human beings do not aim to fail in their endeavours, and yet common problems often re-occur and familiar errors escalate. I believe the reason for this is something— maybe everything—to do with the fundamental acquisition of our learning skills. What we believe we already know and can do serves us well in one sense and badly in another.

I therefore, in the context of 'personal/individual' responsibility for changing and learning, make the following appeal—no more wonderful concepts and 'pure explanations', please!

We are all eternally grateful to recent authors and management change gurus, the best of which, like Peter Senge[14] have provided new and insightful cognitive models to help us to understand our world better. 'Systems thinking'and implications of the 'Fifth Discipline' is a very important contribution to the learning company/organization literature, but like other significant insight it must lead to new/better/more effective actions of individual human beings within organizational life if we are really to see the improvement it promises.

We must avoid the sequel to analysis/paralysis of the organization development perspective so prevalent during the 1970s and 1980s. 'Concept constipation' of the learning company/organization could become a major problem during the 1990s. Of course, we will always need new or different conceptual ways of understanding our organizational lives, but if we are really to change the important things then we must focus on individual responsibility/accountability. For perhaps far too long we have all allowed our intellectual abilities to develop new, more novel explanations of our world which seemed to completely 'outstrip' our action capability to change it. For example, consider the initiatives of total quality management introduced recently in many organizations in the UK and Europe, in both public and private sectors. Learning the concept of TQM is not difficult, nor is convincing people of the benefits, but delivering the requisite behaviours to realize the changes is something else. In TQM, like many other management/organization processes, 'lists' of 'virtuous' instruction and modes of practice are produced for the guidance of all. Just a cursory glance at these lists indicates even to the uninitiated that we certainly 'understand' what we must do. For example, in attending and participating in meetings we are instructed: *Keep to the agenda; listen effectively; don't interrupt; avoid side-conversations; add value when you speak; don't repeat; ask individual for views; criticize ideas, not individuals; trust and earn the trust of others.* How could any intelligent human being disagree with this list? (and this is only part of the instructions given). I find myself, perusing such lists, saying 'Yes! Yes, of course!', but *how* do you do all things effectively and continuously? My experience is that this is not a trivial question. I believe I have illustrated to some degree in the cases studies in this chapter that many suffer the same uncertainty of turning clearly understandable and agreeable instructions of learning into practice.

Finally, I believe emphatically in the concept of the learning company/organization, but for it to become reality we must take responsibility as individuals for ensuring that our personal and interpersonal skills catch up with our temptation to intellectualize every time the going gets tough and explain away our problems. The next time you are faced with a real problem which concerns you personally involving others within your organization, and you would like to learn to help overcome this problem, take a deep breath and pause before pouring out an explanation, ask yourself what is it you are doing (or saying) that may be contributing to the problem. Ask 'another question' of those involved before you 'argue your corner'—you might be surprised at the answer and the final outcome.

'Getting yourself in touch' with the reality of connecting your *intention* with *actuality* is (as for the participants in the case studies) a learning company challenge for us all.

References

1. Argyris, C. and D. A. Schon (1978) *Organisational Learning: a Theory of Action Perspective,* Addison-Wesley, Reading, Mass. and London.

2. Change and learning diagram.

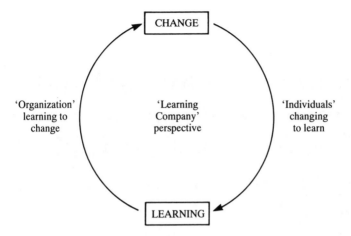

3. Argyris, C. and D. A. Schon (1978) op. cit., p. 8.
4. Argyris, C. (1983) *Reasoning Learning and Action Individual/ Organisational*, Jossey-Bass, San Francisco/London, Chapter 3, pp. 41–64, pp.107–45, p. 362.
5. Handy, C. (1992) a series of short talks, BBC Broadcasts, March 1992.
6. Case 1 taken from real-life situation, Business Management Seminar ('Turning Business Strategies into Operational Reality 1990'). Running a large multinational UK-based company.
7. Case 2 real-life situation taken from Young Manager programme. Multinational company based in UK 1991.
8. This seminar was designed to provide able young managers with an opportunity to explore their personal competency in implementing important 'knowledge' areas of their jobs. Real live cases prepared by the participants are used as a vehicle for learning new implementation or action skills.
9. Argyris, C. (1983), op. cit.
10. Argyris, C. (1987) 'A leadership dilemma: Skilled incompetence', *University of Wales Business Review No 1*, Summer.
11. Argyris, C. (1990) *Overcoming Organisational Defences. Facilitating Organisational Learning*, Allyn Bacon, Boston and London, Chapter I, p. 10. Defensive Reasoning.
12. Lewin, K. (1964) 'Group dynamics v social change', in A. Etzioni and E. Etzioni (eds), *Social Change*, Basic Books, New York.
13. Argyris, C. (1983) and (1990), op. cit.
14. Senge, P. M. (1990) *The Fifth Discipline. Art of Practice of Learning Organisation*, Doubleday, New York.

17
Facilitating individual and organizational change from the inside: the use of internal change agents in the NHS in Scotland

John Edmonstone and Maggie Havergal

Introduction

The National Health Service in the UK is really four quite different organizations, representing the four nations which make up the UK. There are important cultural and organizational differences between them—for example, in Northern Ireland health and social services are managed within one organization, whereas this is not the case in the other three countries. Nevertheless, the four different health care systems face broadly similar problems. This chapter describes a response to immediate managerial problems which also offers one means of building a learning organization in health care.

The changing NHS

There are clear and obvious changes taking place within the management and delivery of health care in all parts of the UK. Primarily, these relate to the creation and development of an internal market between purchasers and providers of care and to a range of related initiatives, including the development of business planning processes and clinical audit; a growing concern for quality; the design and implementation of information systems which link clinical and managerial decision making and the continuing spread of general management. This process has been speeded up by the appointment in all four countries of national chief executives, supported by a management executive 'top team', and offering a corporate lead within a previously disparate and fragmented system. The direction of change can broadly be classified as follows:

From	*To*
A view that the NHS is unique in its issues and problems	A view that the NHS is not so different from other organizations
Long management hierarchies	A flatter, de-layered organization
Professional-based 'tribal' thinking	Corporate thinking
Structural uniformity	Structural diversity
Emphasis on the 'patient'	Emphasis on the 'customer'
Clinical freedom as a basic and central concept	A contractual relationship defining 'bounded' clinical freedom
Rationing of health care by professional decision makers	Greater public debate about care purchasing decisions
National control by distant civil servants accountable to ministers	Management by a corporate management executive closer to the NHS
A concern with process—an emphasis on *how*, things should be done.	A concern with outcomes through enabling loose/tight frameworks

Yet the differences between the countries, and especially between the NHS in Scotland and England, are significant and have been noted by Hunter and Williamson.[1] They suggest that the position in Scotland has historically been akin to a form of 'dynamic conservatism'—an attempt to fight to stay in the same place. They note that the fundamental cultural change implied by the introduction of general management and the internal market were marked by a greater central drive within England, and that overall Scotland simply followed the English lead and merely adapted the changes at the margins, but without demonstrating the same conviction for the changes—a process sometimes known as 'tartanization'. While ascribing some of the reasons for this to a narrower perspective on, and vision of, what change could be, they also note the wider cultural and socio-political differences between the two countries, including an abiding sense of national identity in Scotland and a political consensus significantly to the left of that in England.

A new element was introduced into the picture in Scotland by the appointment in 1989 of the first chief executive. From March 1990 to September 1991 he engaged in a large-scale consultative exercise which comprised:

- a programme of consultative research which asked more than 1000 NHS users and staff what was important about the NHS and the way its services were delivered;
- a series of consultation workshops involving more than 500 senior managerial and professional staff;

- checking-out of ideas generated from these sources at a series of 'sounding-boards'.

From this process emerged the *Framework For Action*[2]—a document which includes:

- a statement of the purpose and values of the NHS in Scotland;
- clarity over the goals of the NHS in Scotland *vis-à-vis* health and health care and the need to empower staff in order to achieve these goals.

The *Framework For Action* was not a standardized and fully worked out action plan, but a reflection of different starting points and different views and approaches among individuals and groups of staff.

The Internal Change Consultant Development Programme

It was against this context that the Internal Change Consultant Development Programme (ICCDP) was developed. The background and original rationale for the programme were:

- the experience of one Scottish Health Board which had developed a comprehensive management philosophy and approach and which had invested in the organization and management development 'infrastructure' necessary to support and promote it. This had included the appointment of local 'change agents'—line managers and professionals seconded into advisory change management roles;
- the advent of resource management which advanced the notion that organization development work should precede, and then work in tandem with, the development of clinical and management information systems. Experience drawn from England identified the need for a local change agent role to support major technological and cultural change;
- the education and training infrastructure within the NHS in Scotland was small in size, fragmented along professional lines and characterized by a 'trainer' rather than a 'developer' orientation.[3] There seemed to be great difficulty in escaping the programmatic trainer mind-set. The ICCDP was conceived in part, therefore, as a means of developing a cadre of developers who would be able to assist with the new agenda associated with the chief executive and the *Framework For Action* and as a means of equipping the NHS in Scotland with the local capacity to support and manage change.

The programme was quite deliberately targeted towards second- or third-level managers who were expected to take on a significant role as an internal change management resource. The exact role was not specified in detail, and it was recognized that such responsibilities might or might not be reflected in job titles and descriptions. It was anticipated that programme participants would be drawn from any professional or occupational background, but needed to possess a track-record of managerial experience and credibility. Personal attributes, such as open-mindedness, a proactive and forward-looking approach and being a career self-starter were deemed equally as important as possession of management qualifications. The most important factor was that individual participants should possess well developed interpersonal skills. The programme facilitators were strongly influenced in this by the research findings of Hamilton[4] on change agent effectiveness. These suggest that desirable individual characteristics are:

- openness and responsiveness to others' needs and concerns;
- being at ease with ambiguity, and ability to make sense of it;
- being at ease with oneself in relation to others.

The programme design concentrated on the generic skills needed in the management of change, although it was seen as highly relevant to people working in such specific areas as total quality management, etc. The numbers on each programme were restricted to 12 and the programme comprised three phases:

Phase 1: A one-week residential workshop designed to equip participants with the necessary consultancy skills to act as internal change agents. During the latter part of this workshop participants decided on the final terms of an organizational change project which they would pursue over the following six months.

Phase 2: Participants met monthly for one day over the next six months in facilitated learning sets. Set meetings involved peer review of project work, personal support and opportunities to supplement earlier learning with mini-workshops on identified topics and issues.

Phase 3: A second residential workshop, largely designed by the participants themselves, and which featured three important aspects:

- further skill, knowledge and technique development which reflected needs emerging from the learning sets and from project work;
- an opportunity for participants to present the results of their project work to their programme 'sponsors' (typically their general managers);
- identification of continuing learning needs and means of meeting them.

An important and central concept in the overall programme design was Revans's 'learning equation'[5] of $L = P + Q$, where learning (L) is the product of both programmed knowledge (P) and questioning insight (Q). Thus, although the programme design did contain programmed knowledge aspects there was also a clear intention to foster questioning insight, both within the workshops and, more especially, through the learning sets, the project work and the self-design orientation of the final week.

Who are the change agents?

More than 60 participants have passed through five programmes to date. The majority of then are line managers or health care professionals (some 44 per cent). A further large group are the resource management project managers (23 per cent). People in human resource management (HRM) roles account for some 19 per cent while the balance are full-time and generic local change agents. Slightly more than half are female and, while age follows the normal curve of distribution, the largest number is to be found within the 31–35 age range. Some 70 per cent are located at provider (NHS Trust) level and are typically drawn from an administrative/business management or nursing background.

Programme outcomes

Programme outcomes have been the subject of an independent evaluation study and can be seen to fall into two areas: immediate, and longer-term.

At the immediate level the most public impact can be seen in terms of the organizational projects. These were generally not clear-cut and systematic descriptions of change management 'success stories', but rather more personal and 'messy' accounts of individual and organizational learning which indicate how participants often had to reframe their intentions and focus as other factors influenced their work. Using crude distinctions between strategic and operational themes, some 60 per cent were concerned with the former and some 40 per cent with the latter. Current management priorities were addressed, such as resource management (19 per cent), quality and customer responsiveness (19 per cent), changes in organization and management structures (16 per cent) and a variety of HRM issues (13 per cent).

A more interesting phenomenon is that of 'chimney-breaking'[6]—breaking out of the vertical career structures which are an aspect of most profession-based organizations. Some 60 per cent of all participants in the five programmes have since changed jobs, some more than once, and most often away from functional/professional management roles and towards general management or new 'hybrid' roles.

The longer-term outcomes are equally interesting. Programme participants have created for themselves the Scottish Change Agent Network (SCAN) as a means of furthering and extending their learning and development. A variety of events and linkages has provided for the continuing existence of a network of developers.

ICCDP and the learning organization

Pedler et al.[7] have identified eleven characteristics of a Learning Company which they have grouped into five clusters. Using this approach, the outcomes of the ICCDP seem to be largely associated with the following characteristics:

1. *Enabling structures*: as a means of legitimizing and encouraging chimney-breaking and making role and organizational boundaries more permeable.
2. *Boundary workers as environmental scanners*: There is ample evidence of ICCDP participants using each other as sources of intelligence, information and advice. SCAN is a formalization of an existing phenomenon.
3. *Intercompany learning*: ICCDP participants cut across different employers and across the purchaser/provider divide.
4. *Learning climate*: Although there is a danger of the programmes being seen as 'cultural islands' where a positive learning climate is a strong feature, the creation of SCAN is a means of sustaining this climate.

In trying to draw lessons from the ICCDP it seems clear that it is possible to take learning organization initiatives by 'piggy-backing' on associated developments such as the *Framework For Action*. Rather than working with an established trainer mind-set, it may be more realistic to start afresh and seek to build a group of developers. ICCDP suggests that it is possible to target talented people by offering learning and career development opportunities for them through working on major organizational concerns. Programme design needs to be founded primarily on the need to identify, develop and support questioning insight at the individual and organizational levels.

Another way of describing the ICCDP is to suggest that participants were actually 'intrapreneurs' with those characteristics identified by Pinchot[8]:

*   *Motivation*   Seeking autonomy, freedom and access to corporate resources. Self-motivated and self-selected.
*   *Orientation*   Action-, not status-oriented.
*   *Confidence*   Self-confident.
*   *Risk-taking*   Like moderate risks.

While one characteristic of learning organizations is that learning and development opportunities are available for *all* staff, this is probably a longer-term goal. Breaking out of negative assumptions, disabling structures and low levels of trust is a first step. The ICCDP can be seen as a programme which sought out intrapreneurs and gave them an opportunity to build an enabling and supportive structure both during the programmes and beyond. As such, it may offer one model for building the learning organizations of the future.

References

1. Hunter, D. and P. Williamson (1991) 'General management in the NHS: Comparisons and contrasts between Scotland and England', *Health Service Management*, **87**(4), 166–70

2. NHS in Scotland/Scottish Office (1991) *Framework For Action*, HMSO,

3. Boydell, T. *et al.* (1991) 'Developing the developers: Improving the quality of the professionals who develop people and organisations', Association for Management Education and Development, London.

4. Hamilton, E.E. (1988) 'The facilitation of organisational change: an empirical study of factors predicting change agents' effectiveness', *Journal of Applied Behavioural Science*, **24**(1), 37–59.

5. Revans, R. (1983) *The ABC of Action Learning*, Chartwell-Bratt, Bromley, Kent.

6. Pascale, R. (1991) *Managing on the Edge: How Successful Companies Use Conflict to Stay Ahead*, Penguin, London.

7. Pedler, M., J. Burgoyne and T. Boydell (1991) *The Learning Company: A Strategy for Sustainable Development*, McGraw-Hill, Maidenhead.

8. Pinchot, G. (1986) *Intrapreneuring*, Perennial Library/Harper & Row, New York.

18
Business schools as learning companies
David Ashton

Introduction

Background

In times of change organizations must learn to adapt or to perish. This simple truism appears more evident today—and for all forms of organization. Hence it is appropriate to be interested in a new approach, which offers a strategic view of organizational adaptation and change. It is also appropriate for management education institutions—the business schools—to show a general interest in any new framework which attempts to develop and operationalize the concept of the Learning Company. Indeed, given the nature of *their* business, business schools themselves *should* show a special interest in the extent to which the ideas of the Learning Company can be adapted to their own kind of organization—which is essentially in the business of learning. This chapter takes a particular interest in the relationship of business schools to the concept of the learning organization, examining whether business schools themselves are able to take advice as well as to give it.

My interests in the competence of business schools in adapting to changing environments began a number of years ago.[1] This has included an attempt to examine the impact of fundamental values on the actual policies and practices of business schools, highlighting particularly the blockages to change which many schools have faced. In addition, the work of Argyris and Schon,[2] on double- and single-loop models of change, has relevance both to a more general concept of a learning company and to strategic decision making and implementation in management education institutions. Turner[3] pointed the way to a new look at organizational learning, by contrasting emerging uncertainties with which organizational life will need to cope with the earlier emphasis on rationality and completeness in the assumptions underlying 'old' organizational learning.

Pedler, Burgoyne and Boydell[4] have pulled together their work and others' ideas on the Learning Company. Their definition of a learning company is 'an organisation that facilitates the learning of all its members *and* continuously transforms itself'. They take a wide view of the membership of a learning company, to include employees, owners, customers, suppliers, neighbours, environment and even competitors. They offer 'glimpses' of the learning company in their book, which is based on specific practices and particular case studies. These glimpses, however, do not add up to a complete picture; neither do the authors provide examples or blueprints of completely successful learning organizations. For them 'the magic of the learning company has to be realised from within—the key word is transformation.'

They do, however, offer eleven characteristics of the learning company, and this chapter aims to take those characteristics and examine the extent to which business schools may themselves measure up against these criteria. From this process we would hope to glean both insight into the organizational strengths and strategic problems of management education institutions themselves, as well as offer, through this example, some kind of critique of the overall Learning Company approach.

Learning company model

Having painted a general background to the Learning Company, and before going on to critique and specific proposals, it may be helpful to present an overall framework offered by the authors of the learning company. They propose that any organization be seen as a learning company, in terms of energy flow between the four points illustrated in Figure 18.1:

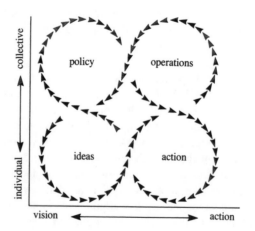

Figure 18.1   Learning circles

So communication ideas flow between the level of the collective/organization and the level of the individual in the organization as well as between what the authors call 'vision' of, and action in, the organization. These four lobes—individual, collective, vision, action—in any organization will be interconnected more or less effectively, with certain features strongly present or absent. These may be seen in terms of energy flow. The overall conception of a learning company is to generate and increase the connectedness and the flow of energy between all four lobes and the interactiveness of the model as a whole. This is done both to help individuals and the organization learn to adapt, and through this process to survive and succeed.

Criteria of the learning company

In order to offer more specific insights into factors making for success and survival, Pedler, Burgoyne and Boydell have produced eleven criteria by which we shall now attempt to measure business schools.

1. The learning approach to strategy
Here the authors suggest that organizations review and modify direction and strategy as appropriate. Built into the processes of strategic formulation and implementation is the notion that managerial acts are seen as conscious experiments. These will often be on a small scale, with feedback loops built into the planning process to enable continuous development. The emphasis in the learning approach to strategy is therefore upon flexibility and feedback.

It is difficult to generalize how well business schools themselves match up to this particular criterion as learning organizations. It is certainly true that business schools have historically been adaptive, innovative, concerned to experiment and to learn from experiments. In many cases, however, experiments which were successful have rapidly become established as routine and dominating products in production-oriented organizations. Encouragement for experiment and innovation may therefore wax and wane according to the relative success of a school in a particular stage of its life. It is also to be doubted whether business schools in practice have given the same degree of overt commitment or approach their strategic planning in as systematic and vigorous a way as the leading companies which those schools advise.

2. Participative policy making
Company policies in the learning company will reflect the values of all members, not just those of top management. Participative policy making makes a commitment to airing differences and working through conflicts rather than burying them. They will also be significantly influenced by views of stakeholders, with all members of the company having some part to play in policy and strategy formulation. Very few organizations match up well against these criteria. Given the nature

of academic communities, business schools may do better than their clients in the commercial world, in terms of the participation of faculties in policy making; however, as has been pointed out elsewhere, business schools are not always in an independent position to behave as if they are autonomous businesses or companies. More often, they may be seen as 'wholly owned subsidiaries', many of whose problems in practice are to do with the difficulties and frustrations caused by implementing 'parent' university policies in the context of business education. It can also be observed that while differences are aired quite widely in all kinds of arenas—for example, in university Senate meetings, boards of studies and so forth—often much less actually changes as a consequence of discussion, compared with the effect of debate (when it takes place) in commercial organizations. Nevertheless, academic traditions may rate the business school relatively highly on this particular dimension.

3. Informating

This is a term which we have borrowed from Zuboff,[5] who has been particularly concerned to examine changing demands on organizations as a consequence of the new power of information technology and the role of the modern knowledge worker. From the learning company perspective, informating is primarily designed to support participation—information is to be used for understanding, not for reward or punishment. It builds on information technology to create databases in communication systems, as well as ensuring that variations in systems and the interpretation of data can be properly undertaken by everyone concerned.

It is likely to be true that business schools do not score that highly as yet—although a lot of experiment is currently taking place in developing individual skills and databases on which decisions can be taken. On the contrary, a lot of time is spent arguing about the significance of data—for example, feedback from students is widely available to staff but is often not necessarily linked to local or strategic decision making. There are some businesses, particularly those which are involved directly in information technology, which have gone considerably further in implementing the 'informated organization', and business schools would do well to attempt to catch up in this field.

4. Formative accounting and control

One of the notions which the learning company approach suggests for the accounting function is that control systems are designed and run 'to delight their customers'. I do not know of many business schools faculties or administrators who are delighted at the present time by the control data that they receive. The exceptions to this are likely to be those private schools who have been able to organize all aspects of their administration and control on a business basis. Again, the 'wholly owned subsidiaries' are likely to suffer from inadequate delayed or irrelevant data, provided more to service the needs of the centre than of the business school itself. Such lack of information both enhances the problems described in the previous section on informating and impoverishes the quality and significance of feedback across the institution. Again, business schools have some way to go even to catch up with the average, let alone the best of their commercial colleagues.

5. Internal exchange

The learning company proposes two main dimensions for internal exchange. First, the facilitation of communication, negotiation and contracting, rather than 'top-down' control as a management style within the organization. Secondly, it emphasizes the need for departments or functions within the organization to be prepared to communicate across departmental and functional boundaries and to work for the organization as a whole. Business schools often do relatively well, because of academic traditions, in the relationship between senior and other staff, reflecting a less hierarchical management style. However, academic and programme groups are as likely as the traditional commercial functions of production, marketing or accounts to over-emphasize departmental loyalties and to resist effective organization across the whole school. Organizational 'chimneys' can be just as damaging in management education as they are in industry and commerce.

6. Reward flexibility

In the learning company alternative reward systems are examined, discussed and tested, together with flexible working patterns which allow people to make different contributions and draw different rewards. Indeed, it is critical, in order for such a company to *learn* successfully, for the nature of reward itself to be examined in some depth.

In many cases business schools have few options when it comes to flexibility of rewards or the adjustment of rewards and reward systems in line with the evolving objectives and priorities of their organizations. Often, pay and conditions are standardized by a national scheme with little local variation, and it is usually assumed that business school academics will be treated in the same way as colleagues in different fields in the same university. Flexibility for rewards therefore tends still to be very much at the 'edges' and is not often consistent with gaining the effective motivation or commitment of the individuals involved. Occasionally there will be special payments for particular extra duties—although the definition of 'extra' is defined differently from one school to another. But in an overwhelming number of cases, national career systems dominate the criteria for rewards primarily associated with promotion, and the individual business school finds it difficult to achieve any degree of local flexibility.

7. Enabling structures

From a learning company perspective, structures must be seen as temporary—

changing in response to a changing environment. Rules and procedures in the organization, while they will be necessary, will, after review and discussion, be frequently changed. In practice, business schools fare here neither better nor worse than many other kinds of organizations. Resistance to change in business schools is more a function of habit, plus the inability to make novel organizational structures work, either where there is conflict with traditional views about careers or the ability to access useful control data from the parent institution.

8. Boundary workers as environmental scanners

In the learning organization, all staff take the opportunity to collect and report on information about what is going on in the outside world. At the same time, the organization receives regular intelligence reports on the world, in order to understand a variety of external trends and examine how they may affect the business.

Although it does it differently from a commercial organization, the business school may well score quite highly on this particular dimension of the learning company. Business school academics tend to spend a significant amount of time outside their institutions—at conferences, involved with research, consultancy, national committee work in their field and so on.

All of this gives a potential for a significant boundary-running contribution to the vital process of environmental scanning. What is to be doubted in most business schools currently is that this information is always sufficiently well organized, or effectively collected, for its potential contribution to strategic decision making in the school to be fully realized.

The barriers therefore are less technical or structural than the willingness to organize the information as well as could usefully be achieved.

9. Intercompany learning

The learning company will use benchmarking in order to learn from the best practice in other industries. It will also consciously involve itself in meetings with competitors and engage in joint ventures, in order to learn as well as to support the development of new products or markets.

Some of the specific criteria associated with this dimension of the learning company are already quite well developed by business schools. There are regular meetings among competitors, and the high degree of idea-sharing is based on a wide sense of academic community, which is shared both by specialists within particular areas in the business school and by academics as a whole.

The specific concept of benchmarking—that is, comparing oneself with the very best in other industries—is a practice not usually undertaken by business schools. Indeed, this touches on the much broader issue of the extent to which management practices developed in other sectors can be usefully applied in higher education. A positive but moderate view would be that many of the best practices learnt from benchmarking could be of interest—although there still needs to be a prior and critical judgement on the extent to which a particular practice can be appropriately and successfully transferred over from the business to the academic culture.

10. Learning climate

Here the learning company stresses a general expectation of continuous improvement—always trying to learn and do better. It also emphasizes an atmosphere of mutual support and interest in learning lessons where mistakes are made.

Again, business schools may score relatively highly compared with average businesses. Historically, teaching quality was not so important, but now individual faculties are most often committed to improving and developing their teaching as well as conducting research. However, many of the specific practices of academic development are based on rather traditional models, some of which may not respond sufficiently to the changing environment and emergent demands on business education.

11. Self-development opportunities for all

The final dimension of the learning company stresses the importance of individuals and their learning needs. For example, they will have their own self-development budgets and there will be many opportunities and resources available for learning on an open access basis.

On this final measure, business schools, in many cases, can score relatively highly, since within the academic tradition self-development is effectively an integral feature. Academic staff are expected to maintain their position as authorities on their specific subjects, which will include a wide variety of opportunities for self-development. In some schools, the processes have become bureaucratized—with individuals haggling about allowances for conference attendance, computer programs and so on. Furthermore, many schools would be reluctant to use the label 'self-development' for such activities. But the general standards, when compared with industry, are still very high.

Conclusions

The Learning Company approach in many ways may best be regarded as bringing together a number of existing practices or frameworks to enable an organization to renew itself and to develop better contact between the outside world of its customers and suppliers and the internal world of its employees and technical skills. Familiarity with much of the material causes the continuing question, 'But shouldn't they be doing this anyway?' to be raised in almost every part of the Learning Company's processes. Any attempt, however, to integrate more closely corporate strategy, with its emphasis on economic concepts, with organizational change and development, with their emphasis upon the human side of enterprise, is to be welcomed. What will be interesting to note in the next few years is whether the Learning Company becomes a standard text for human resource managers, for corporate planners or for chief executives.

The picture that emerges when we attempt to assess business schools as learning companies is, not surprisingly, a mixed one. By certain criteria, business schools look pretty good—in terms of participative policy making, interorganizational learning, the use of staff as boundary scanners and in self-development opportunities. For these dimensions of the learning organization, a number of business school and academic practices would yield interesting and positive case studies, for examination by colleagues in commerce and other public sector organizations.

There are significant weaknesses, however, not least the mediocre condition of the information base and of the control systems within business education. In addition, the schools are as limited as many commercial organizations in terms of their skills in internal exchange, and are particularly handicapped both in terms of lack of flexibility and appropriateness of rewards and their approaches to enabling structures. While some of these limitations can be put down to the consequences of many schools being 'wholly owned subsidiaries' of a larger academic parent community, some of the limitations may reflect a lack of professionalism in the whole approach to the management of management education.

It may well be therefore that a re-examination of all the dimensions highlighted by the Learning Company could be of benefit to any business school. Put into a more general context, business education may now be going into a phase where each organization may need to differentiate itself more consciously from others, may need a more effective process of strategy formulation, implementation and review, and may be concerned to motivate and produce improved performance from academic colleagues at all stages of their careers. Traditionally, business education has been production-oriented; however, its relationship with its customers, both individual students and those organizations which commission research, will need to change over the next few years. Business education will need to think more widely and cooperate more effectively. To do this, many of the dimensions of the Learning Company would be of value to help business schools continue to change and continue to succeed.

References

1. Ashton, D. (1989) 'Are business schools good learning organisations? Institutional values and their effects in management education', *Personnel Review*, **17** (4).
2. Argyris, C. and D. A. Schon (1978) *Organisational Learning*, Addison-Wesley, Reading, Mass.
3. Turner, B. A. (1991) 'Rethinking organisations: Organisational learning in

the nineties', paper presented to EFMD Research Conference, Palermo, October.

4. Pedler, M., J. Burgoyne and T. Boydell *The Learning Company*, McGraw-Hill, Maidenhead.

5. Zuboff, S. (1988) *In the Age of the Smart Machine,* Heinemann, London.

Part III: Further thoughts

19
Learning amoeba: supporting individual managers during rapid change
Malcolm Stephenson

Introduction

The concept of the learning organization raises a number of concerns:

* it requires considerable time, expertise and money to establish and maintain a learning organization;
* many managers are seeking development in order to leave their organization;
* many managers are outside possible learning organizations, e.g. small business owners, unemployed managers, women returners;
* there is much speculation on the need to adapt to rapid change, to encourage small businesses and networks and to take account of new technology and communications. Are learning organizations the most suitable response?
* while the whole may be greater than the sum of the parts, it is individual managers who learn and justify the description 'learning organization';
* positively, the experience of my organization, the Northern Regional Management Centre (NRMC), and others in pursuing open learning approaches, has demonstrated the ability of individual managers to develop themselves, with varying degrees of support.

These concerns may seem unfair, implying that learning organizations were designed to 'cure' all managerial development problems. Nor can advocates of learning organizations (Pedler, Burgoyne and Boydell)[1] be accused of non-interest in self-development. Nevertheless, the concerns are real and have led to the consideration of smaller 'learning units' which would be able to adapt rapidly. The analogy of amoeba sprung to mind, and this chapter explores the analogy to see whether it affords any insights into alternative forms of learning support for managers.

Amoeba

The main characteristics of amoeba are:

- no constant form
- undergo constant change/are fluid
- are microscopic
- reproduce themselves (are asexual)
- absorb nutrients from all sides
- convert their own energy
- flourish or die in different cultures
- are healthy or harmful to their host body
- are non-intelligent

Form and change
The first two characteristics can be seen as concurring with Peters's view of chaos. On a macro scale, company takeovers, management buyouts, privatization, etc. all underline the need for constant change, fluidity and consequently the lack of constant form. Peters argues this in *Thriving on Chaos*[2] and outlines possible solutions, from reorganizing every 6–12 months to centralizing and decentralizing, control and decontrol, all at the same time.

Microscopic
Amoeba are also microscopic. What NRMC has seen is that it is individual managers who learn, and that constant small changes have more impact than one big change. Learning managers who take many small but well defined steps move more purposefully, more assuredly than learning managers who tackle everything on a broad front with minimal impact.

Reproduce themselves
This small step-by-step approach encourages self-development and self-managed learning skills, and these are perhaps the key to managing chaos. They are also the key to taking responsibility and recognizing potential—essential prerequisites for managers in developing their own staff or setting up their own enterprises, (hence reproducing themselves).

Absorb nutrients
As the learning manager learns to take responsibility for self-development so will he or she start to absorb 'nutrients' from all sides. Effective self-developers watch and learn from others, critically evaluate their own and others' performance with reference to the contextual setting, learn from those below as well as above and to the side, and develop their own networks of specialist advisers and sources of knowledge. Also, as home working increases, and especially for consultants and

contract professionals, maintaining many sources of information will be essential for managerial survival.

Convert their own energy
Amoeba possess mitochondrions, which absorb the nutrients and produce energy. A similar process lies at the heart of learning, although it is presumably far more complex. There is a (variable) 'Ingredient X', internally or externally triggered, which energizes or motivates individual managers to learn. Support may provide a stimulus, but will be irrelevant unless the 'Ingredient' can be activated.

Flourish or die in different cultures
There are 'contextual' limits to self-development. Initiatives can be stifled, resources withheld or simply no action taken in a non-supportive environment. This does not alter the fact that initiative lies with individuals, but they do need encouragement to be effective. It perhaps indicates that, for larger firms, the framework or tenor of a learning organization would be advantageous to encourage individual development. It perhaps highlights the known difficulty of finding the appropriate supporting environment for smaller firms.

Healthy or harmful
Amoeba are pursuing their own 'interests', which may or may not coincide with those of the host body. Similarly, managerial self-development is not necessarily in the interests of one's employer. If healthy managerial development is to be encouraged and capitalized upon, and harmful development is to be discouraged, there must be meaningful dialogue with employers. Once more, the relevance of a supportive environment is indicated.

Non-intelligent
Finally, amoeba are non-intelligent. It would be impolitic to stretch the analogy too far! It does, however, highlight the fact that learning need not take place through 'academic' routes; nor is it confined to the manager who can cope with academic study. Amoeba are concerned with survival, their 'Ingredient X', and this has impelled them to learn and to adapt. One of the difficulties for management development is convincing people that it is critical. Linking it (empirically) to the survival of individual managers may be a key.

Insights

In general, the analogy suggests that small 'learning units' could be relevant to many individual managers facing rapid change. However, it also indicates the importance of support. Learning organizations provide one kind of supportive environment, but within this 'culture' it should be possible to have greater individualized support. Indeed, such support may be the *sine qua non* of learning organizations: if learning amoeba are complex, how much more so are learning organizations? Can the concept of 'learning amoeba', of 'learning units' supporting individual managers, be made a reality?

Amoeba in practice

In a management context, a learning amoeba will be, in its smallest form:

a manager with   —X, X being the motivation to learn, for whatever reason(s)
                  —support.

If manager development is to become possible for the majority of managers, then self-development 'capacity' and support must be affordable and accessible. Both these features seem feasible through the use of:

* a self-development 'pack'
* collaborative learning
* mentors

A *self-development pack* is feasible in concept because of the number of 'artefacts' now available for diagnosis, development and support, giving:

* ability to self-assess competence, organizational blockages, learning styles;
* ability to self-develop, considering work-based learning opportunities and using open learning materials and interactive technology;
* ability to gain relevant, in-house support through learning contracts, action sets or by linking to networks.

Collaborative learning is feasible, and a valuable source of motivation, through in-house groups; self-support groups of small firms managers; and groups of managers from a number of firms 'hosted' by a large firm (generally, one to which they are suppliers).

Finally, *mentors* seem to be a critical factor. Mentors can provide the continuing flexible support required for 'lifelong' individual learning, and can 'square the circle' with the culture (organization or, for instance, a small firms market) to enable resources to be obtained and development to be healthy and accessible to all concerned. The frequency, type (academic or general) and costs of mentoring all need to be explored.

These suggestions are only direction pointers but they do indicate that 'learning amoeba'—learning units supporting individual managers in a variety of management contexts—are relevant and possible.

Conclusion

This chapter began with a number of concerns about the relevance of learning organizations to many managers, and possible opportunities for other forms of support. The analogy of amoeba was used to explore the relevance of smaller learning units. Various possibilities have emerged for learning units which could support individual manager development; interestingly, these indicate that the major precepts of learning organizations—encouraging individual responsibility and seeking to provide support—and some of their practices (e.g. mentoring) have wider application, perhaps to all managerial development. Concomitantly, it is individual managers, not organizations, who learn; the learning organization will be strengthened if close attention is paid to the possible 'learning amoeba' within it. This underlies the true locus of learning, while recognizing mutual dependency and advantage.

Whether smaller learning units are viable, both in learning and in economic terms, depends on a balance between an individual manager's capacity for self-development and the amount of support which is necessary and available. In the UK, a 'self-development' approach must be considered if the performance of the majority of managers is to be improved: training resources do not exist for two and a half million managers, especially if lifelong learning is required.

This is an exciting challenge: even more so as it represents pioneering work for the whole higher educational system. The latter will not have the capacity to support lifelong learning with its present college-centred approach. Self-development and collaborative learning will be vital, aided by advances in information technology. NRMC is taking up the challenge with pilot development of a collaborative 'learning community' in the north-east of England. Interesting times ...

References

1. Pedler, M., J. G. Burgogne and T. Boydell (1991) *The Learning Company: A Strategy for Sustainable Growth*, McGraw-Hill, Maidenhead.
2. Peters, T. (1988) *Thriving on Chaos: A Handbook for Management Revolution*, Macmillan, London.

20
Worlds apart?
John Mackmersh

Introduction

Becoming a Learning Company seems to require organizational transformation. I have become increasingly interested in how the thinking surrounding this issue is developing, particularly in connection with the ideas of reductionism and holism.

Organizational transformation, reductionism and holism—let us briefly reflect on *my* understanding of these terms before continuing:

Organizational transformation is the noticeable process by which an organization becomes easily recognized as having different and improved characteristics to those it used to exhibit.

Reductionism When studying science at school I was told that as you studied each discipline in greater detail it moved 'up' the scientific hierarchy. Hence biology (the most messy) became chemistry, chemistry became physics, and physics became mathematics (the most pure). This summed up, to me, what I was later to understand as the reductionist philosophy—the analysis of systems in terms of the constituent parts.

Holism In contrast I later came across the idea of holism and the metaphor of the hologram to describe new thinking in the sciences. The central message of holism seemed to be that the whole is an entity in itself, defying adequate understanding or description by the mere 'naming of parts'. In fact, each part *was* the whole and vice versa. This was heady stuff to someone trained in reductionism and trained to shout: 'Experimental error!' whenever a system behaved other than mechanistically!

The conflict between reductionist and holistic world views has remained with me personally and, I believe, in the development of ideas and actions concerning organizational transformation. At the moment I see much of this development being shaped by the rise of the preferred paradigm of holism. Although much of this makes good sense I offer the following points for consideration.

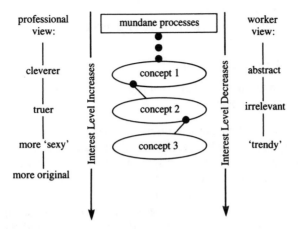

Figure 20.1 Worlds apart

Worlds apart

Are the concepts of organization transformation becoming increasingly abstract, with each new development being a concept in relation to another concept, and therefore becoming more and more removed from the actual concrete experiences of work which most people have? The danger being that the majority of people involved in organizational life are being disenfranchised from the debate about 'what might be' as organizational development (OD) professionals, academics and senior managers define a 'new reality'.

A gap in the OD toolkit?

Some of the new thinking in science is beginning to help us understand how simple repetitive acts can give rise to complexity and beauty (i.e. The Game of Life,[1] Chaos Theory,[2] etc.), but what about the other way round?

If organizations are to transform in a purposeful sense it is essential that the idea of the new organization is not only described at a holistic level, but it must also be shown how the spirit, vision, beauty and wholeness of this new organization will manifest itself in everyday (often mechanistic and mundane) work (the Monday morning briefing, the telephone enquiry, sending a memo, etc.).

Taking a sideways view it would be amusing to ponder the nature of gossip in a Learning Company or how an office affair would be dealt with!

I believe an important role for organizational development professionals working with the Learning Company idea is to develop tools and techniques which help people in organizations to 'hold the tension' between holism and reductionism, i.e.:

Not: holism vs reductionism
But: incremental holism (or holistic incrementalism!)

In defence of reductionism

To help us to hold this tension I believe it is useful to put the world views of holism and reductionism into context:

1. I know that quantum physics offers a 'truer' model of the universe than Newtonian mechanics, but Newton is all I need to become a better snooker player. It is also all I need to help someone else to learn how to play the game. When it is time for me to explore deep space and to take others with me, *then* I'd better brush up on my quantum physics!
2. When I consider my own existence and the richness and complexity of my relationships with others, and the world in general, I find the reductionist viewpoint of life as a well organized chemical reaction hard to swallow.

I also find it amusing to note that some of my most heated debates around the issue of reductionism take place in the kitchen at parties. Here, the holistic/anti-reductionist faction often ends up agreeing that their manner and perceptions are being directly influenced by one chemical, namely alcohol, reacting with another set of chemicals in the brain!

I believe we should not overlook the equal (in context) validity and usefulness of reductionist models in our rush to understand the holistic perspective (an example being the contrast between the eleven-stage model and the energy flow model of the Learning Company described by Pedler, Burgoyne and Boydell.[3]

Worlds apart—an analogy

A stroke of magenta, a dab of vermillion, a patch of crimson. A thick tangle of dried lumps of paint. Move back from six inches to six feet, however, and the form, beauty and meaning of a Monet emerges. What is the nature of this link between the mechanical/repetitive process of applying pigment to canvas and the creation of deeply moving works of art?

Within this analogy are great challenges to anyone working in the creation of learning companies.

Acknowledgements

My thoughts in the above piece have been shaped to date primarily by:

(i) The ideas of the Learning Company expressed by Boydell, Burgoyne and Pedler.

(ii)   Conversations at the first Learning Company Conference.
(iii) Trying to make sense of it all with people who say 'That's all very well and good, but how will it help me to do my job better?'!

References

1. Poundstone, W. (1987) *The Recursive Universe*, Oxford Paperbacks, University Press, Oxford.
2. Gleick, J. (1988) *Chaos*, Cardinal.
3. Pedler, M., J. Burgoyne and T. Boydell (1991) *The Learning Company: A Strategy for Sustainable Development*, McGraw-Hill, Maidenhead.

21
Turning the environment from a threat into an opportunity
John Gunson

Introduction

The environment is one of the major strategic issues facing organizations in the 1990s. All too often, it is seen as a threat to competitiveness or another unwarranted outside interference in the company.[1,2]

The threat tends to come from people seeing and hearing the environment as an unwanted or unsolvable pressure. However, there is a positive side too—a number of large organizations, from the MOD through 3M to Lancashire County Council, have made the environment a central plank of their strategy. Moreover, the number is growing all the time.

Clearly, these organizations adopt this strategy for various reasons: some because of a belief that it is essential for their, and our, survival; some because of the opportunity for competitive advantage, by making or moulding new markets, or by capitalizing on public demands; yet others out of an attempt to make themselves attractive to potential employees or investors. There is a gathering momentum for change, whatever the driving force.

In addition, there is an argument that we need to develop and exploit new technologies in order to have any great impact on resolving environmental problems. Changes to our individual and corporate behaviour are crucial to achieving a sustainable future. For example, what happens when the oil runs out? We need to have developed viable alternatives for transport and all other uses of oil and its by-products.

Organizations, by adopting an environmental strategy, can make a real impact on global issues through their 'stakeholders'. All groups connected with the organization—suppliers, customers, employees and potential employees, investors and/or shareholders, competitors, legislators and the local community (i.e. local to the organization's works or offices)—can be influenced by, learn from, and benefit from, the organization's policies.

If that is the opportunity for the organization, then learning from the environment is a demonstrable and useful way of understanding the issues confronting the organization. We are all part of the world's eco-system, therefore so is our organization. This theme is picked up by the learning experiments described below. These were explored as part of the Learning Company Conference in March 1992, where people experienced being part of an eco-system, and how they could learn by thinking about the longer-term future.

Models

There are two important models to consider as ways of thinking about organizations and their impacts from all angles: the Life Cycle and Organizational Models from the new British Standard for Environmental Management (BS 7750).[3]

In this context, *Life Cycle* means from the *original source* of all inputs *to* the *final disposal* of the product or service by its last user. This differs from the normal product life cycle, which means from product development to end of selling life.

The life cycle model (Figure 21.1) stresses that environmental impact assessment needs to be applied to all stages of the life cycle for any product or service—it is not sufficient simply to audit the process undertaken. The same rigour should be applied to the input and output stages as well.

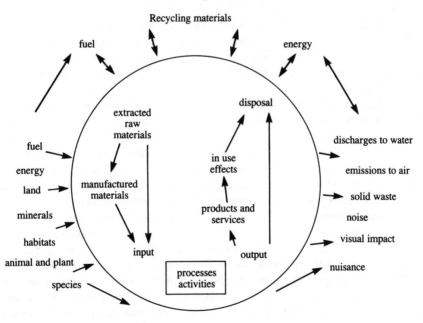

Figure 21.1   Life cycle model

When considering what impact a product or service has on the environment, we should start with all inputs to an organization (including raw materials, manufactured goods, energy, land, animal and plant species, fuel, etc.). Where do we get our supplies from? What conditions are we going to apply to their purchase? How are we going to validate that those conditions are satisfied? How many of those resources are recycled or renewable? Organizations that have changed their purchasing criteria to incorporate environmental parameters have not only found that their competitive position is not compromised, but that they are having a long-term effect on the supply market.

The next stage in the life cycle embraces the processing phase. What energy do we use? What goods do we employ to assist manufacture? What waste products are we generating from the processes? What are the impacts of the processes and their waste products? This is an area where legislation is becoming more demanding, from the European Community, the UK Government and other states, in relation to our exports. Pollution emissions is the most obvious example.

The third stage is the output from the organization, encompassing manufactured goods or services, transport and distribution, packaging, and waste products. How do people use our products or services? How do they dispose of them? What waste from their usage, e.g. packaging, that we can we re-use? What impact (visual, air or water pollution, noise, etc.) do we make on the local or global environment? The EC Packaging Directive and the German government's laws on re-usability are recent demonstrations of this.

To illustrate this concept, here is an activity (the eco-system experiment) which asks people to be trees, crops, mulches or farmers. Trees are asked to stand up and wave their arms like a tree. Crops are asked to sit or kneel on the floor, and move in the breeze, mulches are asked to lie on the floor next to the crops. Farmers sit and tend the system.

This activity can then be used to look at the interconnectedness of the different parts, and people can express how they feel about being one of these. Interestingly, the farmers usually feel the least involved (they aren't allowed to spray chemicals!!). Mulches and crops feel good about their role, even though the mulches acknowledge that they would break down and disappear eventually. Trees are less certain about their beneficial role in the cycle. They can be assured that wind-breaks, shade and leaves for mulch are all important elements.

The organizational model (Figure 21.2) gets people to think about all the other activities that an organization undertakes, e.g. research and development, personnel policies, accounts, pension fund investment, office services and supplies, etc. What environmental objectives do we place on our research and development people? Do we apply the same purchasing criteria to office supplies and raw materials? How do we define such things as recruitment policies or appraisal systems in these terms? What criteria do we apply when we invest our pension fund money? There is also a growing movement among private investors, and

Environmental management systems

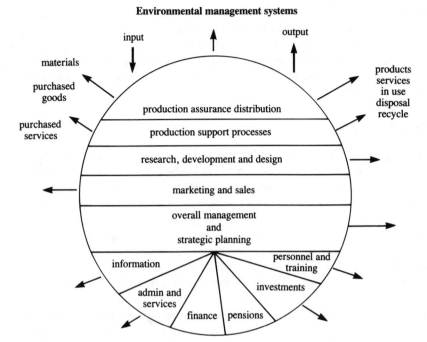

Figure 21.2   Organizational model

therefore investment organizations, to ask questions about the ethical policies of potential investment targets. Ethical or environmental funds are extremely popular.

To demonstrate this model, here is another activity (the co-operative experiment) which involves everyone in a group participating in becoming personal and group visionaries for the twenty-first century. It uses the environment as both a learning tool and a powerful force in encouraging people to develop as individuals, in teams, as part of a whole organization, and finally to influence the wider business community.

People are each given a suitcase of infinite dimensions in order to take five items (physical articles, people, ideas or inventions) to the twenty-first century. They then discuss their ideas in groups of four, and come up with a group list of five items, which they derive from their own ideas or which crop up in discussion as new ones. The whole group finally decides what items to take back to the wider community, as well as discussing their feelings about and during the exercise.[4]

The learning tends to be powerful—people find doing it individually quite hard. Expressing your ideas in a group is risky ('This is going to sound silly!'); however, working as a group enables greater diversity and originality of thought *and* throws up some seemingly unresolvable differences of opinion. Some of the ideas that stick in my mind most vividly from the Learning Company Conference were: the Kew Gardens seed bank, a reverse shredder (to bring back later anything that the world still needed), and maybe a nuclear missile, so that we do not forget what we are capable of creating. Moreover, people found the activity enjoyable and, to a degree, liberating.

Conclusion

My objective in this chapter has been to accentuate the positive (both in terms of thought and action). It is too easy, with the kinds of global environmental threats confronting us, to feel powerless and overwhelmed. I hope that I have managed to offer a different outlook on the environmental context. To confront our situation, we need to find new ways of thinking about and dealing with, our common future.[5]

Where does the learning angle come in? By offering the environment as a learning tool in thinking about the future, the experiments were used to illustrate the two key models. Their purpose was to reinforce the messages of long-term ('cradle to grave') impact. The experiments also aimed to get people involved in their own understanding of collaboration and cooperation as a norm, rather than the more usual competitive situation. Indeed, I see collaboration and cooperation as a creative process, which could be followed up within other organizations.

References

1. Gore, A. (1992) *Earth In Balance*, Earthscan Publications, (USA).
2. Hutchinson, C. (1991) *Business and the Environmental Challenge*. The Conservation Trust.
3. British Standards Institute (1992) BS7750: *Specification for Environmental Management Systems*, EPC/50 of BSI.
4. Steadman, R. (1991) in J. Porritt (ed.) *Saving The Earth*, Dorling Kindersley.
5. Clark, M. E. (1989) *Ariadne's Thread: The Search for New Modes of Thinking*, Macmillan Press, London.

Index